Palgrave Studies in Globalization and Embodiment

Series Editors
Erynn Masi de Casanova
University of Cincinnati
Cincinnati, OH, USA

Afshan Jafar
Connecticut College
New London, CT, USA

This cutting-edge series will address how global forces impact human bodies and the individual and collective practices associated with them. Books in this series will explore the globalization of bodily practices as well as how the interaction of local and global ideas about bodies produces particular forms of embodiment. We are particularly interested in research covering the ways that globalization engenders inbetween spaces, hybrid identities and 'body projects.'

More information about this series at
http://www.palgrave.com/gp/series/15115

Luis Navarro-Ayala

Queering Transcultural Encounters

Bodies, Image, and Frenchness in Latin America and North Africa

Luis Navarro-Ayala
St. Norbert College
De Pere, WI, USA

Palgrave Studies in Globalization and Embodiment
ISBN 978-3-030-06404-4   ISBN 978-3-319-92315-4   (eBook)
https://doi.org/10.1007/978-3-319-92315-4

Cover image: © Liyao Xie

Printed on acid-free paper

This Palgrave Macmillan imprint is published by the registered company Springer
International Publishing AG part of Springer Nature
The registered company address is: Gewerbestrasse 11, 6330 Cham, Switzerland

Dedico este manuscrito a mis padres,
Rebeca Ayala y Luis Navarro,
cuya jornada de vida es mi fuente de inspiración y fortaleza.

PREFACE

My book proposes a new queer transcultural perspective of Frenchness based on its provocative encounters between Latin American or North African male subjects. Whether provided as a cultural description or personified by characters, Frenchness plays a noteworthy role in bodily representations and their formation of queer identities in fiction from both of these areas in the global South. Using the framework of gender, sexuality, and queer studies, queer of color critique, cultural semiotics, transnationalism, and transcultural information media and technology, I analyze queer male bodies who either navigate transcultural spaces or experience cross-cultural encounters in seven works by the following five writers: José González Castillo's *Los Invertidos* (Argentina), Alfonso Hernández-Catá's *El ángel de Sodoma* (Cuba/Spain), André Gide's *L'immoraliste* (France), Mohamed Choukri's *Le pain nu* (Morocco), and Rachid O.'s narratives *Chocolat chaud, Ce qui reste,* and *L'enfant ébloui* (Morocco).

In the Latin American context, the trope of exclusion of the Other is associated with Frenchness as sexually deviant and consequently undesirable. Yuri Lotman's semiosphere helps reveal the ways in which national culture becomes boundary organization that includes or excludes un/wanted individuals—and, more specifically, effeminate male figures. In the North African context, the predominantly masculine public space facilitates cross-cultural encounters with French men, allowing a controversial bond to form between the privileged white European tourist and local impoverished brown boys. I study Homi Bhabha's cultures of survival and mimicry, as well as Marcel Mauss's gift exchange relationships, to show how social conditions prevent or allow the younger participants in these exchanges to develop sexual agency and sites of resistance to global economic power structures. Finally, my book explores homosexual agency and subject formation of a young protagonist thanks to intercultural information media and technology in Morocco. His project analyzes the affective attachment and sensorial connection to a photograph and French television broadcasts developed by an adolescent who manages to turn public space into a realm of intimacy. Ultimately, the character forges a new transcultural identity when he transforms his attraction for racial difference into postcolonial subversion in the soccer-playing field.

De Pere, USA   Luis Navarro-Ayala

ACKNOWLEDGEMENTS

The completion of this manuscript has only been possible because of the collaboration I have enjoyed with numerous scholars and friends, whom I would like to thank. I am deeply indebted to Françoise Lionnet who believed in this project from the very beginning. Her guidance and patience in the French and Francophone Studies Ph.D. Program at UCLA allowed my research to take shape, while her academic rigor and thought-provoking questions helped me to develop it. Our interactions continue to sculpt my intellectual curiosity and my personal take on life.

Similarly, my UCLA professors, Adriana Bergero, Eleanor Kaufman, Andrea Loselle, and Maite Zubiaurre, have modeled my approach to scholarly research. Their demanding seminars and astute reading suggestions are also reflected in my project. Our conversations continue to not only inspire me but also to enrich my professional and personal life. I would also like to thank Efraín Kristal, Dominic Thomas, and Françoise Lionnet for their trust and generosity that made my year in Paris a reality. It was an honor to work at the UCLA Travel Summer Program and at the University of California Study Center in Paris. That year's contribution to my professional development is invaluable. I am profoundly grateful for the opportunity to spend the year as a *pensionnaire étranger* at the Ecole normale supérieure in Paris, where my research benefitted from the insightful feedback from my reading partners, Niamh Duggan, Emily Mclaughlin, Kathryn Kleppinger, Mo Amadeus, Amanda Dennis, and Ben Williams. Our Monday meetings in the Café Gay Lussac were a weekly pleasure.

This book would never have been completed without the support of the Department of French and Francophone Studies at UCLA. Throughout the various stages of the project, I received much-appreciated encouragement from Jean-Claude Carron, Malina Stefanovska, Nicole Dufresne, Kim Jansma, Laurence Denié-Higney, Lia Brozgal, Zrinka Stahuljak, Laure Murat, and Dominic Thomas. I would also like to express my gratitude to the staff of the Royce Humanities Group, especially, Kerry, Fleur, Gina, and Raquel (may she rest in peace—I know she would have been very happy to see it materialize). Their skillful attention to practical details turned challenging administrative tasks into smooth procedures. Finally, my heartfelt gratitude goes to Satik in the Royce Reading Room for providing such a pleasant atmosphere in which to work and write.

I am also thankful to St. Norbert College, particularly the Discipline of Modern Languages and Literatures, the Humanities Division, the Office of Faculty Development, the Office of the Dean, and the Office of the President. Rejoicing from intellectual freedom at SNC has been most valuable for my project. I am especially thankful that their support has motivated me further to develop my role as teacher/scholar. I would also like to thank Connie, David, and Candy from Mulva Library. My work benefited greatly from their generosity and unlimited access to their books, premises, and innumerable cups of coffee.

Finally, I would like to express my special gratitude to my friends and family. Continuous conversations with Jamie Fudacz, Sandra Gamson, Lauren Brown, and Dianne Gunn continue to enrich my work. My book would not have reached its completion without the endless support and encouragement from Alisa Belanger, Michael A. Jones, and my family, la familia Navarro Ayala. Alisa, I am privileged to be your friend. I have learned so much from our conversations; your intellectual generosity is a source of inspiration for me. Michael, your patience and support strengthen me. My family, you nourish my curiosity. Mi familia, alimentan mi curiosidad. Estoy inmensamente agradecido con mis padres, Rebeca y Luis, por la enseñanza de vida que me dan. Este trabajo es para ustedes.

Contents

Introduction: Theorizing Transcultural Queer Bodies and Their Appropriation of Frenchness

The spatial paradigm analyzed in this book displays distinctive male bodies who appropriate two very different representations of Frenchness. Whereas the Latin American imaginary presents the French-inspired *garçonnière*[1] as a private space that allows for homosexual permissiveness, the North African context characterizes the *terrasse de café* as the public sphere, where the transcultural encounter with the French Other leads to masculine transformation through a same-sex encounter. Whether used for work or pleasure, these French spaces enable effeminate male figures to perform their queerness in complete freedom on the one hand. And on the other, Frenchness becomes the locus of meetings between local brown boys and white European travelers, whereby they negotiate new transcultural relationships between themselves and with the broader society around them. Taken together, such interpretations raise the same questions about Frenchness: Is it queer?[2] How and why would French-inspired spaces be associated with queer identity outside of the Hexagon?[3]

Examining France as a nation and an imagined cultural space, this book suggests that the concept of Frenchness plays a significant role in the construction of a queer identity in both Latin America and North Africa. Rather than approach these cultures as a residual depository of European thought, colonization, and linguistic dominance—as has often been demonstrated to prove problematic in queer theory and literary criticism—my research takes a transcultural approach to homo/sexual

© The Author(s) 2019
L. Navarro-Ayala, *Queering Transcultural Encounters,*
Palgrave Studies in Globalization and Embodiment,
https://doi.org/10.1007/978-3-319-92315-4_1

identities and subjectivities. By connecting these two regions from the global South in a comparative mode, my goal is to add to the nascent discussion about bodily image, sexuality, masculinity, marginality, ethnicity, and class within the discipline of queer studies, paying particular attention to the ways in which these sociological factors are associated with France in different cultural contexts. While it has long been acknowledged that France historically considered North Africa to be a queer space permitting promiscuity, it has less often been noted that Latin America looks to France for the same purpose, or that Frenchness has likewise come to represent an imagined queer space enabling sexual explorations in North Africa today. In other words, reversing the gaze of the colonizer, both of these regions in the southern hemisphere have come to view Frenchness as queer.

The notion of Frenchness[4] plays a key role in this study of Francophone North African and Latin American literatures. Emerging research about the similarities between these geographical areas usually adapts Western theories to new contexts using a comparative approach that responds to a national identity paradigm. For instance, in *Performative Bodies, Hybrid Tongues* (2010),[5] Julian Vigo examines how the body serves in both of these regions as an analytical site where nationhood, gender, and sexuality merge to build an interpretation of the social. Like Vigo's work, my project also highlights effeminate male figures, ethnicized bodies and queer subjects—and their daily practical rethinking of the social. More specifically, I focus on homosexual cross-cultural encounters that put society members in each of these regions into direct contact with others from abroad.

In situations where queer subjects cross through transcultural spaces, they find ways to create transversal dialogues inclusive of racial, cultural, age, and sexual specificities, as well as to discover new modes of social engagement. The political terrain of daily life exposes the self-understanding queer in one way or another to the knowledge that potential stigmatization interconnects with a wide array of homogenous social ideologies pertaining to gender, family, consumption, desire, nature, culture, race, and national imaginary—all bound to the male body. In fact, it seems safe to assert that being queer means the need to grapple, if not outright to fight, about these issues on a regular basis. Such a challenging process is often embodied in the figure of the Transcultural Queer, who occupies zones of contact—whether for work or pleasure—that are uniquely qualified to re-conceptualize Frenchness and French influence as they are defined in local cultures from around the globe.

Several questions therefore emerge at the core of this project: What are the social conditionings that give rise to same-sex encounters between two different cultures? To what degree may such encounters facilitate or challenge sexual agency and subject formation in postcolonial societies where Frenchness alternately represents a corruptive influence or a liberating ideal?

Orientalism and Indigenism in the Francophone Context

As a starting point, it is important to remember that contemporary North Africa and Latin America share somewhat similar historical positions in relation to Frenchness: Despite unique cultural and linguistic traits, both regions have remained in continuous contact with French culture, literature or language since the colonial era. Although Latin America's official languages are Spanish or Portuguese, French frequently acts as a second or third language within the literate population, while North Africa's linguistic diversity involves Arabic, Berber, and French. In addition, these regions share a history of invasion by France.

Napoleon I began French colonization in North Africa with the occupation of Egypt in 1789, which gave birth to the modern experience of the Orient as famously defined nearly two hundred years later by Edward Said. In *Orientalism* (1979), Said observes that the Napoleonic expedition motivated a "series of textual children, from Chateaubriand's *Itinéraire* to Lamartine's *Voyage en Orient* to Flaubert's *Salammbo*" (88).[6] In addition to artistic and textual production, the Napoleonic expedition in North Africa also allowed Europe "to know the Orient more scientifically, to live in it with greater authority and discipline than ever before" (22). In June 1830, the French Restoration government sent an expeditionary force to Algeria to capture the capital city. When Louis-Napoleon became emperor in 1851, he saw Algeria as a "special case" and its people "worthy or interest" (2)[7]; after his visit there in 1860, Napoleon III became "obsessed with Algeria and the Arabs" (3), desirous to bring them "the benefits of civilization" as well as "perfect equality" with French citizens. His interests in an Arab kingdom aimed to gain international prestige for France while ensuring posts for his armed forces in the Mediterranean. His *mission civilisatrice* served not only a Christian purpose or a French cultural agenda, but also commercial and military interests. Despite subsequent regime changes, the French would extend their dominion in North Africa to Tunisia and Morocco, which both remained French protectorates until 1956, when they were relinquished during the Algerian War, lasting until 1962.

Although far more briefly, French colonial expansion in Latin America reached one of its most important peaks during the same period. No more than a year after becoming enamored with North Africa, Napoleon III also sent his troops to Mexico. In 1861, Napoleon attempted to establish monarchical rule there in order to strengthen French assets in the region. Since its independence from Spain in 1821, Mexico had struggled against bankruptcy and political disorders. Jay Sexton in *The Monroe Doctrine* (2011) comments that rival factions destroyed "the effectiveness of government and all respect for authority, so that brigandage and outlawry were everywhere prevalent" during that time of turmoil (70).[8] The common belief at the time was that "the political situation in Mexico [would] shortly end in anarchy or else give place to the establishment of a protectorate by some outside power" (ibid.). However, Mexico's political unrest was not necessarily the reason why Napoleon III intervened; instead, it was the failure of the Mexican government to meet the demands of European creditors, among which French investors were particularly alarmed due to interest payments long overdue. Sexton adds,

> France, taking the lead, succeeded in bringing about a concert of the three European nations most concerned with the Mexican dilemma; and on October 31, 1861, Spain and Great Britain signed with Louis Napoleon a convention at London under the terms of which they agreed to act together, employing force if necessary, to secure satisfaction from the Mexican government. (72)

Under the terms of these economic sanctions from the European Convention, the French troops, aided by British and Spanish forces, arrived in the port city of Veracruz. By 1863, they seized the capital, Mexico City, after which Maximilian of Austria was selected "to play the role of Mexican sovereign, and in 1864 [was] proclaimed Emperor. During these years the French [were] establishing themselves in Mexico" (73). In this manner, Napoleon III sought to colonize Mexico with French settlers, to modernize its economy, and to provide political stability. All total, the Napoleonic occupation of Mexico lasted years, until Republican insurgents captured and executed Maximilian in 1867.

North Africa and Latin America thus share a long and fraught relationship with France. As Françoise Lionnet observes, the effort to understand "francophone studies in all its richness," requires that critics identify and examine diverse areas of *francophonie* (French-speaking), which have faced various forms of colonial domination, including "sub-Saharan Africa, the Maghreb, the Mashreq, the Caribbean, and the Indian Ocean" (1253).[9] Given its French invasions in the nineteenth century, Latin America deserves its own unique place in this list. While it is a well-established idea that North Africa contributes to the Francophone literary canon and to the richness of the Francophone world, Latin America has rarely drawn the attention of specialists in this field.

And yet, Latin America has inspired canonical texts, as well as critical notions of the French national narrative since the Renaissance. For instance, Montaigne's *Cannibales* (1588) is based on the French expeditions in South America in the sixteenth century. French explorer André Thévet recounts his explorations of Brazil through the 1550s in his memoirs *Histoire d'André Thévet Angoumousin, cosmographe du roy, de deux voyages par luy faits aux Indes Australes, et Occidentales* (2006). In addition, *L'Histoire de la Compagnie de Jésus* (1874) provides a historical account of the seventeenth-century French Jesuit explorations in Maragnon, Brazil. Beyond these foundational works, French surrealists' visits to Mexico in the twentieth century are narrated by André Breton in *Souvenir du Mexique* (1939), as well as by Antonin Artaud in *D'un voyage au Pays des Tarahumaras* (1945). Brazil then reappears in Lévi-Strauss's anthropological study *Tristes Tropiques* (1955).

These noteworthy texts, among so many others, show that Latin America has long thrived in the French imaginary under a form of Indigenism,[10] not unlike Orientalism as outlined by Said. It has likewise been the object of scientific investigation and imaginary representations of the Other that were designed to mediate and control those perceived as foreign, savage, or simply inferior. Whatever isolated attempts may have been made to break down these dominant trends lasting into the twentieth century (and beyond), Orientalism and Indigenism both function as mirrors which, in the Francophone context, reflect back a certain idea of Frenchness—originally, for the benefit of the colonial power and, increasingly in recent years, as a concept to be renegotiated in postcolonial terms.

Judith Butler's "Performativity": Identity, Parody, and Subversion

If it is true that queer transcultural subjects draw into question societal norms—or, at least, push them to their limits—then it is important to grasp how and why. Judith Butler's extensive work has played a crucial role in the ever-expanding field of Gender Studies, especially in regard to Queer Theory and identity politics. On the one hand, Queer Theory, as a deconstructive strategy, aims to denaturalize heteronormative understandings of sex, gender, sexuality, sociality, and the relations between them. On the other hand, identity politics as commonly practiced in dominant Western societies are based on the assumption that sexual inclinations, practices, and desires are the expression of an individual's core identity. Based on diverse theoretical influences (Foucault, Simone de Beauvoir, Joan Rivière, J. L. Austin, and Derrida, among others), Butler's collected essays reveal the extent to which performativity impacts the construction of identity. Her argument in *Gender Trouble* (1990),[11] states that gender is neither natural nor innate, but rather a social construct which serves particular purposes and institutions. Gender, she says, is the "performative effect of reiterative acts" (33). Repeated in a highly rigid regulatory frame, these acts "congeal over time to produce the appearance of a substance, or a natural sort of being" (33); rather than being expressions of an innate gender identity, acts and gestures which are learned and repeated over time create the illusion of an innate and stable gender core.

Butler's account of the performative character of gender denaturalizes not only what she refers to as the heterosexual matrix (i.e., the hegemonic institutions, identities, and relations), but also identity politics and its founding forms. Her work debunks the commonly held belief that gender is a natural attribute, an internal essence that manifests itself in set characteristics—such as, for example, passivity, nurturance, maternal feelings, and so on in women. Thanks to her seminal work, feminists have countered this sort of essentialism by arguing that gender, like the very notion of the individual, is a social construct. Likewise, this notion explicitly applies to a great number of texts of interest to queer theorists. Notably, the analyses in Chapters 2 and 7 of this book show how two characters, José-María and Rachid, put themselves through a masculinization process in order to erase their feminine attributes, and thus be in agreement with social norms.

Indeed, one important conclusion widely acknowledged from Butler's claim that "genders are truth-effects of a discourse of primary and stable identity" (136) is that sexual categories such as heterosexuality and homosexuality prove to be merely cultural fictions. For Butler, if there is no inner core, there cannot be any such thing as "straight or queer"—at least, not in an essential sense. It follows that some accusations leveled at identity politics suggest that they appear in reality to be complicit in the structures of the meaning that they in fact aim to challenge. In other words, critics tend to agree in theory with Butler, but to carry on in practice without changing their fundamental assumptions about the identity politics of being "queer" or "straight," as a stable state of affairs over time. Butler herself has acknowledged such a dilemma: "identity categories tend to be instruments of regulatory regimes, whether as the normalizing categories of oppressive structures, or as the rallying points for a liberatory contestation of that very oppression" (13–14). It is important to recognize this because the displacement of a political and discursive origin of gender identity onto a "psychological 'core' precludes an analysis of culturally and historically specific systems of power/knowledge and the subjectivities that they engender" (143).

Fleshing out this line of thought in *The Bodies of Women* (1994),[12] Rosalyn Diprose shows that we cannot deny ever reading the gestures, actions, and appearances of others as the expression of who we presume them to be–just as we also tend to classify people in regard to race. Using the example of the immediate assumption that two women passionately kissing are lesbians, Diprose points out the social usefulness of jumping to conclusions: If actions, gestures, and desires are perceived as the representation of the innate self, it becomes possible not only to interpret others, but also to evaluate and categorize them. Undoubtedly, the connection to such a supposed capacity to "know the Other" appears to enable the possibility of self-knowledge. At some level, it allows us to articulate "a sense of ourselves and our position in the world in relation to them" (56). As a result, we can validate, denigrate, punish, or celebrate others' actions, desires, and identity, in addition to our own. This is precisely the experience that characters Dr. Florez and Mohamed Choukri undergo in Chapters 3 and 4 of this book: whereas Dr. Florez is pushed to suicide because his homosexuality is discovered, Mohamed's impoverished looks provoke his social denigration. To some extent, all queer subjects actively attempt to escape such categories, but Transcultural queers must face them in not one society, but two.

According to Diprose, this kind of stigmatization of so-called unnatural actions and identities appears everywhere in society, and functions to reaffirm that which is considered to be natural. As members of a society, we therefore become not only the agents but also the products of disciplinary regimes. Among the negative consequences of policing identity and inflicting punishment are of course homophobia and gay-bashing. In each case, the construction of the other as unnatural or aberrant reaffirms identity as regulatory, and thus, the false impression of an interior gender core leads to the "regulation of sexuality" (136). Such a model of identity is not only integral to the heterosexual matrix but also founded on the so-called stable and dichotomous notion of gender. In the case of transcultural queers, the regulatory power of what is conceived as natural may at times double, while at other times, the transcultural experience lays bare the artificiality of categories, leaving them open to malleability, as is the case for Rachid O. in Chapters 6 and 7.

Throughout my book, this relationship between the notion of an interior gender core and the exterior regulation of sexuality is reconsidered based on the often less individualistic worldviews promoted in Latin America and North Africa, where dominant cultures tend to value family relationships and social ties more highly than personal preferences. While most scholarship in queer studies recognizes the impact of social pressures on the development of self-perceptions, it nonetheless assumes in many cases that self-realization is ultimately a one-person affair. In contrast, my aim is to illustrate how characters evolve within societies that place less emphasis on privacy, distinctiveness, or individuality.

QUEER STUDIES AND SOCIAL THEORY

In response to questions of race, class, and peripheral sexualities within the discipline of queer studies, Michael Warner impressively offered new angles of inquiry in his "Introduction" to *Fear of a Queer Planet* (1993).[13] His analysis points out that the queer is subject to disproportionate social interaction. By beginning with the question, "What do queers want?" and providing the immediate quip "not just sex," Warner immediately sends the queer on a quest to find "new engagements" in society (vii). After thus dismissing the homosexual stereotype that condemns queers exclusively to sex, he explicitly declares that sexual desires in and of themselves imply other wants and ethics. Although "queers live as queers," their conditions are manifested in contexts "other than sex" (ibid.). Hence, from the outset, Warner appeals to queers as social beings in interaction with others. They live in different ways, with implications that expand to every area of their social life; for this reason, it is necessary to think of queer theory as an unpredictable project in elaboration.

Arriving at this point, however, is not a straightforward result of social theory for Michael Warner. He remarks that critical theory in the Marxist tradition has left questions regarding such intersections unanswered, promulgating instead the naturalization of a heterosexual society. He then continues his analysis by providing a critique of the "historical failure" of social theory: He points out that the twentieth century witnessed the birth of social thought which recognizes sexuality "as a field of power, as a historical mode of personality, and as the carrier of utopian imagination" (viii). Yet, he highlights the "second blindness" to queer issues, by which social theory illustrates sexuality "only peripherally or not at all" (xi). Without completely eliminating the efforts of social theory, Warner criticizes how its continuous return to the question of sexuality has failed to recognize precisely why it has done so, maintaining in this manner the marginalization of queer sexuality in its descriptions of the social world. Because of such a deliberate omission, he considers it "manifestly homophobic" and mentions that the "new social movements" treat the lesbian and gay politics model as an "afterthought," reducing dissident sexuality only to a "parallel choice." Homosexuality-as-a-choice fails to challenge the heterosexual order and, hence, remains outside of the realm of power structure. Because of such major flaws within social-theoretical traditions, Warner supports the need to develop a new theoretical language that blends the sexual order with an extensive range of institutions and social ideology. Whereas the concepts and themes of social theory have asserted a heteronormative understanding of society, the new queer engagement will challenge it.

For Warner, the intersections of race and class boundaries must be included in this new delineation of queer studies. Highly aware that the constraints within Gay and Lesbian Studies have been "little understood outside of queer circles" (xi), he maintains that treating the homosexually oriented as a homogenous group simplifies political interest in its members. Continuously interacting with broad social institutions, queers ought to connect to wider demands for justice and freedom. It is important that the new queer commitment does not only revise prior social-theoretical flaws, but also recognizes cultural differences and builds new paths of practical queer reflection within the political terrain of daily life.

Warner develops an impressive list of social-based ideologies that must thus be revisited: notions of gender, the family, individual freedom, public speech, consumption and desire, nature and culture, racial and national fantasy, class identity, intimate life and social display, and deep cultural norms about the bearing of the body. He asserts that "[q]ueers do a kind of practical social reflection just in finding ways of being queer" (xiii), thereby suggesting that they are uniquely poised to redefine such categories thanks to their own life experiences. For the Transcultural Queer, it could be added, these issues are often compounded by the power dynamics of cultural exchange, which mean that each question must be negotiated with historical and political concerns from the international arena in mind, as well.

Utilizing Sedgwick's analysis on "homosociality"[14] as a point of departure for his argument, Warner notes the interaction of class identity and male domination within the queer social environment. He agrees with the developing multicultural critique that presupposes that queer theory continues to evolve based on a foundation established from dominant positions: "whites, males, and middle-class activists of the United States" (xvi). He goes on to explain that the predominance of such men in gay organizing is not a result of deliberate personal discrimination or intentional exclusion, but rather the specificity of the gay movement in relationship to racial or ethnic minority movements. Whereas the latter are based on "nonmarket forms of association" (xvii) like churches, relationships, and traditional places of residence, the former have been "market-mediated" by bars, discos, phone lines, resorts, and urban commercial districts. Hence, such a highly economic structural environment means that the so-called institutions of queer culture (ibid.) have been controlled by those with capital. In his attempt to provide some solution to such an elitist perspective, Warner proposes an "alliance politics": He recognizes that because queer politics do not adhere to the member/nonmember logics of race and ethnicity, there exists an "unresolved dissonance" for queers who also identify with an ethnic minority (ibid.). Consequently, political desire becomes ethnicized when queer subjects deal with the daily intersections of race, class, and dissident sexualities.

Michael Warner's sense of queer practicality indirectly advocates for the creation of a transcultural queer discourse. He points out that there are globalizing arguments about minority interests, just as there are localizing arguments about "quasi-universal interests" (xviii), both of which equally affect queers and heterosexuals by their oppressiveness. Between these ends of the spectrum is what he calls the "the problem of the international sexual politics" (xiii). According to him, as non-Western gay activists become more involved in advancing their own political agendas and as the discourse of human rights is extended to more internationally diversified contexts, Anglo-American queer theorists will have to pay increasing attention to the globalizing tendencies of their social-theoretical languages.

Warner's observations, undoubtedly, become the reverberating appeal for the examination of cultural and racial specificities within transcultural contexts. They point out exactly why a focus on homoerotic encounters with the French Other may serve to broaden our perspective of queer identities and deepen our understanding of their intersections with class and race. As the quintessential white male of the Francophone world, the French Other symbolically represents a dominant partner by worldwide economic and symbolic standards, particularly when he pairs with men from the southern hemisphere. Their interactions in fiction necessarily call for a new engagement with not one, but at least two heteronormative cultural contexts, acting with and against each other.

TRANSCULTURATION

In order to describe the interactions between the French Other and Latin American or North African protagonists, it is especially helpful to borrow the term transculturation as defined by Cuban poet Nancy Morejón in *Nación y Mestizaje en Nicolás Guillén* (1982).[15] She claims that *transculturación* is a constant interaction between two or more cultural components, whose unconscious end—a transmutation—entails the creation of a third cultural entity. This new and independent culture builds on its preceding elements through the process of cultural exchange, where no particular element necessarily imposes itself on another, but each modifies into the other (23). The reciprocal influence here is crucial. Critic Alan West-Durán observes in "Nancy Morejón: Transculturation, Translation, and The Poetics of the Caribbean" (2005) that transculturation "is a form of historical and cultural translation that ingeniously fashions a poetics of historical understanding" (967).[16] Under conditions of brutal difficulty, transculturation is a practice of cultural creativity, a performative philosophical analysis, and an act of social resistance. For West-Durán, the Caribbean (and, more particularly, Cuba) has created plural, sometimes contradictory identities, as well as new ways of acting, thanks to transculturation. He notes that the cultural encounters between Spain and the New World have resulted in a history of brutal conquest, but also creative resistance, which, in turn, has produced communities with a distinctive sensitivity to the influence of politics on the flow of everyday lives.

In this sense, transculturation produces an asymmetry of power relations, which he summarizes as follows:

> Colonial imposition (conquest, slavery, racialist domination), obligatory assimilation, genocide, political cooptation, passive resistance (theft, sabotage, feigning sickness, illegal trade), political subterfuge, tricksterism, and outright rebellion. From the point of view of subjugated peoples, the cultural response can involve mimicry, commercial exploitation, top-down appropriation, and bottom-up subversion (irony, parody, pastiche, carnival, open revolt). (968)

Because transculturation is not a smooth or peaceful process, it can be interrupted, unfold uncertainly, remain incomplete, or simply fail. It also supposes that identity evolves continuously, often over historical periods; likewise, it occurs in a series of different spaces, "public and private, practical and cultural, leisure and work-related" (969). Further, transculturation relates to "material practices: to commodities, objects, and the physical construction of tools, products, images, ideas, and symbols," as well as the "material dimensions of the workplace, home, school, street corner, bar, and club" (ibid.). Although it also has a racial dimension, its ultimate implications go beyond race, as Nancy Morejón declares in the following interview: "I think all Cubans, all those who live here and belong to different races, have an obligation to confront this problem [of racism], whatever color we are, because it is a problem of nationhood" (167).[17] Morejón's take on the racial question, indeed, relies on her clear understanding of the predominant racial *mestizaje* (miscegenation) prevalent not only in Cuba and the Caribbean, but also in most of Latin America.

Although transculturation is not an entirely perfect process, it can still be considered successful when it does not act as a translation that simply repeats an original in another language or culture—but when it becomes an active and resistant force as powerful as creative cultural production. In fact, West-Durán suggests that transculturation will "betray" the original just as translation questions and negotiates Eurocentric domination (973). Further, transculturation implicates listening, being open and emotionally involved with the Other. It becomes "an ingenious form of racial, historical, musical, culinary, and cultural translation, truly and extraordinary philosophical endeavor that epitomizes the openness of listening" (ibid.). Since it exemplifies a philosophy of listening, it disqualifies itself from passivity. That is, it becomes an "active engaged attentiveness that is central to a dialogical ethics and understanding" (974). Consequently, transculturation implies "an unfinished subject, something constantly evolving, changing, adding new elements, a witnessing of new births out of old elements" (ibid.).

Similarly, in "'Logiques métisses': Cultural Appropriation and Postcolonial Representations" (1993), Françoise Lionnet coins the term "*métissage*," which she defines as the process of "forms and identities that is the result of cross-cultural encounters, and that forms the basis for their self-portrayals and their representations of cultural diversity" (104).[18] Lionnet suggests that Francophone women writers delineate the complex interweaving of traditions in a circulation of cultures, where characters manifest a "universal appeal, letting them live their *métissage* in the most original, ingenious, and beneficial ways" (108). She observes that earlier generations of Francophone authors depicted estranging contact between cultures, resulting in a colonized or victim mentality. However, when referring to writers like Maryse Condé, Assia Djebar, and Leila Sebbar, she remarks that they exemplify a dynamic and creative process that is "mobilized by subgroups as means of resistance to the 'victim' syndrome" (109). Lionnet adds that these writers also "use their transformative and performative energies on the language and narrative strategies they borrow from the cultures of the West [in order to] represent their regional cultural realities" (ibid.). They employ techniques that interlace traditions and languages, portraying characters that transform how they perceive their own worlds as well as how the reader, as an outsider, interprets their realities. As a result, Lionnet suggests, the radical realm of the Other will no longer "alienate itself through contact with the West, but rather [portray] a microcosm of the globe" (ibid.).

In this sense, transculturation operates not only as a central theme, but also as a set of narrative strategies in the works that will be examined in my project. Yet, the plays and novels selected for analysis span multiple time periods and mentalities, meaning that they evidence varying degrees of estrangement or transformative contact between cultures. This cross-section of literary production from Latin America and North Africa allows me to concentrate on the more or less successful ways in which characters grapple with historical understanding and regional cultural realities to create a new sense of queer identity. In many ways, the choice to bring together these two regions of the globe also draw inspiration from more recent theoretical lines of inquiry suggested by Françoise Lionnet and Shu-mei Shih in *Minor Transnationalism* (2005).[19] They stress the potential for transnational spaces of exchange, where hybrid cultures can be created without the intervention of the center. I borrow their emphasis on transversal movements of cultures that produce new forms of identification, as well as the recurrent intersections with the local, cultural, and ethnic boundaries that produce new expressions in unanticipated places (8).

Lionnet and Shih make evident that "vertical models of resistance" obstruct "interethnic solidarity and international minority alliances" (4), thus rendering invisible "horizontal communication amongst minorities" (7). According to them, binary model of the global and the local lacks acknowledgment of the "creative interventions that networks of minoritized cultures produce within and across national boundaries" (ibid.). Within this perspective, queer subjectivities could well be interpreted as belonging to a "minoritized culture" where various spaces of contact—physical or virtual, creative or damaging—must constantly be reinvented to account for the needs and desires of those who would otherwise lie on the margins of society due to their sexual preferences or activities. More particularly, as Lionnet and Shih take on questions of authenticity from minorities living within and beyond nation states, they foreground a politics of retrieval as well as a politics of inclusion and exclusion. On the one hand, they claim that a politics of retrieval "allows subaltern groups to reclaim lost and suppressed cultural identifications" (9); and, on the other, they note that a politics of inclusion and exclusion restrains the peculiarities within any given minority group "in the interest of forming a culturally unified front against domination" (10). Such a possibility for this "horizontal approach" (11) allows for productive comparisons that "engage with multiple linguistic formations" (ibid.), a notion that informs the analysis of both Spanish- and French-language literatures here.

There is indeed much shared in common by the racialized and homosexual bodies. Just as "interior exclusion" causes an ambivalence of identification and sense of belonging on the minority who fluctuates between "what the national means and how citizenship is defined" (12), so, too, Warner has shown the political ambivalence experienced by members of the queer community. In addition, the transnational phenomena of migration and travel between the West and the non-West, as well as between the North and the South, often have an especially strong presence in queer communities. Lionnet and Shih expressly note that "the multidirectional travels by the other" have not been sufficiently explored (13), to which it might be added that they take on a doubly important and complicated role when this other engages in homosexual encounters. Additionally, racialized and homosexual bodies are each conceived as a "border subject" when entering the West or the North. As such, the "transnational minority experience" exemplifies the fragmented consciousness of individuals "for whom the private and the public ... the real and the fictional are closely intertwined," displaying postmodern narratives and tendencies that involve "absence and incoherence" (16).

Finally, the "semiosphere," taken from the Lotmanian model of semiotics that forms the framework for Chapters 2 and 3, suggests that the borderline separating the inside from the outside can also be thought of as the line that "both separates and unites the two spaces" (19). Such an understanding of space leads to an infinite multiplicity of possibilities: When delineated within the configuration of the so-called authentic national space, it depicts a "paradoxical view of minority culture as the site of both abjection and incorporation" (ibid.). Because this conceptualization of national culture produces an outside (with exclusion and abjection) as well as an inside (with assimilation and incorporation), it also "puts into question the very marginality of what this space [represents]" (20) for the national imaginary.

All of the chapters in my book indeed reflect the idea that homosexual agency and social identity formation emerge in unexpected places that are marginal in appearance only: The heteronormative society in the second chapter forces the effeminate male body outside and into the French space; the third analyzes how the *garconnière* in Buenos Aires allows for homosexual permissiveness, where the characters live out their fantasies; the fourth chapter studies the agency potential for the exoticized sixteen-year-old Moroccan boy; the fifth looks at an adolescent's fascination with the French muscled body and how it compensates for his lack of professional training as a tourist guide in Morocco; and the sixth and seventh chapters examine how another young man's experiences with a photograph and French television programming in Morocco produce an increasing homoerotic desire that he acts on by willfully creating his own hybrid space in society. Hence, Lionnet and Shih's conceptualization of minor transnationalism—for instance, viewed as the increasingly scattered practices in the nonspaces of boundaries and borders—can serve as a comprehensive and insightful impetus to trace interdisciplinary dialogues on multiple fronts. It can effectively frame questions of ethnicity, class, age, and gender across geographical-national boundaries in the discipline of queer studies, providing new insights into the queer states-of-being-and-feeling in areas like Latin America and North Africa that have long demonstrated minority status for historical reasons.

HOMOSEXUAL TOURISM

Although this project departs from the French cultural and literary context to concentrate on regions in the global South it must recognize the *decentered* presence of France as an imagined space in cultural production from Latin America and North Africa. In this respect, my goal is to reverse the dominant paradigm of the formerly colonized subject who becomes a transnational object in the European culture. While Chapters 2 and 3 indeed examine the travels of a Latin American abroad, Chapters 4–6 look at Frenchmen and French influences at home in North Africa. In these encounters, the local boys are not "foreigners," but rather viewing (and desiring or rejecting) the imagined sexuality of the French from within their own cultures.

In the treatment of what I call the homoerotic encounter with the Other, Jarrod Hayes's chapter entitled "Rading and Tourism: Sexual Approaches to the Maghreb" (2000) in *Queer Nations*[20] enlightens my methodological approach. In his essay, he acknowledges Said's assertion that the Orient exerts sexual attraction on many Westerners, which therefore locates sexual tourism in the context of Orientalist discourses "that often reinforced colonial hegemonies" (23). Once considered a "standard commodity within the context of post/colonialism," Oriental sex becomes available to the mass culture. As such, readers and writers need not necessarily travel to the Orient, for they can also find it at home. As Hayes observes, the diasporas of former colonized peoples into European countries allow Westerners to "find spaces where they can be sexual tourists in their own countries" (24). As a perfect example, he mentions the French cliché which says that if one wishes "to pick up (for pay or not)" a *petit Arabe*, you simply go to the Bois de Boulogne in Paris—and not to North Africa. Because accessibility to "Orient sex" also comes through reading fiction, Hayes points out to the "exotic qualities" in Arabic texts since they are commonly "known for their queer-ness" (26). Thus, he cautions readers not to get trapped in reinforcing colonialism.

In other words, any analysis of Maghrebian literature that aspires to be concerned about representations of nonnormative sexualities also bears the burden of remembering colonialism. For Hayes, this is espe-cially the case in the recurrent criticism that tropes homosexual tour-ism "as essentially exploitative" (ibid.). His insightful observation warns not only against the colonialist implications of sexual tourism but also against conservative assumptions about sexuality in scholarly criticism. In fact, he reveals the double bind that most critiques of homosexual tour-ism are inclined to conceal: "the collaboration between colonialism and compulsory heterosexuality" (27). In addition, Hayes's historical literary account of Orientalism also specifically treats Western sexual repression at home and tourism abroad. He pulls away from the abused Foucauldian discourse that applies knowledge and power to Said's Orientalism, which seems to emphasize an assumed connection between knowing the Orient and having power over it, as well as the sexual implications of colonial penetration. As Hayes succinctly puts it, "[the] Orientalist penetrates/ understands the Orient" (28). He observes that the heterosexualized paradigm of female penetration is also overlooked the existing differences between dominant and marginalized Western sexualities. Simply put, sex-ual exile from the repression of the home culture pushes the homosexual to search for sexual fulfillment abroad, likely to occur in exploitative, sen-timental, and racist forms, reinforcing the paradigm of colonialization.

Hayes of course points out that homosexual tourism has a long and well-documented history. Particularly, in the late nineteenth and early twentieth centuries, Western heterosexuality appropriated Oriental homosex. While conforming to normativity at home, tourists would engage in homosex in the Orient, where they could escape from jeop-ardizing "their heterosexual privilege" (30). Borrowing Rudi C. Bleys's concept of the "ethnographic gaze," Hayes points out that the so-called heterosexual Western tourist is able to explore homosex without risking the heterosexuality of his "gender core" (to use Butler's term), since this gaze provides the opportunity to construct mechanisms of "male homo-erotic tenor without becoming a suspect" (31). Since these experiences occur while traveling, there also exists a "lack of guilt" which Hayes interprets as "unchallenging" to heterosexual privilege; confidently, he believes that until the turn of the twentieth century, the French imaginary considered Oriental homosex to play a "heterosexual role in Oriental discourse" (ibid.). In contrast, the characters analyzed in this study are often overcome by guilt or must find (narrative as well as thematic) strategies to overcome it.

Hayes provides a literary analysis of the several "heterosexual" French writers who explore or show a homosexual experience in the "Orient" in their work; for instance, Flaubert's traveling homosexual experience with the Egyptian boy who served as a "model for Salammbo's dance and for Salomé's in 'Hérodias'" (30) as well as Balzac's lesbian drama in the Orientalized *harem* in Paris in *La fille aux yeux d'or* (1835). The latter novel encompasses not only the Western heterosexual fantasies, but also the polysexuality of the Orient—from female homosexuality to other vices, including male homosexuality. Above all, such an Oriental space in the French capital offered permission to bring homo/sexual tourism home. In opposition, other countries rarely authorized the creation of such a foreign space within their own boundaries, or did so on different terms.

What is perhaps surprising is that a similar process occurs in the early twentieth-century Latin American imaginary. It borrows what I would call Frenchness in order to invent a space where sexual deviance can also conform to the demands of heterosexual normativity. In essence, there exists a type of parallelism: Orientalism for the French corresponds to Frenchness for the Ibero-American imaginary. However, little attention has been devoted to this subject. The exploration on the cultural and intellectual exchange between France and Latin America has yet to obtain serious momentum, and still less attention has been paid to the homosexual representation of Frenchness that I examine here in the Latin American narrative.

For these reasons, Chapters 2 and 3 look at the Latin American imaginary in relation to French space. Building on the intuition that French cultural space is shaped as the Other—and, more particularly, the sexually deviant Other—I analyze Alfonso Hernández-Catá's *El ángel de Sodoma* (1928) in this chapter and José González Castillo's *Los Invertidos* (1914) in Chapter 3. I argue that the nationalist impetus of these narratives uses the idea of exclusion of the Other in order to prohibit marginalized sexualities. Lotman's model of semiotic analysis of culture enables me to show that the main characters are boundary figures; as such, they are placed both inside and outside of national culture, and thus they experience inclusion and exclusion simultaneously. Simply put, the French cultural space seems untouched from traditional Ibero-American norms due to the fact that it harbors homosexuality. Whether the boundary figure walks across Buenos Aires to the French-inspired *garçonnière*, or crosses the Pyrenees to the city of Paris, the "degenerate" physical or imaginary space cannot fully counter the Ibero-American language and values from which these boundary figures are trying to break away.

The parallel idea of escaping the (home) country in search of homosexual realization is further explored in my next two chapters. This time, it is Frenchmen who travel to North Africa in search of homoerotic adventures with local boys. After setting historical context with André Gide's *L'immoraliste* (1902), I analyze Mohamed Choukri's *Le pain nu* (1980) in Chapter 4, as well as Rachid O.'s narratives *Chocolat Chaud* (1998) and *Ce qui reste* (2003) in Chapter 5. Although I treat homosexual tourism as a cross-cultural encounter between French homosexual tourists and local Moroccan boys, my analysis takes most interest in the boys' perspective. I follow a progression of sexual tourism for these boys, from *métier* to *façon d'être*, which allows me to highlight how their own understanding of class and ethnic differences evolves throughout the narratives. This process therefore reveals points of resistance that show potential for the boys' agency and subject formation, where they use their bodies as tools to advance professionally and to compensate for their economic disadvantages on a local as well as global scale.

Moving beyond the question of travel, immigration, and physical border-crossings, Chapters 6 and 7 specifically analyze transcultural information and media technology that produce imaginative growth in the Moroccan protagonist of *Chocolat chaud*, as well as one of Rachid O.'s earlier works, *L'enfant ébloui* (1995). Beginning with Rachid's first contact with the photographed image of a blond-haired, blue-eyed French boy, Chapter 6 studies his intimate moments within the collective setting to illustrate how he manipulates Moroccan social codes to engage in a self-invented form of homosexual awakening through a transcultural encounter. Chapter 7 develops the idea that the initial feelings and affect produced by the first contact with the photograph grow thanks to French televised programming, and eventually materialize into a real encounter with a blond-haired, blue-eyed boy in the soccer field in Morocco.[21]

Together, these analyses show that the transcultural encounters with Frenchmen by those from Latin America and North Africa result in adolescent males using the concept of Frenchness as explicit or tacit permission for sexual experimentation outside of heteronormativity. Perhaps the success of French Orientalism and Indigenism paradoxically left the legacy of Frenchness as a space of sexual liberation in postcolonial societies. Rather than occupy the position of the primitive Other, Latin Americans and North Africans can now look on France as a space that is sexually accessible and on Frenchness as an ideal that corresponds not to economic or political necessity, but to sexual choice.

NOTES

1. *"Garçonnière"* is per definition a male bachelor's apartment in France or its former colonies. This predominantly masculine space has been represented in French literary texts such as Marguerite Duras's *L'Amant* (Paris: Minuit, 1984). However, as I thoroughly elaborate on Chapter 3, my book treats the *garçonnière* as a space which allows for homosexual permissiveness in Buenos Aires, Argentina.

2. I will be referring to terms such as *homosexual* and *queer* interchangeably due to the complex range of sexual practices and identities from the global South analyzed in this book. However, my work uses *queer* in its title and in its methodological approach because its elasticity creates different possibilities, opens up new contexts, and transgresses preconceived scopes of inquiry—as it first did when it came to existence in the 1990s.

3. I use "Hexagon" as synonym for metropolitan France.

4. By "Frenchness" I mean "anything" related to France, be it imaginary or real: literature, culture, or language.

5. Julian Vigo, *Performative Bodies, Hybrid Tongues: Race, Gender, Sex and Modernity in Latin America and the Maghreb* (Bern, Switzerland: Peter Lang AG, 2010).

6. Edward Said, *Orientalism* (New York: Vintage Books, 1979).

7. Eric Anceau, "Napoleon III and Abd El-Kader," in http://www.napoleon.org/en/reading_room/articles/files/471391.

8. Jay Sexton, *The Monroe Doctrine: Empire and Nation in Nineteenth Century America* (New York: Hill & Wang, 2011).

9. Françoise Lionnet, "National Language Departments in the Era of Transnational Studies," *PMLA* 117, no. 5 (October 2002): 1252–1254.

10. Indigenism has been defined in self-contradictory ways by scholars in the field of this specialization, Notably, Alcida Rita Ramos, uses "indigenism" to refer to Indigenous peoples' political claims, which relate to state control, anthropological study, urban issues, etc. (Rita Alcida Ramos, *Indigenism: Ethnic politics in Brazil.* Madison: University of

Wisconsin Press, 1998), 7. However, Indigenism has also been used to describe the essentialization and imagined accuracy of ideas about indigeneity, much in the same way that Orientalism refers to essentialized and supposedly accurate notions of the Orient, despite their imaginary nature. Here, the two terms are intended to pertain to parallel phenomenon by which the Other is seemingly circumscribed and described in European eyes; however, this usage is in no way intended to preclude an appropriation of either term in order to advance the political and sociological goals of those most concerned.

11. Judith Butler, *Gender Trouble* (New York: Routledge, 1990).
12. Rosalyn Diprose, *The Bodies of Women: Ethics, Embodiment, and Sexual Difference* (New York: Routledge, 1994).
13. Michael Warner, "Introduction," in *Fear of a Queer Planet: Queer Politics and Social Theory* (Minneapolis: University of Minnesota Press, 1993).
14. For a full analysis on this concept, see Eve Kosofsky Sedgwick, *Between Men: English Literature and Male Homosocial Desire* (New York: Columbia University Press, 1985).
15. Nancy Morejón, *Nación y mestizaje en Nicolás Guillén* (La Habana, Cuba: UNEAC, 1982).
16. Alan West-Durán, "Nancy Morejón: Trasculturation, Translation, and the Poetics of the Caribbean," *Callaloo* 28, no. 4 (Autumn 2005): 967–976.
17. Gustavo Pérez-Firmat, *The Cuban Condition: Translation and Identity in Modern Cuban Literature* (New York: Cambridge University Press, 1989).
18. Françoise Lionnet, "'Logiques métisses': Cultural Appropriation and Postcolonial Representations," *College Literature* 19–20, no. 3-1 (October 1992–February 1993): 100–120.
19. Françoise Lionnet and Shu-mei Shih, "Introduction: Thinking Through the Minor, Transnationally," in *Minor Transnationalism*, eds. Françoise Lionnet and Shu-mei Shih (Durham and London: Duke University Press, 2005), 1–23.
20. Jarrod Hayes, "Reading and Tourism: Sexual Approaches to the Magreb," in *Queer Nations: Marginal Sexualities in the Maghreb* (Chicago: University of Chicago Press, 2000).
21. All the translations in this book are my own.

References

Anceau, Eric. "Napoleon III and Abd El-Kader." http://www.napoleon.org/en/reading_room/articles/files/471391.
Butler, Judith. *Gender Trouble*. New York: Routledge, 1990.
Diprose, Rosalyn. *The Bodies of Women: Ethics, Embodiment, and Sexual Difference*. New York: Routledge, 1994.

González Castillo, José. *Los Invertidos*. Buenos Aires: Editores Puntosur, 1914.

Hayes, Jarrod. "Reading and Tourism: Sexual Approaches to the Maghreb." In *Queer Nations: Marginal Sexualities in the Maghreb*, 23–49. Chicago: The University of Chicago Press, 2000.

Lionnet, Françoise. "National Language Departments in the Era of Transnational Studies." *PMLA* 117, no. 5 (October 2002): 1252–1254.

———. "'Logiques métisses': Cultural Appropriation and Postcolonial Representations." *College Literature* 19–20, no. 3-1 (October 1992–February 1993): 100–120.

Lionnet, Françoise, and Shu-mei Shih. "Introduction: Thinking Through the Minor, Transnationally." In *Minor Transnationalism*, edited by Françoise Lionnet and Shu-mei Shih, 1–23. Durham and London: Duke University Press, 2005.

Morejón, Nancy. *Nación y mestizaje en Nicolás Guillén*. La Habana, Cuba: UNEAC, 1982.

Pérez-Firmat, Gustavo. *The Cuban Condition: Translation and Identity in Modern Cuban Literature*. New York: Cambridge University Press, 1989.

Ramos, Alcida Rita. *Indigenism: Ethnic Politics in Brazil*. Madison: University of Wisconsin Press, 1998.

Said, Edward. *Orientalism*. New York: Vintage Books, 1979.

Sedgwick, Eve Kosofsky. *Between Men: English Literature and Male Homosocial Desire*. New York: Columbia University Press, 1985.

Sexton, Jay. *The Monroe Doctrine: Empire and Nation in Nineteenth Century America*. New York: Hill & Wang, 2011.

Vigo, Julian. *Performative Bodies, Hybrid Tongues: Race, Gender, Sex and Modernity in Latin America and the Maghreb*. Bern, Switzerland: Peter Lang AG, 2010.

Warner, Michael. "Introduction." In *Fear of a Queer Planet: Queer Politics and Social Theory*, edited by Michael Warner, vii–xxxi. Minneapolis: University of Minnesota Press, 1993.

West-Durán, Alan. "Nancy Morejón: Transculturation, Translation, and the Poetics of the Caribbean." *Callaloo* 28, no. 4 (Autumn 2005): 967–976.

PART I

Frenchness in the Latin American Imaginary

Frenchness: Boundary Figures and Figuring Boundaries in Alfonso Hernández-Catá's *El ángel de Sodoma*

Frenchness as a homoerotic representation is part of the Hispano-American[1] imaginary at the beginning of the twentieth century, as shown in Alfonso Hernández-Catá's *El ángel de Sodoma*[2] (*The Angel of Sodom,* 1928). *El ángel de Sodoma* is a novel that follows the family life of José-María, the oldest brother who, by assuming a motherly role, cares for his three younger siblings, their story taking place in "some city with no name" in Spain. I use Yuri Lotman's notion of semiospheric boundary and its paradoxical double-functionality to establish the main character as a boundary figure, since he is both inside and outside of national culture. I argue that Alfonso Hernández-Catá creates a spatial system where the private and the public merge in order to form a transnational territory. In this narrative, the public is private and the private is public. With no privacy or space for othered bodies or marginalized sexualities in this Ibero-American nation, this novel refers to the dangerous contact with the Other, particularly the French, as homosexually threatening. In what follows, I explore how writer Hernández-Catá seems to use the notion of exclusion of the Other to participate in the nation-building process Latin America undergoes during this period. Here, I align my thought with that of Emilio Bejelin *Gay Cuban Nation* (2001), where he suggests that the homosexual body participates by exclusion in "defining the nation to which it does not belong" (4).[3] I would take a step further and say that the homosexual subject is not only excluded from national culture, but specifically placed within the French cultural space.

© The Author(s) 2019
L. Navarro-Ayala, *Queering Transcultural Encounters,*
Palgrave Studies in Globalization and Embodiment,
https://doi.org/10.1007/978-3-319-92315-4_2

The first section, "Lotman's semiospheric boundary," focuses on the theoretical framework in relation to the Lotmanian organization of space: private/public, inside/outside, center/periphery, multilevel paradigm, and membrane-line behavior. It begins with the notion of the boundary's ambivalent characteristic—whose double-functionality both separates and unites two semiotic spaces—and transforms into a configuration that shows a membrane-like behavior allowing for the continuous interaction of multiple paradigmatic levels.

"The Hispano-Cuban Context: Alfonso Hernández-Catá's *El ángel de Sodoma*" section explores the ways in which the writer blurs the dividing lines between semiotic spaces throughout the novel. I situate the Vélez-Gomara family's house at the center of the narrative's nationalist matrix, with manifold layers superimposed on each other: on the one hand, the geographical location of the house in relation to the city and the sea; on the other, the semiotic configuration of the main character, José-María, in relation to the house, the city, the harbor, and the presumed outside world. The Lotmanian organization of space is essential to identifying these spaces and their boundaries in order to develop the main character's homosexual awakening. However, this process also involves broader questions of gender and identity.

The third section, "Frenchness in the Latin American Imaginary," returns to questions concerning the representation of French space. Within this context, Hernández-Catá uses the French capital, Paris, as the center for sexual degeneracy. Here, I show how the narrative conceals the main character's homosexual desires until he finds himself inside the French space. Given his status as boundary figure, he is pushed from the periphery of national culture, expelled out of the Ibero-American matrix, and obliged to take refuge within the French space. This process illustrates how nationality and sexuality intersect in this work as semiotic values, since the alignment of Frenchness with sexual degeneracy does not correspond to the heteronormative Latin American imaginary.

LOTMAN'S SEMIOSPHERIC BOUNDARY

Yuri Lotman's conception of the semiotic analysis of culture is a useful way of understanding the points which frame Chapters 2 and 3 in this book. The following section seeks above all to explain Yuri Lotman's conceptualization of the semiosphere. I would like to begin by borrowing the following quotation from Lotman's book, *Universe of the Mind* (1990): "The notion of boundary is an ambivalent one: it both separates and unites.

It is always the boundary of something and so belongs to both frontier cultures, to both contiguous semiospheres" (137).[4] As critic Seiji M. Lippit has observed in "The Double Logic of Minor Spaces" (2005), the boundary serves a "double function" for it exists both inside and outside within the Lotmanian organization of space (283).[5] Lippit's conceptualization of the double-functionality aptly summarizes the boundary's ambivalence since, in Lotman's words, "one of [the boundaries'] sides is always turned to the outside" (142). As a semiotic space, the Lotmanian notion of culture identifies one of the boundary's primary mechanisms as "the place where what is 'external' is transformed into what is 'internal'" (136–137).

For Lotman, the notion of the boundary separating the internal space of the semiosphere from the external is not only a rough primary distinction but also the most basic device of semiotic demarcation. In fact, the proper object of investigation for the semiotician of culture begins by dividing the world into "its own" internal space and "their" external space. Jonathan H. Bolton's essay "Writing in a Polluted Semiosphere" (2006) declares that the Lotmanian dividing line, "of course, need not be a particular geographical location such as the border territory between two countries. Lotman defines it more broadly as the 'boundary' between semiotic systems, where people feel a difference between first- and third-person forms, the space between 'my (or our) world' and 'their world'" (325–326).[6] The semiosphere's periphery can be defined as the location where the center's grammar begins to unravel, where it is felt as something foreign and imposed rather than "my own." Lotman comments, "One of the main primary mechanisms of semiotic individuation is the boundary, and the boundary can be defined as the outer limit of a first-person form" (131). He continues, "This space is 'ours,' 'my own,' it is 'cultured,' 'safe,' 'harmoniously organized,' and so on. By contrast, 'their space' is 'other,' 'hostile,' 'dangerous,' 'chaotic'" (ibid.). Within this context, Edna Andrews agrees in *Conversations with Lotman* (2003), "the most external of semiospheric boundaries differentiates the cultural 'we' from all 'others,' regardless of the nature of the space of the 'other'" (46). Lotman offers many examples of how cultures construct everything external as chaotic, evil, and primitive. Correspondingly, Edna Andrews considers that even if we were to imagine that there was no space beyond the semiotic space, "Lotman's conception of the semiosphere nonetheless would require the construction of a chaotic external field" (33). Although these multiple and diverse external spaces are constantly being created and destroyed, they all have the same objective, regardless of the specificities of such definitions: to differentiate the internal space of the semiosphere.

CENTER *VIS-À-VIS* PERIPHERY

Besides the primary distinction between internal versus external space, it is also crucial for my study to bring to the fore the semiospheric constitution of the binary system center/periphery.[7] Lotman declares, "the entire space of the semiosphere ... creates a multi-level system" (138). Considering this citation, it seems especially important to consider the essay "Characteristics and Origins of the Semiosphere" (2003) by Edna Andrews, who argues that according to Lotman, the laws of the semiosphere are binary "and the notion of this binarism and the degree of its application are central issues distinguishing different trends in semiotic theory" (44).[8] Andrews's emphasis on Lotman's law of the semiosphere points to important differences between the center and periphery. Distinctions are also crucial for this chapter? In my attempt to answer the question of the duality center/periphery and its relevance to my study in Chapters 2 and 3, I would like to explore some of the characteristics of the center/periphery dyad as discussed by Lotman.

The first characteristic in the relationship between the center and the periphery is the notion of "asymmetry." The Lotmanian model creates an asymmetric structure in the semiosphere when it evaluates the center as the source of the most developed and structurally organized languages, resulting in an uneven relationship between center and periphery. Along similar lines, no language operates unless it is immersed in the semiosphere; no semiosphere exists without the natural language as its organizing core, although it always remains in continuous fluctuation (Lotman, 127–128). Furthermore, the intrinsic asymmetry of all semiotic space is essential because it creates opportunities for perturbations to the system that inspire change. In this manner, asymmetry acts as the driving force of what Lotman refers to "semiotic dynamism" (134). Finally, Edna Andrews adds that this "dynamicity of the semiotic space" also "proceeds in time and space in a non-linear mode characterized by periods of continuity and explosion" (44).

CENTER: SELF-DESCRIPTION AND METALANGUAGE

The second important characteristic within the dyad center/periphery is self-description, or the development of a metalanguage,[9] which Lotman considers to be the "highest form and final act of a semiotic system's structural organization" (128). This stage happens when grammars are written as well as when customs and laws are codified. According to Edna Andrews, self-description is essential to avoid the dissolution of the semiosphere, since it guarantees that the "code becomes dominant at each of the levels provided as soon as it enters the system" (34). Lotman claims that self-description occurs whether we have in mind language, politics, or culture; for him, the mechanism is the same: "one part of the semiosphere (as a rule one which is part of its nuclear structure) in the process of self-description creates its own grammar;... [t]hen it strives to extend these norms over the whole semiosphere" (128). Thus, metalanguage is placed at the center of the semiotic space of culture.

A partial grammar of one cultural dialect—or, if I may add, one political agenda—may become the metalanguage describing culture by way of its extension into multiple domains. In this manner, a literature of norms and instructions comes into being "in which the later historian will tend to see an actual picture of real life of that epoch, its semiotic practice" (128). This practice is what Lotman refers to as an "illusion" since it is interpreted by contemporaries as persuasive proof that they live in its so-called reality; as a result, they behave in the way prescribed by the metalanguage. Lotman claims, "it will be their reality to the extent that they have accepted the laws of semiotics" (129). As later generations try to reconstruct life from those texts, they likewise come to accept as reality. According to Lotman, if texts generate the norms in the center of the semiosphere, then two chief situations will arise on the periphery: firstly, "the norms, actively invading 'incorrect' practice, will generate 'correct' texts in accord with them" (129); and secondly, entire layers of cultural systems—considered marginal by the prescribed metalanguage—will fail to correspond to the idealized portrait of that culture. They will be declared "non-existent" according to the Lotmanian model of semiotic analysis of culture (129).

Moving Beyond the Binary System: Multiplicity and Membrane-Like Behavior

In addition, it is crucial for the analysis to follow that Lotman chooses not to arrange the semiotic space in terms of binaries alone, moving instead beyond the main center/periphery subdivision. For Yuri Lotman, "semiotic dualism" not only acts as "the minimal form of organization of a working semiotic system" but it must also be "understood as a principle which is realized in plurality since … every living culture has a 'built-in' mechanism for multiplying its languages" (124). Based on Lotman's theory, Seiji M. Lippit maintains that the beginning point for any culture derives from the binary distinction between internal and external space, which exists only as pluralities. Seiji M. Lippit claims that this Lotmanian opposition is typically permeated with specific values, dividing what is "structured and bounded from what is unbounded and heterogeneous" (283). Edna Andrews adds that the semiotic prototype "has proven that well-defined and functionally unambiguous systems never exist in isolation. Rather, they can only become operational and meaningful when perceived as one segment on the continuum of semiotic formations—that is, when they are 'immersed' in semiotic space" (32). What is important to note in Lotman's definition of the semiosphere, as Andrews states, "is that he is shifting away from the level of individual signs and their functions in cultural space toward a higher level of network semiosis and system-level phenomena" (32). Within this context, it could be argued that the entire space of the semiosphere becomes, "transected by boundaries of different levels, boundaries of different languages and even of texts," as Lotman affirms, adding further that "the internal space of each of these sub-semiospheres has its own semiotic 'I'" (138).

How does this system account for the relationships between items that would otherwise remain external to some sub-semiospheres, but that intersect with them due to overlap within these semiotic networks? He proposes the "membrane," defined as "a filtering membrane which so transforms foreign texts that they become part of the semiosphere's internal semiotics while still retaining their own characteristics" (137). According to Lotman, the cultural membrane transforms foreign texts to make them part of the semiosphere's internal semiotics; although they retain their own characteristics (i.e., they remain "foreign"), these texts are absorbed into the semiosphere as "internal" elements, as well. Whereas a biological cell membrane allows for the inflow and outflow of substance, the Lotmanian cultural membrane allows for temporal and spatial coexistence of different cells. Edna Andrews convincingly remarks that the semiospheric boundary resembles a membrane in that it proves "always penetrable … from both directions, internal to external and vice versa. The interplay across these boundaries is inexhaustible" (46). Such an infinite interaction allows for the multiple paradigmatic levels moving and changing spatial dimensions at different rates.

It leads to what Lotman terms the "cultural double."[10] The subject in question may find him or herself in-between two semiotic spaces, at the borderline, facing two distinct cultures, which compose his or her sense of self. In similar fashion, the possibility for intercultural contact corresponds to what critic Amy Mandelker has called a "double-voiced discourse." In her essay, "Lotman's Other" (2006), Mandelker suggests that the "thought about the other ... the need for the *other* (the other person, the other discourse, the other culture)" is a basic condition of existence for Lotman (61).[11] She writes that, rather than providing a reductive system of difference, Lotman adopts an estranged perspective and persistently sees double (ibid.). This idea of "double vision" recalls the initial "double-functionality" of the semiosphere's boundary: its membrane-like behavior not only produces an endless interplay from both directions, but it also allows individuals to experience the ambivalence that both separates and unites semiospheres within the Lotmanian model of culture.

THE HISPANO-CUBAN CONTEXT: ALFONSO HERNÁNDEZ-CATÁ'S *EL ÁNGEL DE SODOMA*[12]

This chapter explores the ways in which Cuban writer Alfonso Hernández-Catá blurs the dividing lines between semiotic spaces throughout his novel *El ángel de Sodoma*. The Lotmanian approach is useful to analyze this work for reasons similar to those that make it pertinent to *Los Invertidos* in Chapter 3. Whereas the text might appear simply to depict sexually deviant behavior in a fictional semiosphere independent from its broader context, the Lotmanian approach shows that this semiosphere intersects with national space, rejecting the main protagonist from the latter. Much like Dr. Florez in Chapter 3, *El ángel de Sodoma*'s main character, José-María Vélez-Gomara, straddles the boundary between what is inside and outside of national culture.

THE VÉLEZ-GOMARA HOUSE IN THE LOTMANIAN MULTILEVEL SYSTEM

I place the Vélez-Gomara family's house at the center of the narrative's nationalistic matrix, with manifold semiotic spaces that overlap with each other, resulting in a blurring of the boundary lines. My analysis seeks to illustrate how the Lotmanian paradox of double-functionality operates in Hernández-Catá's Vélez-Gomara family home.

CENTER/PERIPHERY

This section explores the dyad center/periphery as the first layer in the Lotmanian multilevel system in *El ángel de Sodoma*. From the outset, Hernández-Catá situates the Vélez-Gomara family residence at the center of the narrative, whereas it occupies a peripheral space at the outer edges of the city. As a result, it corresponds to Lotman's paradoxical double-functionality, whereby a single object may be found in two places conceived as distinct and opposite to one another: the center and the periphery.

The description of the house is indeed crucial in relation to the city's geography. Hernández-Catá introduces this space as follows:

> La casa de los Vélez-Gomara [que] era muy antigua y había sido varias veces ilustre por el ímpetu de sus hombres y por la riqueza atesorada bajo su blasón,... mantenía ... el escudo grabado por sus antecesores en piedra, [ya que formaba] el estandarte secular del Ayuntamiento [y] constituía uno de los orgullos de la ciudad. (47–56)

> (The Vélez-Gomara house [which] was very old and had been illustrious on several occasions for the strength of its men and the treasure found under its seal,... kept ... its coat of arms printed on stone, [since it formed] the city hall's insignia [and] constituted one of the prides of the city.) (47–56)[13]

The Vélez-Gomara house is an illustrious building that has lodged impetuous and energetic men. The coat of arms represents not only the Vélez-Gomara family, but also the entire city since it is also part of the city hall's insignia; thus, the identities of the city and of the Vélez-Gomara family are intertwined. This historical relationship of course impacts the eldest son's identity.[14] Given the status of his family as landed aristocracy, José-María seems at first glance to suffer from no lack of reference points to determine his identity. On the contrary, he can find them in multiple sources, the coat of arms working much like a symbolic version of the Lotmanian cultural membrane, which allows for continuous interplay across semiotic spaces, in this case moving between the private and public realms.[15] Here, I would like to stress the significance of the first semiotic phenomenon in Hernández-Catá's novel for it will recur in the remainder of my analysis. In fact, the identity correlation between these two semiotic actors will be fully developed at a later point; for now, what is important for this section is to establish the first multilayered formation in the dyad center/periphery. And since the Vélez-Gomara house's coat of arms corresponds to the city hall's insignia, we could attest that the house represents the city's civic core.

If the Lotmanian cultural model places the center as the source where customs and laws are codified in order to extend them outward, then the Vélez-Gomara family plays a crucial role in the citizens' lives by nature of its role in the city's founding lineage. It is important to stress that the codification of laws and norms, as well as the identity correlation between the city and José-María, are meaningful semiotic constructions whose source of origin lies at the center of the novel *El ángel de Sodoma*. Whereas Dr. Florez contributes by profession to a legal field that condemns his behavior in *Los Invertidos* in Chapter 3, this chapter explores how José-María belongs by blood to the influential family that establishes the exemplary norms rejecting his homosexuality in *El ángel de Sodoma*. Chapter 3 also analyzes how author José González Castillo uses the social relationship between father and son to show how sexual degeneracy might manifest across generations. In contrast, this chapter studies how writer Hernández-Catá focuses on hereditary traits that provide a direct bond determining inclusion and exclusion. He therefore attacks homosexual desire all the more adamantly as unacceptable in the Hispano-Cuban context (based on an essentialist argument), although the semiotic spaces within the novel complicate this reading.

Periphery

Besides having its façade toward the city's center, the Vélez-Gomara house is situated on the city's periphery. The writer continues to describe the house, "Toda de piedra, enclavada en una ciudad prócer, con ventanas abiertas al mar" (Built entirely of rocks, rooted in a city of national character, with windows open to the sea) (48).[16] As this description indicates, the Vélez-Gomara family lives in a fortress-like building, whose founding rocks are of national character. In addition, this structure has also windows that face the sea; thus, it is geographically located on the city's periphery. These windows, "con sus cristales rotos trepidaban nerviosas, participando del estremecimiento aventurero de las campanas, de los trenes, de los buques" (with their broken glasses, would vibrate, nervously, participating in the adventurous shudder of bells, trains, and ships)

(49). Even at such an early stage in the novel, Hernández-Catá introduces the house in a highly ambivalent position—for although it has a strong foundation, its geographical location on the city's periphery causes it to shudder. That is, the Cuban writer seems to warn us that the Vélez-Gomara's home suffers from continuous exposure to what the exterior represents—a threat to not only the house architectural structure, but to the political system placing it at the heart of the city's history.

Of course, the harbor near the home likewise represents a borderline space. The harbor is initially mentioned in *El ángel de Sodoma* when José-María goes there to meet his brother, Jaime, as he returns from Nautical School. The scene reads, "Cuando el buque se reclinó a reposar en el muelle, les devolvió un ser [que] casi había desconocido ... era un Jaime nuevo" (When the ship docked in the harbor, an almost unknown person re-appeared ... it was a new Jaime) (78). Without specifying where Jaime arrives from, the narrative offers one certainty: Because he has been exposed to the outside world, he returns with a new identity, like a stranger to his own family. If the harbor is first associated with feelings of strangeness, it is later transformed into an exotic and dangerously attractive location.

> José-María fue, sin saber por qué, hacia los muelles.... Una orgía de luces entre las cuales ... el negro cielo de tormenta prestaba ... novedad de aventura. Algo de pueril fiesta veneciana habría alegrado su ánimo si un *no sé qué* de turbio, *de neblinoso en los cuerpos y en las intenciones*, no diese a cada paso trémulo sentido de riesgo (124–125, emphasis added)

> (José-María went, unknowingly, to the harbor.... An orgy of lights among which ... the blackened stormy sky seemed to bring ... a new adventure. Something of a childish Venetian carnival brought him happiness as if a blurry *je ne sais quoi*, with *nebulous bodies and intentions*, would not give each trembling step with pleasure approaching to some sort of risk) (124–125, emphasis added)

Inexplicably attracted to the quay, José-María seems taken with its vague charm, as the landscape's sexual appearance begins to tempt him. As he continues to walk on the seashore, he sees,

> tres marineros cogidos por los brazos [que] venían tambaleándose al compás de una canción alcohólica y lúbrica.... José-María se detuvo lleno de un terror infinito y delicioso. El grupo se acercó, cruzó, se alejó,

mientras él, sin aliento, prestó a romperse ... en una medrosa suspensión de casi toda su vida.... Después, en una sola carrera, huyó hasta su casa. (125–126)

(three sailors who were holding each other by their arms and tumbling to the beat of an alcoholic and lewd song.... José-María stopped, filled with an endless but delicious terror. The group approached, crossed, walked away, while he, breathlessly, began to break ... in a fainthearted suspension from his entire life.... Then, in one single race, he rushed home.) (125–126)

Although *El ángel de Sodoma* refers continuously to the main character's homosexual desire, this passage constitutes the sole instance when José-María will witness others overtly displaying homosocial behavior within the city's public space. Although the city seems accustomed to homo-social behavior among sailors, the queer character is shocked by it. He is not only excluded from participating in the interactions among members of this group, but also frightened that such homosocial bonding could reveal his secret desires. As captivating as the three navy young men might be, José-María decides to escape from them by running home. In this manner, the peripheral space represented by the harbor—whose initial strangeness transforms into a lewd landscape—thus eventually turns into an alluring mystery that tries to trap queer José-María.

MULTILEVEL BOUNDARY SYSTEM

The following section continues to explore the Vélez-Gomara family residence. However, its focus shifts to the house as a space in a semiotic network. The first of the semiotic layers I would like to discuss is the house as a refuge for José-María. Escaping from the threat that the three navy men represent, José-María runs home for protection. "[A]l entrar, abrazó y besó a [sus hermanas], con la efusión vital de quien acaba de escapar a un gran peligro. ([U]pon entering, he hugged and kissed [his sisters], in such a vital effusion of someone who has just escaped from a great danger) (128). This search for refuge in the place where he was born and raised makes allusion to Gaston Bachelard's oneiric house in *The Poetics of Space* (1958).[17] The French critic suggests that one of the maternal features of the oneiric house is to protect and to maintain the man "through the storms of the heavens and through those of life"

(6–7). Could we therefore argue that the Vélez-Gomara home is precisely this type of refuge for José-María?

It could indeed be argued that this house plays a maternal role in offering protection to the queer character and his sisters. "Bastábales cerrar la puerta, olvidar un poco ..., aislarse de la ciudad obstinada en gravar su orfandad con excesivas obligaciones de estirpe ... y para conservar aquella dicha niña, reían." (José-María and his sisters would close the doors, forget a little ..., isolate themselves from the obsessed city that seemed to insist in reminding them about the problems ... so that they would maintain that happy child, they would laugh.) (72). Just as the solitude available at home appears to protect the children from the antagonistic city, all that remains outside its confines could also be viewed in Bachelard's terms. He affirms that snow covers all tracks, blurs the road, muffles every sound, and conceals all colors in the outside world of the oneiric house during a storm (40). At first glance, the house seems to provide a shelter from the city, but this feeling of security quickly dissolves as José-María begins to analyze his own situation.

Once at home, apparently safe from the dangers that the city represents, José-María enters into a new and more dangerous semiotic space: his own mind and body. The Vélez-Gomara house then loses its maternal characteristic and turns into a destructive force, or a "non-place," for queer José-María. As Alejandro Mejías-López claims, José-María follows "a fashion typical of other *modernista* characters, as he [José-María] spends hours analyzing himself" (5).[18] Searching to understand his sexual attractions, he asks himself "cien interrogaciones henchidas de asco y de lástima" (a hundred despicable and shameful questions) that would provoke on him "una angustia irrevocable [que le revelaba] un revés repugnante" (an irrevocable anguish [that would reveal] a repugnant inversion) (Hernández-Catá, 96–99). As the house progressively engulfs him in a self-perception of disgrace, José-María embarks upon the following psychological battle of gender construction: "Tendré que modificar esta constitución física mía [con] piel impúber,... de carne y de formas indecisas entre los dos sexos.... [¡]Quitaré de mi nombre aquel María invasor, y seré José, José nada más, para siempre!" (I will have to change this physical constitution of mine [with] childish skin,... of flesh and shapes that are indecisive between the two sexes.... I will eliminate from my name that intrusive María, and will become José, just José, forever!) (101–129). Whereas his family name ties him to the center of the city, his given name leads him astray from social norms. By imagining that he could let a part of his personality drop along with the second half of his given name, José-María demonstrates the conscious will to change an aspect of his identity that follows him wherever he goes—whether at the harbor, or at home.

Realizing that sexual ambiguity is reflected in his own body, José-María initiates a struggle that would not only eliminate all feminine traces but also enhance his masculine qualities. His self-imposed process of gender construction is vividly summarized by Alejandro Mejías-López as follows:

> The novel recounts in painful detail his attempts to erase any trace of femininity and enhance the qualities he—and society—assumes to be signs of the masculine ... he works out every morning until his muscles begin to grow and show; he learns how to smoke and walk with a cane; he sunbathes often and foregoes shaving everyday in order to have a "rougher" look; he wears less fine clothes; and ... yet, after all that work, José-María then decides to look for the "cure" for sex in sex itself. He goes to a brothel and, when that fails to work, he convinces himself that a conventional marital path (having a girlfriend, getting married, and having children) will "save" him. After dating Cecilia for some time, he realizes his mistake and ends their relationship. (6)

Since the expected heteronormative male gender construction fails in José-María, and he struggles to conceal his intrinsic feminine characteristics, the reader begins to realize that this character will likely admit to being a sexual invert. Such inversion surfaces when he enacts the "*madrecita*" (little mother) role by imitating his mother while doing the house chores. Identifying himself with his mother echoes the Chodorovian mother–daughter relationship that stresses the daughter's observation of the mother as contributing to her gender identification.[19] José-María's gender identification shows after his father's burial.

> José-María presidió el entierro.... Al volver a casa y quedarse solos, para resistir la marea del llanto, dijo: Lo primero que ha de hacerse es limpiar esto como Dios manda. [¡]Da asco! Jaime se encogió de hombros y, abandonándose ... en sueño, se echó en el cuarto último. Cuando despertó, Amparo, Isabel-Luisa y José-María daban los últimos toques a una limpieza que había durado más de cuatro horas. –[¡]Menudo baldeo le habéis dado, hay que ver! Parece la casa otra –dijo. Y no sólo lo parecía; lo era.... Dijérase que Santiago [el padre] había muerto, y que, libre de

su corpulencia ensuciadora y holgazana, ella [la madre], con las arañas de sus manitas tejedoras de orden, dirigía, por primera vez del todo, el hogar. (57–58)

(José-María presided over the burial.... Upon returning home and find-ing themselves completely alone, and in an attempt to resist from crying, [he] said: The first thing we must do is clean this mess like God would command. It's disgusting! Jaime shrank his shoulders and, abandoning himself ... asleep, went to the last room. When he awoke, Amparo, Isabel-Luisa, and José-María were finishing a cleaning that had lasted longer than four hours. –What a job you've done, amazing! It looks as if I've awaken in another house, he said. And it did not just resemble another house; it was.... One could even say that Santiago [the father] was indeed dead, and that, finally free from his idle and robust body, she [the mother], with her industrious spider hands, orchestrated, for the first time ever, the entire household.) (57–58)

As the eldest son under the Hispano-American patriarchal society, José-María finds himself socially obligated to preside over the funeral march. Upon returning home, unseen by the city, he continues to play a newly dominant role in his family. This time, however, his goal is to carry out a female-gendered activity: house cleaning. While the two sisters and José-María spend hours cleaning the house—as if their mother, with her industrious "spider" hands, were orchestrating the entire process for the first time—his youngest brother, Jaime, goes directly to the most isolated room to sleep. In this respect, Jaime shows more similarities with their idle father, previously known for his massive, filthy, and slothful body. Whereas he succeeds in using the home to isolate himself from others, José-María identifies with this maternal space and uses it as a common area to socialize with other members of his family.

Of course, the parents themselves need not correspond to traditional gender patterns in the novel. Critic Juan Carlos Galdo observes, "Un padre débil, alcoholizado e incapacitado para la acción ... se contrasta con una madre menuda físicamente pero de un comportamiento activo que la acerca a las concepciones de 'lo masculino.'" (The alcoholic and weak father's inability to action ... is in contrast with the mother's indus-trious behavior which approaches her to masculinity) (27).[20] Further, Emilio Bejel suggests that the gender-role inversion in José-María's parents is the possible cause of his sexual preference, claiming that the "genetic causes" of José-María's homosexuality derive from his "inverted Oedipal upbringing" (75).[21] As the eldest son of the Vélez-Gomara family, José-María becomes a type of depository for his parents' reversed roles. Above all, he is able to take on both kinds of traits depending on their appropriateness in any given situation, as shown when he switches roles during his father's burial: from masculine gender role during the funeral procession to female-gendered activities in the privacy of the domestic sphere. Thus, he navigates between the public and private spaces with versatility, despite his own reserves concerning his sexuality.

PRIVATE AND PUBLIC SPACES

It is generally assumed that the individual and private realms of the home stand in contrast to the national and public domains of the city. However, it is noteworthy to emphasize here the paradoxical relationship expressed by the Lotmanian boundary that both separates and unites such semiotic spaces. Just as the private and public blur with one another within the Lotmanian analysis of culture, the same effect occurs in Hernández-Catá's novel. Since the city's coat of arms is engraved at the entrance of the Vélez-Gomara residence, the public space of the city fuses with the private space of family. Much like the city's core identity corresponds to the Vélez-Gomara family's, so, too, José-María's identity is interwoven with that of his community. Everywhere he goes, he is esteemed as the eldest son of the family.

> Tomó un coche en la plaza y ordenó al cochero: –Echa por la carretera del Oeste, hasta después de las tres vueltas. –Sí, señorito José-María. Ignoraba que el cochero lo conociera, y se sorprendió. Se sorprendió más cuando, aquí y allá, muchas personas se volvían para saludarle y por doquier elevaba su paso un murmullo de simpatía: "Es el señor de la casa del escudo." "¡Es el mayorazgo de los Vélez-Gomara, bueno si los hay! (207–208)

> (He took a car at the square and ordered the driver: –Take the West road, after the three turns. –Yes, my boy José-María. He was unaware that the driver knew him, and was astonished. His surprise increases when, everywhere they would drive by, most people would turn to greet him and to show a profound gratitude: "He is the '*señor*' from the house with coat of arms." "He is the eldest of the Vélez-Gomara family, what a presence!) (207–208)

Although José-María engages in soul-searching to understand his feelings at the harbor, the other residents in his hometown view him essentially as a member of an illustrious family, rather than an individual. His reputation remains intrinsically linked with the city's self-perception. Alejandro Mejías-López adds that the family name itself serves the same functions as city monuments and legends, suggesting that "the family name helps preserve the town's own identity through its connection to a glorious past that it refuses to relinquish at any cost ... [and] that fixes the meaning of the community's identity and guarantees the survival of the *patria*" (4–5).[22] Within this context, José-María becomes a public figure; yet, the semiotic space of the individual fuses with that of the community, producing the Lotmanian union of the private and public spheres.

From Public to Private Space

The final expression of this semiotic fusion occurs when the public domain penetrates the privacy of José-María's room. While the narrative reflects *naturalista* tendencies in the literature of its era, there are no intimate moments for José-María in the so-called privacy of his room. Even when he is alone at night, the public discourse invades his thoughts. In each instance where Hernández-Catá describes José-María's insomnia, the young man "no se atrev[e] a asomarse a su propia alma por [revelar] ... un revés repugnante" (does not dare to look into his own soul which [reveals] ... a repugnant inversion) (95, 98). This anguish increases as the protagonist reflects on comments from senior banker Bermúdez Gil, who tells him,

> Estoy satisfecho de tu conducta, y si tu padre viviese también lo estaría. Honras su nombre, sí. Lo dicen todos. José-María se estremeció. Un sonrojo interno le daba impulsos de gritar: [¡]No, no lo honro! Precisamente para no deshonrarlo tengo que apretar los ojos y los puños de noche.... [¡] Ah, si ustedes supieran mis torturas! Por mi conducta, hasta ahora, sí, lo honro: He sido buen hijo, buen hermano.... Entre todos los pecados posibles el suyo sería el más hediondo, el más denigrante. Hasta la deshonra tiene matices. (113–115)

> (I am satisfied with your behavior, and your father would be as well, if he lived. You honor his name, undoubtedly. Everybody says it. José-María shook. An interior blushing provoked him to shout: Not true, I do not honor him! And to avoid dishonoring him I must shut my eyes and my fists at night.... Ah, if you knew my torture! Because of my behavior, I still honor him: I've been a good son, a good brother.... Amongst all possible sins, his would be the most revolting, the most degrading. Even dishonor has nuances.) (113–115)

Here, José-María becomes the most efficient employee at the local bank, inspiring the owner to congratulate him. However, Bermúdez Gil speaks, on behalf of the entire city, becoming in this way a sort of spokesperson for its population. Although his praise relates to José-María's excellent performance on the job, the senior banker reminds him that his impeccable conduct and significant contributions continue to honor his family's legacy. Constantly, he is admired for his ancestry, becoming the city's pride.

Nevertheless, rather than feeling empowered by such accolades, José-María laments his lineage. He becomes conscious of his own homosexual desires and knows the city must not discover them: he must not dishonor his family name. As the eldest child, it is especially important for him to lead an exemplary life. Yet, as his homosexual desires become more difficult to tame, the city's protection turns into a form of surveillance that appears to keep his desires continuously in check. Especially at night, while he tosses and turns, unable to sleep, the city becomes a panopticon that invades his most intimate moments. Unable to fantasize about his attractions to men, he concentrates instead on his own inadequacy. In this manner, the public domain penetrates the privacy of his bedroom, and, more oppressive still, his psyche.

INSIDE NATIONAL CULTURE

Rather than just being inside the narrative of national culture, José-María enjoys a status of privilege. Thus far, it is clear to us that José-María is the eldest child of the family lineage that founded the city; and as such, it is safe to situate him inside the city's culture. When orphaned, he and his siblings are, in fact, adopted by the entire city, since "el consejo de familia lo constituyó la ciudad entera" (the family council is constituted by the entire city) (59). Yet, José-María is not merely a citizen among others, capable of developing his lifestyle unnoticed. On the contrary, he is continuously reminded of his Vélez-Gomara lineage wherever he goes. At work, senior banker Bermúdez Gil trusts him unconditionally with highly charged commissions and loans, chiding him, "Por Dios, Vélez ... Si necesita usted más, ya sabe. Fui amigo de su padre, y en la casa usted es lo menos empleado posible: sépalo. Ea tome.... [¡]No faltaba más!" (For God in Heaven, Vélez ... If you need some more, just tell me, you know that. I was your father's friend; and at this home, you are not considered an employee: you ought to know that. Here, take it.... Nothing else to add!) (145). Likewise, his lineage is also celebrated by even the most impoverished inhabitants of the city. "[L]os mendigos ciegos le conocían los pasos y lo bendecían al acercarse. En todas partes se celebraba su llegada" ([B]lind homeless knew his steps and would bless him as he approached them. His arrival was celebrated everywhere) (205). In this passage, which is almost reminiscent of biblical rhetoric about Jesus's foot-steps venerated by the homeless and the blind, José-María transcends mere celebrity in the nationalist context to attain a quasi-sacred character. Such virtually religious devotion to José-María falls apart due to his homosexual self-awareness. His sexuality pushes him to the margin of national culture, resulting in the disintegration of his initial status of privilege. As a self-aware queer outside the nationalist ideal, José-María turns into a boundary figure, experiencing both inclusion and exclusion simultaneously.

Outside the National Paradigm

As might be expected, José-María first learns about his homosexual desires through contact with the outside world. More particularly, I am interested in the Other as José-María's differentiating mechanism con-cerning the learning of his homosexual desire within the Lotmanian net-work semiosis. Hernández-Catá specifically mentions the "vices" that he internalizes from others,[23] "Los segundos [síntomas de la desgracia] los trajo Jaime de su viaje a tierras remotas, a modo de contrabando indómito comprado y escondido en su alma, hasta entonces dócil, en uno de esos puertos donde confluyen las razas y los vicios de varios con-tinentes" (The second [symptoms of disgrace] were brought by Jaime from his trip to far-away places, trafficking his bought and hidden soul, until then docile, in one of those harbors where races and vices from sev-eral continents intersect) (127). Employing highly xenophobic and racist language, Hernández-Catá seems in agreement with the social hygien-ist discourse of the period. In particular, he makes allusion to the dis-course employed by the highly popular work of Cuban social hygienist Céspedes. When Hernández-Catá categorically evokes races and vices that find their origins on several continents and come into contact in the ports visited by Jaime, the Cuban writer seems to provide a fictional illus-tration of the theoretical work by Céspedes.

Emilio Bejel provides the following outstanding summary of this sci-entist's findings: "Regarding the racially marked with the gender-marked identities, Céspedes classifies the 'pederasts' according to 'the black, the mulatto and the white,' and also with the Chinese, whom he calls a 'wretched race that vegetates.... Like a vegetating plague of mushrooms on a rotten organism" (30). Although José-María's only brother, Jaime, is nowhere in the novel portrayed as sexually deviant, he is the only figure (and apparently the first) in the Vélez-Gomara lineage to have traveled beyond their native city and returned. Interestingly, the "bad seed," although coming from the exterior, is brought back by one of the members of the Vélez-Gomara lineage since it is in contact with the Other that Jaime exposes his older brother to "contagion."

In addition to importing the "contagion" of homosexual tendencies through his travels, Jaime exposes his older brother to this vice by taking him to the circus. If the port causes preliminary exposure to homosexuality, then the circus is the place where he becomes infected with it. The Vélez-Gomara lineage founded the city that has remained uncontaminated from all the vices from the outside world; but because this city is a port, it could also be argued it is at risk from exterior "threats." Yet, despite these outside influences, there is no actual invasion of this illness from the exterior in the novel. Interestingly, the "bad seed," although coming from the exterior, is brought back by one of the members of the Vélez-Gomara lineage since it is in contact with the Other that Jaime exposes his older brother to "contagion." After all, it seems no coincidence that Jaime becomes romantically involved with a girl who works at the circus and who is also aboard the ship that transports all of them into the city. In sum, the two brothers react differently to the same stimulus.

> José-María [es] arrastrado por el hermano menor [al] circo ... él estaba intranquilo y su malestar acrecentase [del] descubrimiento ... que sólo una figura perduraba en su retina y en sus nervios: la del hombre ... [¡]La del hombre joven y fornido nada más! (75, 90–92)

> (José-María [is] dragged by the younger brother [to the] circus ... he was nervous and his restlessness increased to realize ... that only one figure remained in his mind and in his system: that man ... That young and well-built man, nothing else!) (75, 90–92)

As Alejandro Mejías-López observes, "It is at the circus that José-María faces his own sexual desire for the first time" (5), adding, "[to José-María's] surprise, first, and horror soon after, he discovers that his desire is not directed at the woman his brother brought him to admire, but to her male partner on stage" (5). The circus, then, acts as the explanatory aegis of the Other, the space that allows those of variable sexualities to come to self-realization.

In José-María's case, the circus turns into a negative epiphany that awakens his homosexual desires, turning his world upside down. Although no one from the city seems to be aware of his homosexual awakening, it is precisely this self-discovery that turns José-María into a boundary figure. For this reason, it might be best to describe the new identification that he imposes a self-marginalization. This term recognizes that his outward existence need not change in order to have profound consequences on his sense of self and his social status.

Further, this self-marginalized identity solidifies when José-María expresses feelings of self-rejection, revealed when he laments his male-to-male sexual desires, as follows:

> Cien interrogaciones henchidas de asco y de lástima se cruzaban su mente … [¿]De cuál antepasado le venía la degeneración? [¡Se sentía] un monstruo, un lirio de putrefactas raíces! … Y, poco a poco, el resucitar en el alma y en la piel la impresión reveladora que el hércules del circo le sacó del secreto de la carne y del alma, una angustia irrevocable lo oprimía … y acometido de una debilidad inmensa, sintiéndose completo en las dos mitades sexuales que cobijaban sus dos nombres, ocultó la cabeza en la almohada, y se puso a sollozar sin ruido. No lloraba por él sino por sus antepasados [mientras continuaba] la creciente ola de menosprecio con que se juzgaba. (96–104)

> (A hundred questions filled with disgust and shame would cross his mind … Where did this degeneracy come from? [He felt like] a monster, a lily of putrid roots! … And, little by little, when his mind and skin would awake to the revealing impression of the muscled man from the circus, an irrevocable anguish suffocated him … and surrendered to an immense weakness, he felt complete in the two sexual halves that embraced his two names, he hid his head under the pillow, and began to cry in silence. He was not crying for himself but for his lineage [all the while] increased the contempt with which he judged himself.) (96–104)

As this passage suggests, his new peripheral situation in relationship to national culture derives not only from his self-denunciation, but also from his alienizing physical appearance which fails to match the normative nationalist body. As a result, José-María himself represents the physical marker of the Other—not by racial or ethnic composition, but by his physical fragility. Similar to Oscar Wilde, "whose own physical make was of an opposite sort [to a British or Irish national type], an infinitely less appetizing, desirable, and placeable one" (242), as observed by Eve Kosofsky Sedgwick,[24] José-María Vélez-Gomara's physical appearance fails to correspond to the Ibero-American nationalist body type.

In fact, the only physical description of José-María in the narrative, which appears while he occupies a public space in the city, suggests that, by traditional standards, he bears an effeminate demeanor, such as: "Pálido, aguileño, de piel marfilina y ojos verdes, destacaba del grupo de caras contraídas por una tristeza ocasional su belleza tímida y frágil, de flor" (57). According to these sentences, José-María's slight frame stands out from the sad appearance of the rest of the group. Here, we have a young man whose pale, ivory-looking skin with green eyes unveils a timid and fragile beauty, like that of a flower. Comparing José-María to a flower unquestionably eliminates his virility. Hence, the main character in *El ángel de Sodoma* appears to be an "effeminate" man. As such, he does not fit the nationalist model of masculinity during the period. Emilio Bejel comments, "[the] repudiation and rejection of the 'unmanly' man [shows] how the 'effeminate man' (as well as the 'manly woman') is constructed in Cuba to delineate the limits of the Cuban nationalist discourse; this is an excluded being that participates (by exclusion) in defining the nation to which it does not belong" (4). The unmanly man, then, is excluded from any nationalist design; and José-María's particularly fragile physical characteristics turn him into an alienated figure, but one that reinforces national heteronormative standards. Similarly, Juan Carlos Galdo points out that José-María changes social status due to his "unmanly" traits. He observes, "Su condición distintiva, la de ser 'el mayorazgo de los Vélez-Gomara' aparece desplazada por la individualización de José-María como un 'ser' homosexual, es decir 'su clasificación patológica prima sobre su linaje patricio'" (José-María's distinctive condition for being the 'eldest of the Vélez-Gomara' appears displaced before his individualization for being a homosexual 'subject,' that is to say, his pathological classification displaces his aristocratic lineage) (26).

Outside of National Culture (Final Stage)

As José-María becomes more mindful of his marginal status and his exclusion from the nationalist design, he comes to another realization: it might be possible for him to build a new life for himself in sexual freedom. Once again, it is his younger brother Jaime who leads the way in bringing hope for a new life to José-María. Jaime abandons his former life as a member of the Vélez-Gomara family in the city and changes his full name upon becoming a pirate in Jamaica, which allows José-María to consider doing the same. Since he has already failed to correct his sexual deviance in the attempt to honor his surname, he instead decides to pursue life beyond the city.

> [Dejar] el pueblo mezquino para ir … hacia el ancho mundo donde el nombre de mayor alcurnia es brizna en el viento.… La idea, para José-María nueva, de que se pudiera cambiar de nombre, le produjo primero estupor y luego una perspectiva lejana y confusa de esperanza. El nombre aquel por el que llevaba tantos años sacrificándose.… Urge huir: dentro de poco me lo conocerán todos.… Todavía sentía el valor preciso para volverse a asesinar al monstruo pero las consecuencias del escándalo, la certeza de malbaratar en un solo minuto las precauciones de tantos años de disimulo, le aconsejaron huir. (175–191)

> ([To leave] the small-minded town in order to go … to the vast world where the most noble name is breeze in the wind.… This idea, new to José-María, about changing his family name, caused on him anxiety at first and then a distant and confusing idea of hope.… That name for which he had sacrificed himself for so long.… I must leave: everybody will soon find out.… He still had enough strength to turn around and kill the monster but the consequences of the scandal, the certainty to destroy, in one minute, the precautionary measures from all of those years of concealment, advised him to leave.) (175–191)

If José-María plans to change his name and adopt a new sexual identity, he must leave the miserable town that has become a repressive space. As his secret becomes more difficult to hide, he consolidates his thoughts about leaving, yet remains extremely fearful that his homosexual desires could be revealed and, thus, provoke the scandal of dishonoring his lineage. Interestingly, he must not just "leave" (*partir*) but "escape" (*huir*) the town: what begins as a concerned paternalistic city when the Vélez-Gomara children become parentless turns into an overpowering panoptical eye whose construction of heteronormative discourses, which entail agencies of control and power, aim for one clear objective: to eliminate the homosexual subject from the national territory.

The Lotmanian analysis of culture therefore allows us to understand José-María's role in national culture at two levels: first, it shows the paradoxical relationship of the semiospheric boundary's double-functionality (which determines what is both internal and external); secondly, it reveals how the overlapping dyads of the center/periphery, private/public, and inside/outside interact in narrative, especially in the development of a conflicted subject who remains attached to differing semiotic values in each realm. José-María's self-denunciation displaces him from the center to the periphery of national culture, resulting in a new self-imposed marginality. In turn, this peripheral position highlights the ways in which his body composition fails to fit the nationalist ideal and, thus, ultimately expels him outside of the nationalistic Ibero-American matrix.

Frenchness in the Latin American Imaginary

It is by identifying the boundaries that separate internal semiotic spaces that we can best understand the idea of the exclusion of the Other, or as undesirable citizens in *El ángel de Sodoma*. While the authenticity of the representation of French space in this text is far from established, my focus falls rather on the purpose of such representations in the Latin American imaginary at the turn of the twentieth century. I argue that Hernández-Catá uses the so-called French space to imply degeneracy, promiscuity, immorality, and Otherness. The Lotmanian language is a useful tool to understand the idea of national culture in relationship to what Lotman refers to as the boundary's primary mechanisms. It allows individuals to feel a difference between first- and third-person subjects by forming the space between our world and their world. The space associated with the self is considered cultured, safe, and harmoniously organized; by contrast with their space, which becomes othered, hostile, dangerous, and chaotic.[25] Hernández-Catá also indeed seems to differentiate the cultural we from all others, since his definition of the outside world corresponds to Lotman's chaotic exterior.

El ángel de Sodoma depicts a tumultuous outside world and a city fearful of vices that might originate overseas. What is perhaps most intriguing about this text, however, is its focus on the specificity of Frenchness as homosexually threatening. Within this context, this writer excludes the Other (the French as well as the homosexual) and participates in the nation-building process. While Emilio Bejel has astutely pointed out that the exclusion of the homosexual body assists in describing the nation to which he does not belong (4), it may also ironically entail the explicit inclusion of France—or, at least, French stereotypes—in the socially recognized space that constitutes the outside world.

Hispano-Cuban Context

Within this context, Alfonso Hernández-Catá suggests that homosexual subjects should suppress their desires, or seek asylum elsewhere. He uses the French national territory—and, more specifically, Paris—as the sole place where homosexual degeneration belongs. Whether in public or in private, José-María cannot find a place for himself. As a result, the nationalistic society surrounding him not only expels the sexually inverted protagonist out of his native city, but forces him to travel to the French capital, an exclusive destination in every sense of the term. According to Uva de Aragón, the City of Light "gravitated strongly over the *modernistas'* mind" (58).[26] Hernández-Catá indeed introduces it like a welcoming promised land, "Paris, nombre-promesa para cualquier buscador de cualquier alcaloide de vida, lo acogió con esa sonrisa" (Paris, promise-name for any individual in search for any type of life, welcomed him with that smile) (217). This personification of Paris turns the city into a knowing accomplice to his unconventional lifestyle.

As José-María begins to experience a new identity in sexual freedom, the reader is also invited to enjoy his anonymous walk in the city.

De la estación al hotel reflejáronse en sus ojos las imágenes desconocidas y empero familiares del Sena, de la Catedral de las dos torres truncas, de la grúa paralítica que es la Torre Eiffel y del jardín ilustre de las Tullerías. La cándida sorpresa de que su Vélez-Gomara no significase [nada] en el hotel …, complacióle. (217)

(From the train station, his eyes reflected unknown images but his enthusiasm increased with familiarity of the Seine, the Cathedral with the two incomplete towers, of the paralyzed crane of the Eiffel tower and the illustrious garden of the Tulleries. The warm surprise that his Vélez-Gomara did not mean [anything] in the hotel …, pleased him.) (217)

This joy increases as he continues to explore the many pleasures Paris offers—when he purchases soaps and fragrances—and restrains his desires but still rejoices at the view of the amazing threads, warm silk, and soft elasticity of pantyhose on display. The countless possibilities in Paris turn him into a new being.

Se bañó como jamás en su vida se había bañado: en una inmersión larga, llena de ensueños sin forma.... [E]ra un goce de sentirse liviano ... bajó a comer y ... echóse a la calle. Sentíase seguro.... [S]ubió a su cuarto y se transformó, maravillándose de la magia. [¡]Era otro! ... [S]e vió íntegro, terso y túrgido el cuerpo de que tantas veces se había avergonzado, la cara iluminada por la sonrisa (220–222)

(He showered like he never did before: in a long immersion filled with unclear dreams.... [I]t was the pleasure to feel lightweight ... he descended to eat and ... went out to the street. He felt self-confident.... [H]e returned to his room and saw himself transformed, completely marveled. He was somebody else! ... [H]e saw himself complete, smooth and pleased with the body that had previously produced shame, his face was lit up with his smile) (220–222)

The self-assured José-María in Paris no longer resembles the fearful and timid young man who left his native city. The anonymity of the modern urban landscape allows him to enjoy life on a daily basis, as the fragile body he felt so ashamed of in his native city turns into a complete being, which makes him smile for the first time in the narrative.

Furthermore, the discovery of sexual freedom in Paris strengthens his new sexual identity. In particular, Alejandro Mejías-López observes, "the narrative spatializes the freedom that José-María finds by embracing his sexual identity" (8). The novel recounts,

Gustaba de situarse [a ver] el ritmo desmoralizador de la música e interesándose por los jóvenes de belleza profesional ... José-María penetró también, impelido por extraño aplomo. El mozo [que] era alto, hercúleo ... sacó una hoja de papel y escribió con lápiz en ella. Cual si tuviera larga *práctica*, José-María comprendió la maniobra y, en el apelotonamiento de la salida, el billetito estuvo, sin que nadie se diera cuenta, en su mano. (Emphasis added, 223–227)

(He would like to sit [to watch] the disturbing rhythm of the music and would get interested on the young men with professional beauty ... José-María penetrated as well, empowered by some strange energy. The young man [who] was tall and muscled ... took out a piece of paper and wrote on it. As if he was experienced in the *métier*, José-María understood the movements and, in the commotion of the exit, the little note ended up in his hand, without even noticing.) (Emphasis added, 223–227)

In this subtle exchange by which José-María enters the world of prostitution, Paris empowers him to express his homosexual desire and, thus, becomes the "capital of sin" which "radiates 'degeneration,'" in Carlos Galdo's words (27–30). Little prior to attending this rendezvous,

José-María receives a letter from his boss and brother-in-law in his native city, reminding him about the honor associated with his lineage. This renewed guilt causes José-María to commit suicide by throwing himself in front of a metro train. Through the language of the letter, the semiotic space of his hometown invades Paris, transforms into the overpowering panoptical eye he had previously known, and pushes him to kill himself.

Conclusion

In sum, my second chapter's protagonist commits suicide after his homosexual desire is revealed within the so-called French space. I will thoroughly elaborate on the function of suicide in the Hispano-American narrative in the next chapter. For now, it is essential to highlight the significance of the French space: It promises a safe haven from traditional Ibero-American values, but fails to maintain the autonomy necessary to carry out that promise due to the overlapping nature of semiospheres, which pass from one region of the world to another along with boundary figures.

Notes

1. I will use "Hispano-American" interchangeably with "Ibero-American" when I refer to the story taking place in *El ángel de Sodoma*. I will use the term "Latin American" when I refer to both writers.
2. Alfonso Hernández-Catá, *El ángel de Sodoma* (Madrid: Mundo Latino, 1928).
3. Emilio Bejel, *Gay Cuban Nation* (Chicago and London: The University of Chicago Press, 2001).
4. My understanding of the "semiosphere" corresponds to Lotman's description which reads, "we could talk of a 'semiosphere' ... as the semiotic space necessary for the existence and functioning of languages,... a cluster of semiotic spaces and their boundaries, which, however clearly defined these are in the language's grammatical self-description in the reality of semiosis are eroded and full of transitional forms. Outside the semiosphere there can be neither communication, nor language." Yuri Lotman, *Universe of the Mind: A Semiotic Theory of Culture*, trans. Anne Shukman (London: I.B. Tauris & Co Ltd., 1990), 123–124. See the chapter entitled "Semiotic space" from his book *Universe of the Mind: A Semiotic Theory of Culture*, trans. Ann Shukman (London: I.B. Tauris & Co Ltd., 1990).

5. I would like to thank Seiji M. Lippit for his seminal essay that inspired my conceptualization of this part of my project. Seiji M. Lippit, "The Double Logic of Minor Spaces," in *Minor Transnationalism*, eds. Françoise Lionnet and Shu-mei Shi (Durham and London: Duke University Press, 2005), 283–300.

6. Jonathan H. Bolton, "Writing in a Polluted Semiosphere: Everyday Life in Lotman, Foucault, and de Certeau," in *Lotman and Cultural Studies*, ed. Andreas Schönle (Madison: The University of Wisconsin Press, 2006).

7. Although Lotman himself does not delineate a "clear-cut" illustration between these two concepts, I attempt to provide my own understanding of such differences. See Yuri M. Lotman, Part 2, "The Semiosphere" in *Universe of the Mind* (1990), 123–204.

8. Edna Andrews, *Conversations with Lotman: Cultural Semiotics in Language, Literature, and Cognition* (Toronto: University of Toronto Press, 2003).

9. Here, I am borrowing the juxtaposition of the terms "self-description" and "metalanguage" from Edna Andrews, who writes in *Conversations with Lotman* (2003), "One of the remaining defining characteristics of the semiosphere ... is self-description, or the development of a metalanguage" (33). Subsequently, she provides a synthesis of the terms as laid out by Yuri Lotman. My use of the terms, however, corresponds to Edna Andrews's as she uses them interchangeably.

10. This term refers to the nomads who after settling on the borderlands of Kievan Russia, become agriculturalists and form alliances with the Russian princes in order to campaign against their own nomadic kin. Lotman writes, "they were called 'our *pogany*' (*pogany* meant 'pagan' as well as 'foreign,' 'incorrect' or 'unclean'). The oxymoron 'our *pogany*' epitomizes the situation of boundary" (1990, 137).

11. Emphasis on original. Amy Mandelker, "Lotman's Other: *Estrangement and Ethics* in Culture and Explosion," in *Lotman and Cultural Studies: Encounters and Extensions*, ed. Andreas Schönle (Madison: The University of Wisconsin Press, 2006), 59–83.

12. There is some debate about the nationality of Hernández-Catá: although he grew up in Cuba, he studied university in Spain, where his parents lived. After completing his diploma, he worked as a diplomat for the Cuban Embassy until his death. See, for example, the works of Uva de Aragón and Emilio Bejel. Jorge Febles perhaps states it best when he affirms that Hernández-Catá was "*ni cubano ni español*" (neither Cuban nor Spaniard), but rather a true "*hispanoamericano*" (78). Jorge Febles, "Sobre la estética naturalista y la ficción erótica: el narrador comprometido en dos textos de Hernández-Catá," *Letras Peninsulares* (Spring, 1989), 65–80.

13. All translations in this book are my own.
14. Following the patriarchal Hispano-American tradition, males are expected to honor the family's name.
15. See the complete analysis on my take on the Lotmanian cultural membrane in this chapter, the section entitled "Moving beyond the binary system."
16. My emphasis on the italics.
17. Gaston Bachelard, *The Poetics of Space*, trans. Maria Jolas (Boston: Beacon Press, 1994).
18. Alejandro Mejías-López, "Reframing Sodom: Sexuality, Nation, and Difference in Hernández-Catá's *El ángel de Sodoma*," www.lehman.edu/faculty/guinazu/ciberletras/v16/mejiaslopez.html.
19. See Nancy Chodorow, "Gender as a Personal and Cultural Construction," *Signs* 20, no. 3 (Spring 1995): 516–544.
20. Juan Carlos Galdo, "Usos y Lecciones del Discurso Ejemplar: A propósito de *El ángel de Sodoma* de Alfonso Hernández-Catá," *Chasqui* 29, no. 1 (2000): 19–32.
21. For a complete analysis of this term, see Emilio Bejel, *Gay Cuban Nation* (Chicago: The University of Chicago Press, 2001), 75–76.
22. His italics not mine.
23. Other critics such as Bejel, Galdo, and Mejías have done a superbly thorough analysis on the trope of Otherness in the novel's entirety.
24. Eve Kosofsky Sedwick, "Nationalisms and Sexualities in the Age of Wilde," in *Nationalisms & Sexualities*, eds. Andrew Parker, Mary Russo, Doris Sommer, and Patricia Yaeger (New York: Routledge, 1992), 235–245.
25. See my take on Lotman on this chapter.
26. Uva de Aragón, *Alfonso Hernández-Catá: un escritor Cubano, salmantino y universal* (Salamanca: Universidad Pontífica de Salamanca, 1996), 58.

References

Andrews, Edna. *Conversations with Lotman: Cultural Semiotics in Language, Literature, and Cognition*. Toronto: University of Toronto Press, 2003.

Bachelard, Gaston. *The Poetics of Space*. Translated by Maria Jolas. Boston: Beacon Press, 1994.

Bejel, Emilio. *Gay Cuban Nation*. Chicago: The University of Chicago Press, 2001.

Bolton, Jonathan H. "Writing in a Polluted Semiosphere: Everyday Life in Lotman, Foucault, and de Certeau." In *Lotman and Cultural Studies: Encounters and Extensions*, edited by Andreas Schönle, 320–344. Madison: The University of Wisconsin Press, 2006.

Chodorow, Nancy. "Gender as a Personal and Cultural Construction." *Signs* 20, no. 3 (Spring 1995): 516–544.

De Aragón, Uva. *Alfonso Hernández-Catá: un escritor Cubano, salmantino y universal*. Salamanca: Universidad Pontífica de Salamanca, 1996.

Febles, Jorge. "Sobre la estética naturalista y la ficción erótica: el narrador comprometido en dos textos de Hernández-Catá." *Letras Peninsulares* (Spring 1989): 65–80.

Galdo, Juan Carlos. "Usos y Lecciones del Discurso Ejemplar: A Propósito de *El ángel de Sodoma* de Alfonso Hernández-Catá." *Chasqui* 29, no. 1 (2000): 19–32.

Hernández-Catá, Alfonso. *El ángel de Sodoma*. Madrid: Mundo Latino, 1928.

Lippit, Seiji M. "The Double Logic of Minor Spaces." In *Minor Transnationalism*, edited by Françoise Lionnet and Shu-mei Shi, 283–300. Durham and London: Duke University Press, 2005.

Lotman, Yuri. *Universe of the Mind: A Semiotic Theory of Culture*. Translated by Anne Shukman. London: I.B. Tauris & Co Ltd, 1990.

Mandelker, Amy. "Lotman's Other: Estrangement and Ethics in Culture and Explosion." In *Lotman and Cultural Studies: Encounters and Extensions*, edited by Andreas Schönle, 59–83. Madison: The University of Wisconsin Press, 2006.

Mejías-López, Alejandro. "Reframing Sodom: Sexuality, Nation, and Difference in Hernández-Catá's *El ángel de Sodoma*." http://www.lehman.edu/faculty/guinazu/ciberletras/v16/mejiaslopez.html.

Sedwick, Eve Kosofsky. "Nationalisms and Sexualities in the Age of Wilde." In *Nationalisms & Sexualities*, edited by Andrew Parker, Mary Russo, Doris Sommer, and Patricia Yaeger, 235–245. New York: Routledge, 1992.

CHAPTER 3

A Tango Performance: Inverts and Flowers in the *Garçonnière* in Buenos Aires

To the argument developed previously, this chapter continues to treat queer bodies as boundary figures who experience inclusion and exclusion simultaneously. This time, however, I focus on José González Castillo's *Los Invertidos*[1] (*The Inverts, 1914*). *Los Invertidos* is a play about Dr. Florez, a married man who has a homosexual affair with his best friend, Mr. Pérez, in Buenos Aires, Argentina. Here, too, Frenchness is essential to understand the role of the *garçonnière* in Argentinean society at the turn of the twentieth century. I explore González Castillo's use of the French space where homosexual behavior is openly allowed. This narrative is situated amid a period of nation-building throughout Latin America, which is reflected in the author's concern regarding national culture. Building on Lotman's paradoxical double-functionality from Chapter 2, the Argentinean author continues to appear doubly anxious about the question of membership at the national level in two respects: the definition of nation itself and national identity.[2] Although González Castillo fails to provide an actual exemplification of the ideal nation, the Lotmanian model is a useful way to understand the nation's inside in terms of its outside. The idea about the exclusion of the Other will determine how this writer portrays belonging and, thus, the type of individuals accepted—or not—by the nationalist agenda.

It is precisely within this paradigm of exclusion that the representation of the French space becomes significant to the Latin American imaginary. In order to contextualize representations of the French, I focus first on

© The Author(s) 2019   55
L. Navarro-Ayala, *Queering Transcultural Encounters*,
Palgrave Studies in Globalization and Embodiment,
https://doi.org/10.1007/978-3-319-92315-4_3

the boundaries that separate and, thus, define semiotic spaces within the Latin American matrix; then, I examine how González Castillo builds Frenchness. Corresponding to Chapter 2, the present analysis also considers how the Lotmanian organization of space is helpful in understanding the nationalist model in which the writer unveils the following traits: First, the main character, Dr. Florez, becomes a boundary figure because of his homosexual desire, which justifies his expulsion from his territory. Second, the author insists on situating homosexual behavior outside of national culture and within the French transcultural space of the *garçonnière* in Buenos Aires, Argentina.

In the section, "Dr. Florez's House: The Private Becomes Public," I suggest that the audience's task is to break the dividing line between the private and public spaces in order to expose the Argentinean bourgeoisie as sexually deviant. This section explores how such a revelation occurs within two bourgeois spaces in Buenos Aires: the main character's office and the *garçonnière*. As a space of overlapping thematic and, therefore, semiotic layers, the *garçonnière* becomes an extension of the office: what begins as a theoretical discourse about homosexuality in Dr. Florez's place of work seems to be put into practice in the *garçonnière*. That is, the author chooses the French cultural space of the *garçonnière*, among the many foreign cultural representations in Argentina of the period, in order to reveal the pivotal moment of the main character's overt homosexual affair. This thematic layering brings to light the theoretical discourse about homosexual behavior and the writer's anarchist ideologies: whereas his discourse involves terms like contagion, degeneracy, threat, and vice, his ideologies lead to a class struggle and thus situates the play in the genre of the theater of ideas.

The second section, "Frenchness in Latin America," sheds light to the appropriation of the French cultural space. In the Argentinean context, González Castillo turns the French cultural space of the *garçonnière* in Buenos Aires into a "homosexual brothel," whereas writer Hernández-Catá in Chapter 2 uses the French capital itself as the center for sexual degeneracy.

Finally, the conclusion of this chapter explores Lotman's concept of nonexistence and the question of suicide in relation to the nationalist culture proposed by González Castillo and Hernández-Catá. This particular analysis brings together recurring thematic and semiotic layers throughout Chapters 2 and 3: Both narratives construct a national culture and determine its membership in accordance with what some critics have called *"hispanoamericanismo."* By revisiting the idea of exclusion of the Other, the French, and their parallel term, homosexuality, regain significance and become undesirable to the Latin American imaginary, bringing forth the Lotmanian model of analysis of culture in *Los Invertidos* and *El ángel de Sodoma.*

José González Castillo's *Los Invertidos*

If, for Lotman, the boundary's function is to control the external, filtering its movements toward the internal, then it carries essential implications for the construction of personal space. As Lotman notes, the semiosphere tends to distinguish "'one's own' from someone else's" (140). In this light, González Castillo's blurring of the dividing line between the private and the public invites the differentiation of a semiotic cultural space particular to the character. In his play, González Castillo embarks upon the mission of cultural definition, *à la Lotman,* while Argentina undergoes a process of nation-building. The author separates the first person from the third person in order to transcend the "most external" boundary between self and other, as well the internal boundaries of national culture. For him, cultural definition corresponds to the double-functionality invoked by Lotman's semiospheric boundary, as the entire space of the semiosphere is transected by boundaries. This chapter explores the ways in which González Castillo breaks these dividing lines between the private and public spaces in order to depict the Argentinean bourgeoisie as sexually deviant.

Dr. Florez's House: The Private Becomes Public

The first of these private spaces is the main character's house as a private sphere.[3] The play opens up with the following description of Dr. Florez's office, which immediately situates his milieu within the haute-bourgeoisie of Buenos Aires: "[there is a] private office at Dr. Flórez's home, richly decorated. To the left side, there is great balcony, through which crystal doors would allow us to appreciate the buildings from across the street. On the walls, there are several paintings and panoplies with various coats of arms hanging. To the right side, there is a Moroccan desk set, with ivory statues" (González Castillo, 11).[4] The careful description of the luxury found in Dr. Florez's office allows us to appreciate not only the structures of economic power, but also his family's status in Argentine society from the very beginning of this play. Although this is the office where the lawyer works, he does not appear in the opening scene; we see Julián, his sixteen-year-old son, who "*copia en limpio*"[5] (polishes) his dad's report. Because the father is absent, the son occupies his father's position by working at his desk. As a result, I would argue, he dominates not only the desk but the entire office. Following the patriarchal tradition, the son will eventually inherit all of his father's possessions in exchange for the commitment to carry on the patriarchal lineage. Given this scenario, González Castillo seems to warn the audience about the danger of the "bad seed." Could we fear that the sixteen-year-old is at risk of "contagion" related to his father's sexual preferences? Could we suppose that, inheriting his father's genes, Julián would eventually be as dangerous and corrupt as his father?[6] Before proposing answers to these questions, I would like to return to the emphasis placed on the affluence of the Florez family, clearly illustrated in the house they inhabit.

In addition to the luxury found in the office, several key details indicate that the rest of the estate is as spacious and sumptuous. Julián works in this room completely undisturbed by Petrona, the family's servant, who arranges several chairs and documents in another room. When Dr. Florez enters the office, he is not seen by his son and is only noticed after he speaks. Surprised by his voice, Julián says, "¡Ah! ... papá. ¡Buenas tardes!" (Ah! ... dad. Good afternoon!) (14). Then, Clara, Dr. Florez's wife, comes in but once again she fails to notice when her husband returns home, asking if he was in the room. To which he confirms his recent arrival. Later on, by herself in the office, Clara asks Petrona about the children's whereabouts. The servant replies, "La niña se ha acostado. El niño estudia en su pieza" (The miss is in bed. The young boy studies in *his* room) (58).[7] If the servant arranges several chairs without interfering with the son's work and the father arrives unnoticed by his son, then the office must be a very spacious room indeed, where anyone might be able to hide at any moment. In addition, Clara's dialogues show that the Florez house is a very large bourgeois estate, where each member seems to move freely in complete privacy. It is precisely within this broad space that González Castillo's anarchist ideologies come into play in this drama of ideas. I suggest that, despite the isolation of the characters within their lavish home, the author provides no space for intimacy to the sexually deviant in the Argentine nationalist context.

That said, González Castillo clearly recognizes the notion of privacy as it began to develop in Western societies in the nineteenth century. In the Argentinean context, González Castillo seems to agree with critic S. J. Kleinberg, who notes that middle and upper classes were the only sectors in society that could practice the concept of privacy in their homes. Kleinberg observes that working-class rooms accommodated many functions. For instance, the kitchen would also operate as the eating, sitting, and socializing room. The working-class rooms' main function was to integrate rather than to segregate family members. Kleinberg adds, "Working-class homes lacked the spatial separation which enabled the middle class to create soothing environments and private worlds. Doors and windows remained open to the streets, so that everyone saw, heard and smelled what went on in their neighbours' homes" (154).[8] Kleinberg's observations on crowded conditions, shared facilities, and open windows mean that working-class neighbors knew the intimate details of each other's lives. Such living conditions prevalent in the West could also be thought of as existing in Argentina. It is therefore significant that González Castillo decides not to depict a working-class home as described by Kleinberg, but quite the opposite. The Argentine author insists on portraying the Florez's estate as a spacious and luxurious space, with separate rooms designed for specific purposes and for each family member, providing a sense of privacy. As Graham Allan's "Insiders and Outsiders: Boundaries around the Home" (1989) describes, this Argentinean home is "an essentially private sphere [which] comprises both a physical setting and a matrix for social relationships" (141).[9]

Dr. Florez's House: The Public Becomes Private

This section addresses how the public becomes private. I argue that the public domain enters the privacy of Dr. Florez's household through his profession as a lawyer. I analyze the theoretical discourse about homosexuality in Argentina, starting with the opening of the play, which opens up with sixteen-year-old Julián, who is *"copiando en limpio"* (polishing) a report his father has been asked to prepare regarding a man accused of killing his male lover in an outrage of jealousy. For now, what is significant to note is the order in which the two actions occur in this scene: First, the son seems to *"copiar en limpio;"* then, he reads with difficulty—while his reading attracts the attention of the old family servant, Petrona.

I believe that the author's choice for the expression *"copiar en limpio"* about the son's performance has two important implications: On the one hand, we are told from the very beginning of the drama that the sixteen-year-old boy has access to his father's work statement; and, on the other, we learn about this boy's age. These two facts are inseparable for I believe that the boy's age plays a crucial role in this drama: because it is understood that at sixteen years old a human being has not yet reached full maturity, we could think of Julián as "vulnerable" as he is exposed to his father's occupation. There is therefore the suggestion of what I consider to be an *"actividad sucia y contaminante"* (contagious, dirty activity) introduced to this family by the father. In order to build this argument, I would like to borrow from Gustavo Geirola, who states, "El hijo ... está 'pasando en limpio' el informe pericial, lo cual remite inmediatamente a una producción de 'escritura sucia' generada a partir del padre a una *re*producción escrituraria por parte del hijo" (The son ... is 'copying out the final draft' which immediately brings attention to the production of some 'dirty writing' generated on the father and moves to a written *re*-production on the son) (77). Geirola's comment suggests that the *"escritura sucia"* (dirty writing) which originates from the father, could also turn into a *"reproducción escrituraria"* (writing reproduction) initiated, in this instance, by the son. Clearly, such reproduction could occur—González Castillo seems to warn us—if Julián continues to be exposed to his father's writing. But is he simply reproducing a legal document? If writing is a type of legacy, what kind of *re*writing should this play's audience expect from the son? Another *"escritura sucia"*? Will Julián be capable of "cleaning" not only his father's writing but also his own?

The responses to these questions may be elucidated by a deeper understanding of how Julián reads. First and foremost, his reading exemplifies common knowledge regarding theories about homosexual behavior in Argentina. According to David William Foster in "José González Castillo's Los Invertidos and the Vampire Theory of Homosexuality" (1989), Julián is "reminding the audience of some of the prevailing concepts of the day concerning homosexual activity" through the course of his reading (21).[10] I would take a step further by affirming that Julián's reading is a type of "acknowledgement parallelism" between the prevailing concepts of the day, the audience, and the author himself. That is, I consider that such a reading is some sort of recognition, a type of awareness performance. It therefore represents a type of alliance between different parties who share a common understanding of the types of homosexual activities that occur in Argentina at the turn of the twentieth century. These parties are, in fact, the audience and González Castillo as the author, who crafts the reading content to reflect his understanding of existing economies of homosexuality in Argentina at the turn of the twentieth century. The report that falls in Julián's hands reads as follows:

> El procesado ... constituye uno de esos ... casos de inversión sexual ... No aparecen en él, después de un prolijo estudio orgánico, las deformaciones fisiológicas,... pero sus hábitos, marcadamente femeninos,... sus mismas predilecciones por todas esas futilezas que constituyen el encanto de las mujeres, la inflexión de su voz, suave y acariciadora. (11–12)

> (The processed subject ... is one of those ... cases of sexual inversion ... After a meticulous biological study, he does not show any physiological deformations,... but his very prominent feminine mannerisms,... his preferences for all those trifles that are known to be loved by women, the inflection of his soft and caressing voice.) (11–12)

As Julián's shows when he reads this passage aloud on stage, Dr. Florez's report contains multiple public discourses about homosexual behavior, which filter through the eyes of the son, into the private sphere of the Florez family home. My interest in citing this passage is not to analyze it in its entirety for this would interrupt my argument; instead, I propose to highlight the words relevant to the theories contemporary to González Castillo—or in Foster's terms, "to the prevailing concepts of the day concerning homosexual activity" (20). The mixture of discipline-specific vocabulary in this passage shows the normative framework for the social semiosphere in which the characters have learned to thrive economically. Words such as "the processed" and "judge" make reference to the legal discourse; "pathology," "organic analysis," and "physiological deformations" make allusion to biological discourse; "ancestral tendencies" and "morbid heredity" make allusion to genetics; as "habits" and "insufficient physical and moral education" refer to pedagogical discourse.[11]

Why does author González Castillo begin this play with such a detailed account of the theories about homosexuality? Why is it precisely the sixteen-year-old who recites such a loaded and dangerous discourse? Would this be appropriate knowledge for those reared with a careful upper-middle-class upbringing? More than a mere reminder to the audience, this meticulous approach (*senda de persuasion*) adopted by the author exposes the Argentinean ruling class as continuously risking homosexual contagion. That is, as the curtain opens up, the first scene perceived by the audience is a sixteen-year-old being in close contact with both the threat of homosexuality and the discourses designed to control it. "Al levantarse el telón aparecerá Julián,... hijo mayor del doctor Florez, trabajando sobre la mesa-escritorio de la derecha. Simula que copia en limpio un informe pericial de su padre ... Leyendo con dificultad" (Julián will appear on stage when the curtain opens,... as the eldest son of Doctor Florez, he will be working on the desk to the right. He pretends to copy out his father's report ... He reads with difficulty) (11).

Julián's task shows many levels of engagement with the text: He is not only physically involved in the writing process but also cognitively, as he tries to make sense of these challenging discourses. And yet, as a subtext, González Castillo's anarchist ideologies also appear on stage right from the very beginning of *Los Invertidos*. As a creator of the thesis genre, he uses direct tools of persuasion to convey his message, showing the audience the type of education that the oligarchy provides its youth right at the nucleus of their home. A task as benign as assisting his father with his job could, in fact, turn into a very threatening activity for the eldest child in this otherwise prim and proper family.

This scene shows how the author injects the public discourse about homosexuality into the most important and private room in order to distribute it all throughout Dr. Florez's residence. Despite numerous comments alluding to the size and riches of the house, González Castillo decides to show only the office on stage. How do we interpret the author's choice to place the family drama entirely in the workplace? This question brings to light the concept of class/gender divisions within the domestic sphere, according to which the distribution of domestic space entails that the father, the economic base of the whole family structure, has the most power and the most space within the household (Kleinberg, 148).

We are indeed given the impression that Dr. Florez's office is not only the Florez family's economic stronghold, but also the most powerful and spacious room in the house. I believe that the anarchist author, remarkably watchful of his own militancy, chooses the prominent lawyer's office as the membrane through which he infiltrates the public discourse of homosexuality and disperses it to more intimate places within the Florez house. Similar to a blood transfusion, in which the blood reaches the heart and then, through the arteries, it spreads everywhere in the body, the discourse about homosexuality enters directly into the most important social space in the home, then permeates all the individuals living there as they enter the office and have contact with that discourse. Rather than distribute the discourse to the "society-body," they attempt to contain it within the household. González Castillo seems to ask: Are Petrona, Dr. Florez, Clara, and Mr. Pérez exposed only to the discourse or to the "real" contagion of sexual inversion?

THE *GARÇONNIÈRE*: THE PRIVATE BECOMES PUBLIC

In addition to Dr. Florez's household, González Castillo depicts the *garçonnière* as the other private area where the Argentine bourgeoisie enjoys its material wealth. Although both spaces illustrate bourgeois status, it is important to note about the functional differences between them: On the one hand, the house is usually perceived—to borrow Graham Allan's words—as "the routine site of family life [where] family here is usually taken to be narrowly defined, that is typically a couple ... and children" (148); on the other, the *garçonnière* is essentially a bachelor's apartment, which is, in Adriana Bergero's terms, "ergonomically disposed to reaffirm social spaces in the sexuality of the city and to accommodate sexual fantasies in a private darkness that ha[s] a very public side to it" (325). González Castillo aims to expose elitist homosocial private spaces as masking sexually deviant behavior, such as the setting of the *garçonnière*. As an example of private space, the *garçonnière* represents one of the most impenetrable and exclusive places within Buenos Aires society. In her convincing analysis entitled "The *garçonnières* and the Sex of Power" (2008), Adriana Bergero states that, contrary to cabarets, which were public spaces, *garçonnières* in Buenos Aires "spatialized the symbolic capital and power of the elite" (318). In other words, they represent first and foremost a statement on class difference, rather than sexuality.

When analyzing the tango song, "Portero, suba y diga" ("Doorman, Go Up and Tell Her," 1928), written in collaboration by Eduardo de Labar and Luis César Amadori, Adriana Bergero observes that the melody's protagonist has followed his lover to her living quarters, in the hopes of a passionate encounter; however, he stops when he sees that the woman crosses the "threshold of the apartment belonging to a *niño bien*" (elite young man). The disenfranchised lover is conscious he cannot penetrate the bourgeois building. In consequence, he asks the doorman to "go up and tell that ingrate/that I have come/to charge her with treachery." By using the doorman as a messenger, these tango lyrics show us that "the *garçonnière* belongs, in effect, to a class of private exclusive spaces jealously protected against any incursion from the street" (Bergero, 319). Contrary to cabarets and working-class homes whose easy access gives way to free interaction, the Buenos Aires *garçonnière* is a space protected from the public domain. It is therefore all the more significant that González Castillo overturns this exclusivity by exposing the *garçonnière* to the public in *Los Invertidos*. How does the author present one of the most emblematic spaces of the privileged in Buenos Aires at the turn of the twentieth century?

Similar to Dr. Florez's home, the *garçonnière* proves sumptuous and spacious, or, as David William Foster affirms in "José González Castillo's *Los Invertidos* and the Vampire Theory of Homosexuality" (1989), "as exaggeratedly Wildean as possible" (23). The play introduces this set as follows:

> Sala de una *garçonnière* elegante. Puerta al fondo derecha. A la izquierda, especie de apartement, con un piano, divanes, etc. En la lateral izquierda puerta que se supone conduce a un dormitorio ... el alumbrado ... debe ser compuesto por brazos eléctricos con lámparas. (31)

> (Living room in an elegant *garçonnière*. A door to the right. Some sort of an apartment, with a piano, shelves, etc. to the left. Next to the left, another door that is supposed to lead to a bedroom ... the lighting ... must be composed of lamps with electric branches.) (31)

The bourgeois sophistication of Pérez's *garçonnière*, as illustrated by the piano and electric lamps, resembles an extension of the Florez's family home. What happens in each space is nonetheless very different: whereas the Florez's home is introduced as a family setting, the Pérez's *garçonnière* appears to be a "homosexual brothel," in Foster's terms, appreciated precisely because it offers a refuge away from family.

Indeed, González Castillo introduces the *garçonnière* with the following tango performance played and danced by three queer characters: "Juanita, a twenty-year-old male with a beautiful face, sits down by the piano and executes a tango—while Emilio, a tasteful playboy, contemplates another 'invert' dancer who performs with exaggeratedly feminine movements, Princess of Bourbon" (31). Yet, as Adriana Bergero comments in *Intersecting Tango* (2008), the *garçonnière* is never a neutral place, never a site for dialogue between diverse social actors; rather, it is a space where "only equals [are] welcome for the reciprocal reassurance of 'the masculinity of elite men'" (322). In other words, the languages of power are clearly defined by the *garçonnière*, for it represents the *caballero*'s place of heteronormative sexuality and economic affluence. Why does González Castillo include characters who are otherwise sexually and economically powerless in such an elitist space? What is the role of the queer tango performance in what was arguably one of the most virile places in Buenos Aires during his time? In the realm of the narrative, there is no public source of authority to sanction or punish this digression from the rigidity of social norms. Yet, paradoxically, *Los Invertidos* anticipates the reception it will face from its implied audience. Through this paradoxical approach, González Castillo's play corresponds to Yuri Lotman's semiospheric ambivalence. That is, González Castillo blurs the dividing line between the private and public spaces in literary practice, just as Lotman both separates and unites multiple semiotic spaces in his cultural theory. It is precisely this paradox that makes the Lotmanian model relevant to understanding *Los Invertidos*. Ultimately, the way in which González Castillo defines the national belonging of homosexual men depends upon his portrayal of their "membrane-like" behavior[12] inside the *garçonnière*, a private space inverted to become public, as well.

CLASS STRUGGLE IN *LOS INVERTIDOS*

This section explores how a class struggle plays out in relationship to national and foreign influences in *Los Invertidos*. In many respects, González Castillo associates the working class with national identity, whereas he ties foreign influences to the bourgeoisie. Choosing to represent the *garçonnière* as a stronghold of the bourgeoisie, in such close proximity with the foreign, makes me believe that the highly respected space of the *garçonnière* in Buenos Aires plays an essential role for writer González Castillo when crafting *Los Invertidos*. The author is able to synthesize his anarchist politics. His choice to use it as a setting where the Argentine ruling class behaves like a "band of stereotyped fairies" (Foster, 22) becomes a means by which he develops his theater of ideas. It appears that his goal in staging overt homosexual behavior in one of the most impenetrable spaces in Buenos Aires might have been to overturn the respectable public image of those in positions of power. In his efforts to support the plight of the working class, González Castillo succeeds above all in providing an antagonistic portrait of the bourgeoisie as relatively emasculated and absolutely self-indulgent.

Although this drama focuses on its wealthier protagonists, its few interventions by working-class characters attest to the anarchist beliefs of the author, who makes no pretense to hide his preference for them. Depicted as truthful and loyal, the only two servants to appear are Petrona and Benito. Although both prove equally important as representatives of the working class, I will focus primarily on Petrona, since she plays a crucial role at the climax of the dramatic action thanks to her complete knowledge of the family's sexual history. When Petrona first appears on stage alongside Julián, who works on his father's report in the office, its heavily charged discourse attracts her attention. She dares to interrupt him by asking, "¿Qué es eso niño?" (What is that my boy?). After he responds that it is his father's report, she adds, "Como tiene tantas palabras raras y no entendía ni jota." (As it contains so many rare words, I didn't understand a thing.) (12). Despite this disclaimer, her curiosity pushes her to continue with additional questions.

When Julián tells her that he is working on a case regarding a person that the medico-legal discourse refers to as an "hermaphrodite, a sexual invert with congenital anesthesia," her so-called ignorance returns. "Si no me habla en cristiano no le v'y a entender." (I won't understand you if you don't speak to me in Christian language.).[13] Julián responds that the report is about an individual who is at once both a man and a woman. Petrona's astonishment, regarding such complex terminology for commonly known behavioral problems, is interesting to examine. She claims, "[¡]Bah! ... Los médicos y los procuradores siempre le han de inventar nombres raros a las cosas más sencillas ... En mis tiempos se les llamaba mariquita, no más, o maricón, que es más claro ... Pa que tantos términos ... [¡]Yo he conocido más de cien!" (Bah! ... Doctors and lawyers always end up inventing odd names for the simplest things ...[14] In my old days, we used to call them "*mariquitas*" nothing else, or "*maricón*" which is much clearer ... How come so many terms ... I've known more than a hundred!) (Ibid.).

In turn, Julián is surprised to learn that the family's old servant, so seemingly unaware of her surroundings, holds information concerning family members with unrecognized sexual preferences. For that reason, he asks where she has met these "mafroditas." She responds, "En donde ha e' ser, pues ... En el mundo.... Usted qué se cree, hay más mafroditas que lo que se parece ... Mire: se lo voy a decir, sabe, pero no lo vaya a repetir,

porque se podría saber ... y el pobre pertenecía a la familia de su papa"
(Where do you think ... well ... in this world there are more "*mafroditas*" than you could imagine, what do you think ... Look: I'll tell you,
my boy, but, don't repeat it to anybody because it could be found out ...
and the poor man used to be a member of your dad's family) (13). As
these utterances indicate, Petrona controls the power of knowledge
about sexual aberration within the family and seems reluctant to share it.
As talkative as she appears to be concerning matters of daily life, she is
more cautious when dealing with family secrets. This discretion notwith-
standing, she tells Julián about "that" uncle (Dr. Florez's cousin) who
was known as "Lilli" and who used to look more like a woman than a
man: with woman's powder, some perfume, a fan, and "who knows," she
says, "we may have also seen him dressed as a woman, the swine ... he
really disgusted me!" (13). Because she feels like a member of the family,
Petrona expresses shame when discussing Lilli. She even seems relieved
for his suicide, claiming, "He killed himself ... almost all the *mariquitas*
that I've known have done the same, they've killed themselves ... like a
punishment sent by God" (13). If there were any doubt regarding her
motivations for condemning transgendered behavior, then this comment
puts it to rest by spelling out the religious convictions behind them.

Despite her disapproval, the servant is willing to divulge this secret to
sixteen-year-old Julián. I interpret this choice not as an act of betrayal,
but a warning and an acknowledgment of the tacit rules usually gov-
erning patriarchal lineage in Latin America. Since Petrona has worked
with the family for generations and helped raise Dr. Florez, often finding herself privy to their private lives, she occupies a position of unlikely
authority, as an heir to the Florez family secrets. Her decision to share
such a shameful family stain with Julián reflects awareness that under the
Hispano-American patriarchal model at the turn of the twentieth century, Julián, the eldest and only male child, will become the head of the
Florez household. As such, he should know the truth in order to take
pride in it—or to hide it, in which case, he must learn how to protect the
family from any possible consequences—as it seems Petrona could teach
him to do.

Amid this conversation with Julián, Petrona is the first to enlighten the
audience about Dr. Florez's homosexual behavior. When asked about his
whereabouts, she maintains, "casi siempre sale solo ... o con ese señor
Pérez ... Estaban juntos en el colegio ... Y era un peine, el tal Pérez ...
más sinvergüenza cuando muchacho" (he usually goes out alone ... or

with Mr. Pérez … They went to school together … And, Mr. Pérez, he was a bad influence … he had no shame when he was younger) (13). As soon as Julián interrupts because he dislikes her way of talking about his father's friend, she adds, "Yo no hablo mal de nadie … digo lo que es" (I'm not bad-mouthing anybody … I'm just saying how it is) (ibid.). Knowing that he could be disappointed by what she might say or not say, should he attempt to prod her further, Julián tells her, "No diga tanto, pues … en todo se ha de meter …" (Don't speak too much, then … you meddle in everywhere … (14). She responds, "Está bien … ya me voy … [';]En todo se ha de meter!' [¡]Yo no me meto en nada, oh! [¿]Pa qué me pregunta, también[?]" (It's ok … I'll get going … "You meddle in everywhere!" I don't meddle anywhere! Why are you asking me, then?) (ibid.).

In these first lines dedicated to the character, the audience distinguishes an enthusiastic older lady, also very sharp and wise. Although her behavior seems not to follow conventional patterns, she speaks reverently in regard to Dr. Florez. In this context, she suggests a double-standard, by which she forgives her boss even if he behaves "awkwardly," while she disparages his friend, Mr. Pérez. In fact, she goes as far as to express disgust for him—not unlike Lilli—but it seems to stem above all from his "poor influence" on Dr. Florez, of whom she feels possessive. After all, she is fully conscious that Mr. Pérez has been her employer's friend since childhood when they attended the same boarding school. In sum, the opening scene demonstrates that she chooses when, how, and to whom to disclose information. However, insensitive or capricious her judgments may appear to audience members holding various social views across time; Petrona cannot be considered merely a working-class servant who accepts any and all behaviors from her employer with indifference. On the contrary, her profession is a chief reason why she believes herself aptly placed to judge the Florez family with both caring and discernment. The opening scene, then, provides us with an intuitive and thoughtful servant who knows when, to whom and about what type of information she should disclose. As the sole container bearer of the truth about the aberrations of the family sexual history (at least, in her own eyes), Petrona has complete power over and controls the transmission of confidential knowledge. In this manner, she also becomes the protector of masculine sexuality in the Florez family.

Beyond the narrative, Gustavo Geirola's "Sexualidad, Anarquía y Teatralidad en *Los Invertidos* de González Castillo" (1995) proposes that the Argentinean author reflects an official concern for masculine sexuality in *Los Invertidos* as such: "desde el caso de ... Flórez, su hijo y sus amigos, la obra se preocupa por la transmisión [y crisis] de la masculinidad" (beginning with the case of ... Florez, his son and his friends, the work is concerned with the transmission [and crisis] of masculinity) (79–80). In particular, Petrona behaves like a watchful guardian, careful to avoid indiscretions on her part that could potentially harm the family's reputation in the bourgeois milieu. To the extent in which the viewing public finds her self-assured knowledge convincing, and her defensive strategies effective, Petrona becomes a means for González Castillo to siphon power away from the bourgeoisie to the working class.

Anarchist Beliefs and a Drama of Ideas

In their essay "José González Castillo: Cine Mudo, Fábricas y *Garçonnières*" (1991), Aníbal Ford and Nora Mazziotti provide an insightful analysis of González Castillo's anarchist ideas and his preference for the drama of ideas. They argue that González Castillo is an "anarquista, perseguido y exiliado, [quien] acompañó las luchas obreras de principios de siglo" (anarchist, persecuted and in exile, [who] supported workers' struggles at the start of the century) (77), while befriending "chorros, prostitutas y vagabundos" (homeless, prostitutes, and tramps) (79). Ford and Mazziotti also point out that the author favors taboo spaces that illustrate the urban chaos of Buenos Aires, where the changes produced by modernity are reflected in spaces at odds with each other, such as the *garçonnière* and the sweatshop. While this opposition undoubtedly holds true, it must be added that other spaces complement each other, including the *garçonnière* and the lawyer's office in *Los Invertidos*.

I suggest that the author chooses these bourgeois settings for his play in order to reveal hypocrisy and moral corruption among the select few, as well as to construct an argument *a contrario* (opposite) that condemns their economic privilege. In this respect, *Los Invertidos* might be interpreted as using a didactic tone to instruct its audience; however, it adopts above all the trappings of legal discourse by giving dramatic form to the case-building language of lawyers. The fact that the opening scene illustrates the intimate setting of a lawyer's home shows, as well, the relationship between drama and legislation—two essential characteristic elements to anarchism. Ford and Mazziotti declare that González Castillo's intersection of drama and legislation can be interpreted as denouncing "[una] forma de injusticia de una sociedad que para los resentidos, para los culpables o humillados sólo responde con leyes rígidas, con cárceles que aumentan la corrupción, con asilos de niños arrancados a sus madres 'pecadoras' [y] con la beneficencia hipócrita" ([a] form of injustice against a society to which the resentful, incarcerated or humiliated only responds with strict laws, incarcerations that increase corruption, with orphanages of children removed from their "sinful" mothers [and] with a hypocritical welfare system) (84). Within this context, the author's alliance with marginal members of society also shows his preference for a drama of ideas in *Los Invertidos*, which likewise carries a significant influence in his other plays.[15] It is precisely through the semiotics of legislation and the drama of ideas, as a genre, that González Castillo's play demonstrates membrane-like behavior, by which the author puts traditional Argentinean values in contact with more alternative lifestyles, associated with the French.

It would of course prove ineffective for an anarchist author to take a naïve position that haphazardly seeks to persuade others that his political leanings constitute a viable alternative to traditional government. More than merely evoking the controversial subject of homosexuality, González Castillo warns the Argentinean nation about the immorality of the ruling class by deploring this sexual preference as morally degenerate. In other words, he uses this social debate as a means to reinforce class strife, in search of allies among the working poor who would be otherwise likely to share more traditional values.

It is worthwhile to remember that Argentina in particular was experiencing a national identity crisis due to massive European immigration and drastic changes produced by rapid industrialization at the beginning of the twentieth century. The ever-changing alliances formed in this period of socioeconomic and political turmoil left González Castillo poised to write at the intersection of overlapping semiotic spaces, as self-contradictory as his stance might appear to some contemporary readers. His anarchist beliefs situate him siding with the poorer sectors. Here, we find ourselves at the possibility of adding another topic of study—in which case, we would be adding another semiotic layer to the Lotmanian network of the semiosis of culture—and so I would simply like to emphasize the significance of the continuous reproduction of the multileveled formations when considering the Lotman's model. However, continuing with the location of the complex multiple relationships in González Castillo's work, I align my thought with that of Ford and Mazziotti's who aptly note that the play brings together seemingly distinct semiotic levels to forge unexpected combinations of thought.

Tal vez alguien lea en la obra de González Castillo hibrideces, transla-
ciones, convergencia de niveles aparentemente disímiles. Pero todo esto es
la cultura misma, el intento de dar sentido a los cambios y las transformaciones, no como respuesta funcionalista, sino desde los mismos cambios y
las transformaciones que se producen en la Argentina de la etapa. (80)

(Perhaps some may read hybridities, translations, and convergences of
apparently dissimilar levels in González Castillo's work. But all of this
is a reflection of the culture of his time, the effort to make sense of the
changes and transformations, not only as a functionalist reaction but as a
participant of the changes and transformations taking place in Argentina of
the period.) (80)

As Ford and Mazziotti point out in this passage, González Castillo seems
adamant to contribute to the future nation-state through these combinations of ideas. Given the scope of the changes taking place at the time,
his work aims to influence long-term thinking about the dynamics of
power in Argentinean society.

Such an infinite reproduction of manifold thematic levels reflects a
twofold realization: González Castillo's anarchist ideas and preference
for the drama of ideas aiming to show the class struggle that overturns
the bourgeoisie's public image, succeeding in depicting the working class
in a positive manner on the one hand; and on the other, all the unanswered questions that have originated from the unstoppable multiplica-
tion of the thematic layers in *Los Invertidos* behave as the driving force of
what Lotman calls "semiotic dynamism."[16] As such, they will continue to
intersect with each other, reproducing infinite interpretative possibilities
and additional semiotic spaces within González Castillo's play.

DR. FLOREZ AS A BOUNDARY FIGURE

If the semiospheric boundary line both unites and divides, as Lotman
suggests, then the same principle applies to representation in this work
by González Castillo. He may in fact have preferred writing drama of
ideas theater partly because it lends itself to supporting an ideological
agenda even while inspiring reflection and further debate. Above all,
he seems to have believed it to be his nationalistic duty to alert society against what he perceives as a destabilizing and threatening sexual
inversion that occurs in the otherwise prestigious French space of the

garçonnière. The main character, Dr. Florez,[17] experiences both inclusion and exclusion simultaneously. On the one hand, he experiences inclusion within Argentine society since he belongs to the upper echelons of its ruling class and influences law-making policies as a lawyer. On the other hand, Dr. Florez falls prey to exclusion to the extent in which he must seek partners outside the national context, in the metaphorically French space of the *garçonnière*.

By showing Dr. Florez (as representative of the ruling class) is contaminated with homosexual desire behaving in such an overt manner in the *garçonnière*, the anarchist writer seems to embark on a mission to cast doubt on his masculinity and to debunk the doctor's reputation by descrediting his masculinity. And once outside the sexual norm, Dr. Florez becomes a polluted agent that must be eradicated from the nation. In this manner, we can attest to Lotman's double-functionality of the semiosphere in *Los Invertidos*. By successfully blurring the dividing line between the public and private spaces, we can observe that the Latin American writer also shows that transforming Dr. Florez as a queer character he also becomes a boundary figure: Dr. Florez experiences inclusion in the national culture—where he acts as a leader in the legal profession—and exclusion from that very same culture, which considers the *garçonnière* to be foreign.

As analyzed in the previous chapter, the outside world is chaotic and sexually deviant. Similarly, González Castillo also exploits the idea of an unruly outside world, which symbolizes a threat to national culture, and the Argentinean writer seems concerned with fending it off. *Los Invertidos* suggests that the bourgeoisie becomes a corrupt class due to its continuous contact with foreign cultures. Before proceeding, it is important to stress the significant role that France has played throughout Latin America since its independence movements in the nineteenth century. During the nation-building period, and national identity crises that ensued, this region underwent continuous battles to delineate what character would be created by the postcolonial countries breaking away from Spain. With this in mind, France contributed one alternative source of inspiration in terms of philosophy, literature, and culture. Factions openly debated the kind of citizens that the nation should value or shun from society. Thus, González Castillo makes his position obvious: The Argentinean bourgeoisie, who has imported excessive French cultural iconography, has also brought homosexuality to Argentina through contact with the French.

Frenchness in the Argentinean Context

José González Castillo uses Frenchness in the shape of the *garçonnière* to contextualize *"le mal qui vient de plus loin."* This evil from abroad has already infiltrated Argentina because of the bourgeoisie. Members of the Argentinean bourgeoisie, in their fascination with French culture, have produced sexual degeneracy, and, as sexual degenerates, they also pollute society in the nation-building process.[18] Adding to this thematic layer, this section specifically deals with the *garçonnière*'s pivotal role as the space where Dr. Florez's sexual deviance is uncovered. Moreover, their promiscuity is not always single-sex based: Dr. Florez's wife, Clara, is lured to the *garçonnière* to engage into an adulterous affair with Mr. Pérez, but soon realizes this is not a bachelor's apartment since those who frequent it are a band of "stereotyped fairies."

In a particularly tense scene, their intention to engage in adultery is discovered. Surprised that queer characters are not allowed in the apartment because there is "a real woman" with Mr. Pérez, Clara, who is hiding, eavesdrops on their conversation. "Ah ... so you are cheating, huh ... ? Let's see what happens when Florez finds out!" (41). To which Pérez reacts violently, "Can you be quiet?" (Ibid.). Suddenly, Dr. Florez appears at the door, wanting to come inside to assist Mr. Pérez with the headache he tells the visitors that he is experiencing. Mr. Pérez's negative response aggravates the situation, as the queer friends sarcastically tell Dr. Florez that Mr. Pérez is in excellent company with "a real woman." When Mr. Pérez confirms their comment, "Florez is paralyzed, confused. Then, he seems to react ... quavering with jealousy;... he makes gestures showing a terrible internal battle and then leaves abruptly" (42). On their way out of Mr. Pérez's *garçonnière*, the others shout as loudly as possible, "I love scenes of jealousy like these ... Let's get out of here!" (ibid.). Such scandalous behavior provokes indignation and disgust in Clara who runs out of the premises, shouting at Mr. Pérez: "I don't need your explanations ... Degenerate! ... I've heard it and seen it all ... You disgusting pig!" (41–45). Despite her apparent lack of scruples for extramarital affairs, Clara is repulsed to learn that two men in her life engage in sexual encounters with other men.

Clara's newfound awareness of her husband's homosexual affair in the *garçonnière* has implications for two aspects of politics: the gendered division of space and the writer's anarchist beliefs. If, as S. J. Kleinberg's "Gender Space: Housing, Privacy, and Domesticity in the Nineteenth-Century

United States" (1999) observes, "space usage exemplified hierarchies of gender, with male spaces such as the library being preserved from female intrusions" (148), then Clara's admission to the *garçonnière* violates the hierarchy of gender to which Kleinberg refers. Interestingly, Clara's intrusion and her violent reaction does not draw into question the concept of bourgeois masculinity, since these male love partners are instead represented as a "band of stereotyped fairies." Because she is portrayed as a heterosexual woman safeguarding the masculinity of her family's men, Clara also gains strength to overpower any of the marginally male homosexuals she encounters there. Her violation of male-dominated space causes the demise of the queer characters, most notably her husband, Dr. Florez.

As I have previously discussed, one of the *garçonnière*'s main roles is to protect the elite's masculine sexuality and economic affluence from public view—and, I would add, from gendered disturbances. Although Clara first enters this space with the intention to gratify the masculinity of Mr. Pérez, she becomes a witness to the homosexual behavior that occurs even within such a highly respected space. Rather than engaging in an adulterous affair, she ends up angrily trapped in a web of treachery and hypocrisy, a change that ironically still reassures Mr. Pérez's virility, since he finds himself at the center of this multidirectional love triangle. Within this context, the anarchist writer overturns the national/sexuality dyad. While Clara moves away from being a potential contributor to the sexual satisfaction of a prominent community leader, she stays inert, merely observing homosexual behavior. This unanticipated turn of events places her in parallel with the play's audience. Whether this juxtaposition creates a double-perspective, "the public from 'outside' and Clara from 'inside' [the play]" (80),[19] or strictly a coincidence that the character and viewers discover a dramatic plot twist at the same moment, the writer conveys shock as an expected reaction under the circumstances. All three parties—Clara, the audience, and the writer himself—join up for the same purpose: to form an alliance in order to destroy the bourgeoisie's public image. Thus, Clara's role as an intruder is to expose the French cultural space as one where sexual degenerates congregate.

Upon discovering the relationship between Mr. Pérez and Dr. Florez, Clara shoots Mr. Pérez, then immediately gives the gun to her husband, blames him for his lover's death, and forces him to shoot himself. As some critics have argued by virtue of the metonymy of her name, Clara brings clarity to the drama. She pulls the closet lives of the other figures out from their secret place into the light because there is no space for these corrupting agents in Argentinean society. She seems to know that someone ought to purify the family's name so that its shame will never fall on Julián, her six-teen-year-old son at risk of homosexual infection. In a double homicide, she cleanses her family name from the possible contagion of sexual degeneracy.

Comparable to the protagonist's suicide in Paris from the previous chapter, Dr. Florez's death also occurs in the *garçonnière*. Both of their deaths happen after their homosexual desire is revealed within the so-called French space. Whether that boundary figure travels across town to a French-inspired hideaway, or across the ocean to a modern city, the corruptive geographical or architectural space cannot fully withstand attack from language and social norms in the places that those boundary figures hoped to escape.

The parallel idea of escaping the (home) country in search of homo-sexual realization is also found in the next two chapters. In Chapters 4 and 5, for instance, it is the Frenchmen who travel to North Africa in search of homoerotic adventures with exoticized brown young bodies. More particularly, I focus on homosexual tourism as a cross-cultural encounter between French homosexual tourists and local Moroccan boys. This dyad allows me to highlight class and ethnic differences—and look at the points of resistance that show potential for the teenagers' agency and subject formation in Chapter 5. Chapters 6 and 7 analyze transcultural information and media technology and its produced imag-inaries on local teenagers. Here, I analyze the Moroccan boy's first con-tact with the photographed image of a blond-haired, blue-eyed French boy. This encounter creates the protagonist's interest and affection for the French boy on the one hand; and on the other, it awakens a homoe-rotic desire, which opens the way for my continued discussion of homo-sexual agency and subject formation, introduced in Chapter 6.

CONCLUSION

According to the essay "Sobre la estética naturalista y la ficción erótica" (1989) by Jorge Febles, suicide "has a pedagogical function" (77). If this affirmation holds true, then what is the pedagogy of the suicides depicted in these narratives? Again, the Lotmanian model offers an instructive the-oretical tool to think through a cultural question of critical importance. As outlined at the beginning of this chapter, Lotman makes specific reference to the coding system that originates in the semiosphere's center—where norms are generated and produce layers of cultural systems considered marginal. If they are still unable to correspond to the idealized portrait of that culture as time evolves, then they will be declared nonexistent. Following this pattern, *Los Invertidos* and *El ángel de Sodoma* narrate the lives of two characters who experience homosexual desire but prove unable to lead an open homosexual life. They manage to carve out a life on the culture's periphery, but both end up choosing to become nonexistent when they commit suicide. In this context, suicide is a reflection of the homophobic discourse to which both of these narratives belong. It is best exemplified in the "city without a name" found in Hernández-Catá's novel, which appears not unlike the "uncertain place in the Spanish region of La Mancha" where Don Quixote's plot unfolds. This use of intertextual reference to evoke nonspecificity of place corresponds to the idea about Hispano-Americanization promoted by Latin American intellectuals at the beginning of the twentieth century. By directly invoking the most distinguished literary master in the Spanish language, Hernández-Catá is calling for the creation of an Hispano-American alliance.

There can be little doubt that Hernández-Catá and González Castillo were active participants in the nation-building process that took place throughout Latin America in their era. Their texts took shape against the backdrop of cultural invasion by the French, as well as increasing economic imperialism from the British and North Americans. Whether intentional or inevitable, their implied stance on foreign cultural influences participated in those debates. Juan Carlos Galdo's "Usos y Lecciones del Discurso Ejemplar" (2000) considers that the discourse in *El ángel de Sodoma* is of strictly *hispanoamericanista* origin. For him, this "city without name" is meticulously linked to a differentiating model that aims to distinguish Latin America from other regions. He proposes that this is a heraldic city, meaning a utopian space, which can extend to any desired jurisdiction of Hispanic communities (30). From this perspective, the homosexuality shown in both of these narratives draws a sociopolitical map where the identity of a community carries out the panoptic mission to denounce elements considered undesirable. The notion of a unified region that is characterized by heterosexuality seems inspired by "cultural mentors of Latin American *modernismo*," as Sylvia Molloy explains in "Too Wilde for Comfort: Desire and Ideology in *Fin-de-Siècle* Spanish America" (1992),

Wilde ended up being the disturbing phantasmatic construct of many, certainly haunting Martí and Darío. Yet I will go one step further and propose that this anxiety may be, and indeed should be, contextualized in a larger cultural framework. In other words, I want to argue that Darío and Martí are voicing a collective anxiety, one with which their Latin American readers will identify,... the notion of national, even continental heterosexual health. (191–197)[20]

In other words, Darío's and Martí's preoccupation with Wilde derives from the homophobic discourse that was widespread throughout Latin America at the turn of the century. José González Castillo and Alfonso Hernández-Catá participate in this tradition, especially because they associate French spaces with homosexuality.

As numerous critics have stated, Paris, not Madrid, Havana, Buenos Aires or any other Latin American city, is "the corrupt city par excellence" (Bejel, 32). This specificity of Paris as the corrupting center—and, taking a step further, the very notion of Frenchness as a homoerotically charged—posed a threat to heteronormative institutions amid the process of nation-building in Latin America. Here, the definition of membership is done by a twofold negation of the Other—reinforcing critic Juan Carlos Galdo's observation when he writes, "We are not like the French" (28); and thus unveiling both of these narratives' message: homosexuality does not belong to the Hispano-American identity but to the French.

Notes

1. José González Castillo, *Los Invertidos* (Buenos Aires: Editores Puntosur, 1914).
2. I realize I am on shaky ground, since each of these terms leads to interminable and unavoidable questioning—as any effort to fix the limits of these fields leads to new discursive possibilities.
3. I am using this idea as it is fully developed by Graham Allan, when he discusses the private and public spheres in nineteenth-century England. See Graham Allan and Graham Crow, *Home and Family: Creating the Domestic Sphere* (London: The Macmillan Press, 1989), 141–158.
4. All translations in this book are my own.

5. The literal translation of "*copiar en limpio*" is to "copy in clean"—which means to edit from the first draft, to polish it. I will address this sentence thoroughly in the following section of this chapter.
6. This is a question that I consider to be tightly intertwined with Julián's sentence, where he is "polishing" his father's report; and thus, that I will analyze together.
7. My emphasis on the possessive article "his" room.
8. S. J. Kleingberg, "Gendered Space: Housing, Privacy and Domesticity in the Nineteenth-Century United States," in *Domestic Space: Reading the Nineteenth-Century Interior*, eds. Inga Bryden and Janet Floyd (Manchester and New York: Manchester University Press, 1999), 142–162.
9. Graham Allan, "Insiders and Outsiders: Boundaries Around the Home," in *Home and Family: Creating the Domestic Sphere*, eds. Graham Allan and Graham Crow (London: The Macmillan Press, 1989).
10. David William Foster, "José González Castillo's *Los Invertidos* and the Vampire Theory of Homosexuality," *Latin American Theatre Review* (Spring 1989): 19–29.
11. For a complete analysis concerning homosexual behavior in Argentina, contemporary to González Castillo, see Francisco De Veyga, "El amor en los invertidos sexuales," *Archivos de Criminología y Psiquiatría* 2 (Buenos Aires, 1903): 333–341; José Ingenieros, "Patología de las funciones sexuales–Nueva clasificación genética," *Archivos de Criminología y Psiquiatría* 9 (Buenos Aires, 1910): 3–80. For more recent works, see Donna Guy, *Sex and Danger in Buenos Aires: Prostitution, Family, and Nation in Argentina* (Lincoln: University of Nebraska Press, 1991); and Jorge Salessi, "The Argentine Dissemination of Homosexuality, 1890–1914," *Journal of the History of Sexuality* 4, no. 5 (1994): 337–368.
12. See my analysis on Lotman's term on Chapter 2: It argues that although the beginning point for any culture is based upon the binary distinction of internal versus external space, the Lotmanian cultural membrane allows for the infinite interaction of the multiple paradigmatic levels moving at different rates and changing their spatial dimension.
13. My emphasis on the translation: speaking in "Christian language" means to use "simple" language, as it is spoken and understood by everyone, especially working-class people.
14. As stated previously, all the translations provided here are my own. Here, I would like to underscore the fact that the Spanish used by Petrona shows contractions and semantics done only by the unschooled, working-class individuals in Argentine society; and hence, my choice to provide an incorrect English grammar and syntax.
15. For instance, *El hijo de Ulises* and *La mujer de Agar*.
16. See my own take on Lotman's analysis on Chapter 2.

17. An argument similar to the one developed here in respect to Dr. Florez could be built regarding several queer portraits present in the play, notably a feminine boy, a transvestite, and a bisexual man.

18. Here, I would like to make a parenthesis: As I have previously discussed, González Castillo's play as a reflection of multiple relationships, convergences, and conflicts, which also produces an overlapping of the multiple thematic layers. With this in mind, I previously explored the *garçonnière* not only in relation to the dyad private/public, but also as the space where homosexual behavior is openly revealed.

19. Gustavo Geirola, "Sexualidad, anarquía y teatralidad en *Los Invertidos* de González Castillo," *Latin American Theatre Review* (Spring 1995): 73–84.

20. Sylvia Molloy, "Too Wilde for Comfort: Desire and Ideology in *Fin-de-Siècle* Spanish America," *Social Text* 31–32 (1992): 187–201.

REFERENCES

Allan, Graham. "Insiders and Outsiders: Boundaries Around the Home." In *Home and Family: Creating the Domestic Sphere*, edited by Graham Allan and Graham Crow, 141–158. London: The Macmillan Press, 1989.

Allan, Graham, and Graham Crow. "Introduction." In *Home and Family: Creating the Domestic Sphere*, edited by Graham Allan and Graham Crow, 1–13. London: The Macmillan Press, 1989.

Bejel, Emilio. *Gay Cuban Nation*. Chicago: The University of Chicago Press, 2001.

Bergero, Adriana. *Intersecting Tango: Cultural Geographies of Buenos Aires, 1900–1930*. Translated by Richard Young. Pittsburgh: The University of Pittsburgh Press, 2008.

De Veyga, Francisco. "El amor en los invertidos sexuales." *Archivos de Criminología y Psiquiatría* 2 (1903): 333–341.

Foster, David William. "José González Castillo's *Los Invertidos* and the Vampire Theory of Homosexuality." *Latin American Theatre Review* (Spring 1989): 19–29.

Ford, Aníbal, and Nora Mazziotti. "José González Castillo: Cine Mudo, Fábricas y Garçonnières." In *Los Invertidos*. José González Castillo. Buenos Aires: Editores Puntosur, 1991.

Galdo, Juan Carlos. "Usos y Lecciones del Discurso Ejemplar: A Propósito de *El ángel de Sodoma* de Alfonso Hernández-Catá." *Chasqui* 29, no. 1 (2000): 19–32.

Geirola, Gustavo. "Sexualidad, Anarquía y Teatralidad en *Los Invertidos* de González Castillo." *Latin American Theatre Review* (Spring 1995): 73–84.

González Castillo, José. *Los Invertidos*. Buenos Aires: Editores Puntosur, 1914.

Guy, Donna. *Sex and Danger in Buenos Aires: Prostitution, Family, and Nation in Argentina*. Lincoln: University of Nebraska Press, 1991.

Ingenieros, José. "Patología de las funciones sexuales–Nueva clasificación genética." *Archivos de Criminología y Psiquiatría* 9 (1910): 3–80.

Kleingberg, S. J. "Gendered Space: Housing, Privacy, and Domesticity in the Nineteenth-Century United States." In *Domestic Space: Reading the Nineteenth-Century Interior*, edited by Inga Bryden and Janet Floyd, 142–161. Manchester and New York: Manchester University Press, 1999.

Lotman, Yuri. *Universe of the Mind: A Semiotic Theory of Culture*. Translated by Ann Shukman. London: I.B. Tauris & Co Ltd, 1990.

Molloy, Sylvia. "Too Wilde for Comfort: Desire and Ideology in *Fin-de-Siècle* Spanish America." *Social Text* 31–32 (1992): 187–201.

Salessi, Jorge. "The Argentine Dissemination of Homosexuality, 1890–1914." *Journal of the History of Sexuality* 4, no. 5 (1994): 337–368.

PART II

Exoticization of Brown Bodies: Strategic Confusion in North Africa

CHAPTER 4

Travels in North Africa: Orientalism or Frenchness?

To what degree are homosexual subjects able to live out their fantasies despite the normative demands of society? By juxtaposing the trope of the exclusion of the Other with the French Other, the Latin American project excludes homosexuals from its territory and places them within French cultural space. Whereas the Latin American narrative tends to associate France with a queer space that promotes sexual deviance, the French themselves have often considered North Africa to be a homoerotic playground. Unlike boundary figures who leave Latin America for Europe in search of greater sexual freedom, Frenchmen who travel to North Africa in search of exotic brown boys in homosexual adventures bring with them a significant cultural cachet and strong socioeconomic power. Tales of the homosexual tourism industry indeed reveal an ongoing struggle to deal with the dyad of the privileged French tourist and marginal Moroccan boy. Yet, focusing on the perspective of local boys makes it possible to trace their potential resistance to exploitation in such cross-cultural encounters. After a brief overview of sexual tourism in the French literary tradition, I therefore examine how Moroccan writers represent homosexual tourism in Morocco through the viewpoint of these young characters.

With this in mind, the first section focuses on André Gide's account of homosexual tourism in the groundbreaking novel *L'immoraliste* (1902), where the main character's extended stay in the North African city of Biskra shows how the encounter with the exotic boy occurs according

© The Author(s) 2019
L. Navarro-Ayala, *Queering Transcultural Encounters*,
Palgrave Studies in Globalization and Embodiment,
https://doi.org/10.1007/978-3-319-92315-4_4

to his perspective as a privileged tourist. The second section focuses on Mohamed Choukri's autobiography, *Le pain nu* (1980), where I under-score the local boy's perspective in order to illustrate the flip side of homosexual tourism as a cross-cultural encounter. My analysis stresses the controversial bonds created in spite of the politically charged con-texts that surround the male characters in these novels due to wide age gaps between them. Despite challenging socioeconomic conditions, the young protagonist shows some initiative to develop (sexual) agency, which remains latent or becomes realized depending on the assistance he receives from additional members of their social milieu.

My reading of homosexual tourism in North Africa addresses the ways in which class and ethnic differences impact relationships in a predom-inantly masculine public space. It treats the streets and cafés as points of contact for boys and male youth whose encounters prove insep-arable from the financial hardships that they experience in Morocco. I suggest that the writers' choice to raise a collective voice on the mat-ter breaks the silence that most often surrounds this taboo in North Africa and that the Moroccan government has hereto chosen to ignore. Mohamed Choukri is joined by writer Rachid O. in the next chapter to call attention, as they both seem "moved by a sense of urgency and responsibility" (23), as Françoise Lionnet describes authors from colonial backgrounds in her study of postcolonial autobiography in *Postcolonial Representations: Women, Literature, Identity* (1995).[1]

Beyond Survival? Agency Development

My approach to study the three Moroccan boys chosen for Chapters 4 and 5 stems from "cultures of survival" as defined by Homi Bhabha's in his chapter entitled "The postcolonial and the postmodern: The ques-tion of agency" in *The Location of Culture* (1994).[2] I am interested on Bhabha's reference to counterhegemonic strategies that shy away from a generalizing series of negative ontologies. He considers such inde-terminism to be an indication of the "conflictual yet productive space" that allows for a reinterpretation of what is commonly regulated cultural signification (171). He reminds us that the individuals who have expe-rienced subjugation or domination are those from whom "we learn our most enduring lessons for living and thinking" (172). Their social mar-ginality begins not only to emerge in "non-canonical cultural forms" but also to transform "our critical strategies." This process encourages scholars "to confront the concept outside *objets d'art* or beyond the canonization of the 'idea of aesthetics'"; hence, there will occur an engagement with culture as an "uneven, incomplete production of meaning and value, often composed of incommensurable demands and practices, produced in the act of social survival" (ibid.). It is precisely within this context of social survival that I understand the Moroccan boys' participation in homosexual encounters with European tourists in these narratives. My attempt is not only to point out at the affective experience of their social marginality, but also to treat their cross-cultural encounters with the French Other as a "mark of the conflictual yet productive space" (ibid.) that society may occupy in literary accomplishments.

If, as Homi Bhabha states, culture "reaches out to create a symbolic textuality, to give the alienating everyday an aura of selfhood, a promise of pleasure" (ibid.), then Mohamed's involvement in homosexual meetings with Europeans moves beyond canonized aesthetics and the tragic victimization of the local boy. Although the character might live out a fragmented story, his is also a culture of survival, since it does not necessarily occur "in the ordered *musée imaginaire* of national cultures with their claims to the continuity of an authentic 'past' a living 'present'" (ibid.). In other words, the transmission of cultures of survival as defined by Bhabha can only be achieved through the complexities of social structures and interpersonal relationships that often fall outside normative expectations. In their introduction to *Queer Studies: An Interdisciplinary Reader* (2003),[3] Robert J. Corber and Stephen Valocchi more broadly affirm that the subject "does not exist prior to social structures but is constituted in and through them, and thus it is neither autonomous nor unified but contingent and split" (3). The relationship between social structure and individual agency is indeed paramount in order to discern the nature of power, the stability of communities, the role of institutions and culture, and finally the history of the organization of social life. Chapters 4 and 5 look at the ways in which it may prevent or enable agency among young postcolonial subjects in development.

Homosexual Tourism in the French Literary Tradition

Recent work has focused primarily on the perspective of the European traveler in French literature in search of homoerotic adventures in the Orient during the nineteenth and early twentieth centuries.[4] My approach centers on social class and ethnic differences in André Gide's

L'immoraliste in order to extend our understanding of their role in cross-cultural encounters between the European traveler and the local Arab boys in North Africa within this novel. Michel, the protagonist, and his wife, Marceline, embark on a healing pilgrimage from North to South. Herself in perfect health, Marceline encourages and assists her convalescent husband throughout this trip. When they finally arrive in Biskra, she realizes her husband spends very long days in bed; thus, she decides to bring Arab boys to entertain him in their lodgings. The once dying French traveler quickly seems to absorb the adolescent visitors' strapping health. He then experiences an invigorating desire to live and leave his quarters in order to explore Biskra. His wife decides to take him to the city park, where he quickly realizes there are men everywhere, stating, "Presque pas d'étrangers, quelques Arabes; tous circulent. [Ils] passèrent; puis survint une troupe d'enfants" (Not many foreigners, some Arabs; all of them went in circles, they passed by; then, a group of kids followed) (43).[5]

Michel finds the park stunning, with an alluring shadow projected by the trees along the river and beautifully colored by the local soil, which is a clayish pink. Completely intoxicated by this sensuous colors in the park, Michel discovers that his wife is the only reason why he does not feel fully recovered. He declares, "ce qui me gênait, l'avouerai-je, ce n'étaient pas les enfants, c'était elle. Oui … j'étais gêné par sa présence" (and there again came my discomfort; but which annoyed me, I must confess, was not the kids, but her. Yes … I was annoyed by her presence) (43). What seems to bother Michel is the fact that his wife sticks to him not just like a shadow, but more like super-ego who represents social norms and judgment. "[P]arler aux enfants, je ne l'osais pas devant elle…. Rentrons, lui dis-je; et je résolus à part moi de retourner seul au jardin" ([T]alk to the kids, I wouldn't dare before her…. Let's go back, I told her; and then, I decided to return to the garden alone) (ibid.).

Dehumanization of Arab Boys

With renewed physical strength, Michel decides to liberate himself from his wife in Biskra. He returns by himself to the city garden, where he hopes to experience once again the revitalizing intoxication provided by the setting. As soon as he reaches the park, he is approached by local boys, for they anticipate receiving coins in exchange for any services provided to French tourists. As the Frenchman sits on a bench, unable to pick up his shawl, "un grand garçon de quatorze ans, noir comme un Soudanais,... s'offrit de lui-même. Il se nommait Ashour. Il [lui] aurait paru beau s'il n'avait été borgne" (a tall fourteen-year-old boy, black like a Sudanese,... offered himself. His name was Ashour. He would have been beautiful if he had not been one-eyed) (45). Michel's emphatic description on Ashour's physical characteristics denies full humanness to the local boy. Although exotic, this blackish-brown body "like a Sudanese" is treated as damaged goods which do not fully satisfy the observer. The division of this body into body parts (i.e., tall, young, black, and one-eyed) objectifies the boy, stripping off his individuality and personality—whose only existence seems to aim to the full satisfaction of the Frenchman. In this context, Elisa Puvia and Jeroen Vaes observe accurately in their article "Being a Body" (2013) that "the objectified becomes instrumental or useful for the observer, for example, to fulfill one's sexual desires ... [and that] the tendency to chronically and pervasively focus on one's physical appearance can translate in perceiving the objectified as not fully human" (485).[6]

What initially begins as a denial of humanness, but still remaining an "imperfect" blackish-brown Sudanese-like body, *L'immoraliste* later provides descriptions with an overt dehumanization of Arab boys when they are compared to domesticated animals. Moving beyond physical features, these representations initially refer to personality traits, as if the French traveler were individualizing the boys and noticing special talents or attributes to them—when, in fact, what he does is to dehumanize the local boys he meets in the street by turning them into cats or dogs. Comparing the *"petit Arabe"* to a cat, *L'immoraliste* reads, "Quand il riait, il découvrait des dents très blanches; il lécha plaisamment sa blessure; sa langue était rose comme celle d'un chat. Ah! qu'il se portait bien. C'était là ce dont je m'éprenais en lui: la santé. La santé de ce petit corps était belle" (34) (When he laughed, he showed very white teeth; he licked his wound pleasantly; his tongue was pink like a cat's. Ah! He was well-behaved. That's where I became besotted with him: his health. The health of this little body was beautiful) (34).

An additional description compares the Arab boy to a dog, "Le petit Bachir, qui manquait rarement de venir le matin, prit mon châle; [n] ous étions presque seuls dans l'allée; je marchais lentement, m'asseyais un instant, repartais. Bachir suivait, bavard; fidèle et souple comme un chien." (43) (The little Bachir, who seldom missed coming in the morning, took my shawl; we were almost alone in the alley; I walked slowly, sat down for a moment, went back. Bachir followed, talkative; faithful and docile like a dog.) (43). Referring to the French language online Larousse dictionary, the adjective *"souple"* is defined as malleable or complaisant. If we are to take complaisant, as someone who is willing to please others, we could assume that Michel is thinking of young Bachir as someone who is also willing to please him—in whatever form or shape that pleasure takes. It could simply be the pleasure of acting as a companion in Michel's morning walks, when they cross several new alleys is Biskra or as malleable or willing to perform *unnamable* acts, which would require some of the bodily maneuvering skills attributed to the definition of *"souple"* in the Larousse dictionary: someone who possesses easiness in moving his/her body, to impose him/her several positions which would entail diverse movements (*Qui a beaucoup de facilité pour mouvoir son corps, lui imposer des positions, des mouvements divers*).[7]

Further, if to dehumanize is to deprive individuals of positive human qualities, comparing Arab boys to domesticated animals epitomizes the dehumanizing images in which "ethnic and racial others have been represented, both in popular cultural and in scholarship" (252), as Nick Haslam claims in his article "Dehumanization: An Integrative Review" (2006).[8] Haslam asserts that ethnic others have been historically described as barbarians without culture, self-control, moral awareness, or intelligence. Another consistent representation is the comparison of people to animals. Nick Haslam adds,

> In racist descriptions Africans are compared to apes and sometimes explicitly denied membership of the human species. Other groups are compared to dogs, pigs, rats, parasites, or insects. Visual depictions caricature physical features to make ethnic others look animal-like. At other times, they are likened to children, their lack of rationality, shame, and sophistication seen patronizingly as innocence rather than bestiality. (252–253)

The patronizing tone used in *L'immoraliste* to refer to fourteen- and fifteen-year-old boys is clearly expressed in Haslam's accurate observation about the process of dehumanization. The children Michel meets in the street are treated in a patronizing manner, "as innocence rather than bestiality," to put it in Haslam's words. These ethnicized and racialized children must not be treated as children, exclusively; they are not Arab adult men who, through the process of dehumanization, would be treated as cognitively incompetent or as innocent Arab children. These racialized Arab boys are already children, and as such, they must undergo a process of further dehumanization. Although apparently sympathetic, Michel, in fact, dehumanizes these Arab boys by denying them any attributes to the human species, turning them into docile domesticated pets. As Fabio Fasoli et al. indicate in their essay "Not 'just words'" (2015), "[d]ehumanization involves the denial of human characteristics and attributes to others" (238).[9] This attests the sense of superiority portrayed by the French traveler, and hence, it reiterates the complex process of dehumanization, which Fasoli et al. observe that it "occurs when people perceive others as belonging to a lower order of humanity" (ibid.).

Biskra: A Gift Exchange Culture?

Becoming aware of the attraction he represents for the locals in Briska, Michel, the protagonist in *L'immoraliste*, promises himself "un autre jour, de descendre tout seul au jardin et d'attendre, assis sur un banc, le hasard d'une rencontre heureuse" (another day, to return to the garden alone and wait, while sitting on a bench, for the chance of a happy encounter) (59). During this period of increasing attraction towards the male park-goers, Michel begins to neglect his wife; he takes solitary strolls through the city and the park with the sole objective to meet the local boys. As he engages in conversation with them, they enter into a trading system.

> Certains m'accompagnaient au loin [chaque jour j'allongeais mes marches], m'indiquaient, pour rentrer, un passage nouveau, se chargeaient de mon manteau et de mon châle quand parfois j'emportais les deux; avant de les quitter je leur distribuais des piécettes; parfois ils me suivaient, toujours jouant, jusqu'à ma porte; parfois enfin ils la passèrent. (53)

> (Some of them would accompany me very far [every day I would stretch my walks], would indicate to me a new pass upon return, taking care of my coat and my shawl at times; and at times, I would carry both; before leaving them, I would hand them out some coins; sometimes they would follow me, still playing, to my door; and sometimes they finally entered.) (53)

We see that the European visitor obtains services (i.e., taking the coat and shawl) while the local boys receive gifts in return (i.e., coins). The anticipated outcome of these meetings for both parties reflects how the factors of class and ethnicity play a crucial role in cross-cultural encounters. Although homosexual contact is not specifically mentioned in the novel,[10] Michel's realization that he prefers these boys' company, rather than his wife's, has a two-sided effect: He not only becomes self-aware about his homoerotic tendencies, which seem to be more blatant as he prolongs his stay in Biskra, but he also recognizes that his privileged status as a French visitor facilitates the meetings. The fact that the attractive Arab boys would run small errands in exchange for a few coins offered by the much older Frenchman transforms these otherwise banal promenades of a patient in recovery into potential examples of sexual tourism in Gide's *L'immoraliste*.

The verb tenses in the original French imply ambiguities. On the one hand, the imperfect tense describes a concrete set of permissible events that occur in the public space. These are expectations in a cross-cultural encounter between an older Frenchman and North African boys. As a European in North Africa, Michel expects that the Arab boys follow him, indicate new passages in the city, and take charge of the cloak and the shawl; in return, these boys anticipate that the Frenchman would hand out coins. On the other hand, the simple past tense used in the last phrase from the quote above deliberately leaves events up to the imagination of the reader, who envisions *forbidden* and *unnamable* acts (emphasis added) between the protagonist and the Arab boys who enter the private sphere of his home, "enfin ils la pass*èrent*"[11] (my emphasis on the conjugation). Indeed, it is tantalizing to read a three-and-a-half-page description about Arab boys in the park that abruptly concludes with such a finalizing indoor period that remains unnarrated: The narrator mentions in passing that some of these boys accompanied him home without providing a detailed account of what, in fact, may have transpired inside that more intimate space.

Michel's convalescence turns into sexual play, and he falls into the stereotypical pattern of an early twentieth century white explorer, for he now embodies the "sexual traveler in the Orient," as critic Jarrod Hayes points out when he discusses sexual tourism in *Queer Nations: Marginal Sexualities in the Maghreb* (2000). Hayes states that the Orient becomes the point of homoerotic traveling not only for homosexuals, but also for nineteenth-century European heterosexuals, who seem to develop a desire to explore non-normative sexual relationships once they venture outside their familiar surroundings in Europe. Once in the

Orient, they pursue encounters involving "sex with a stereotype" (46) rather than consciously challenge cross-racial or class-related boundaries, they appear to have maintained the predetermined image of the native and to have preferred making "love with the cliché" (ibid.). Along these lines, Jarrod Hayes suggests that Jean Genet can also be considered a sexual tourist, who "had two long-term relationships with North African men … The first, Abdellah Bentaga, son of an Algerian man and … [t]he second, Mohammed El Katrani, a Moroccan" (41). The experience of having "sex with a stereotype" is explicitly illustrated in Genet's following interview with Hubert Fichte, which, in Hayes's words, best "describes a Moroccan trick with the racist stereotypes" involved in sexual tourism:

> G: –I was in Morocco. I met a young 24- or 25-year-old Moroccan man, very poor. He came up to my room every day. He stayed in my room. *He left my money alone. He didn't touch anything.* Do I admire him for that? No. I think *it was a ploy.* In short, I admire him for having tricked me to such a degree.
>
> H. F. –Later, you brought him to France?
>
> G. –Of course, and he was very clever, I don't regret having brought him to France. *In Arab countries, in Third-World countries, a young boy,* as soon as he meets a *white guy* who pays him a little attention, can only see in him a potential victim, *a man to rob, and that's normal.* (42, emphasis added)

Beyond self-victimization or the possibility for migration to Europe as the ultimate profit from sexual tourism, Genet's sexual encounter with the ethnic Other suggests above all a profound racist stereotype. The European traveler anticipates deceit and robbery from the local boy while engaging in sexual contact. He feels that he was duped into trusting the young man who never touched his money only to learn later that he was robbed of his affection in order to gain access to the economy of his more developed nation. Why would the white European explorer take such risk to engage in sexual tourism in North Africa? Some critics provide a possible answer in their understanding of the relation between sexual repression at home and tourism abroad. In *Sexual Dissidence* (1991), Jonathan Dollimore comments,

[T]he homosexual is involved with difference … Sexually exiled from the repressiveness of the home culture …, homosexuals have searched instead for fulfillment in the realm of the foreign. Not necessarily as a second best…. That this has also occurred in exploitative, sentimental, and/or racist forms does not diminish its significance; if anything, it increases it. Those who move too hastily to denounce homosexuality across race and class as essentially or only exploitative, sentimental, or racist betray their own homophobic ignorance. (250)

By contextualizing sexual tourism from the perspective of the European homosexual traveler—as the experience of a man who is the victim of homophobia at home and, thus, must seek human fulfillment and satisfaction elsewhere—Dollimore seems to question the legitimacy of certain positions from which homosexual tourism is critiqued. Here, the most essential notion to retain is that national and racial boundaries tend to carry an inordinate weight within relationships founded on homosexual tourism, regardless of the individual mind-set of its participants. Whether they wholeheartedly embrace stereotypes or fight against them only to fear feeling cheated in the end, European travelers and their lovers must all confront a presupposed imbalance of power at play behind their relationship.

While much has been written about the striking similarities between the white traveler/local boy dyad and its parallels to the binary colonizer/colonized, my approach seeks to move beyond the colonizer's homoerotic gaze by highlighting instead the local boy's perspective of the encounter with the European Other. Instead of dealing primarily with the colonialist implications of Western gay texts that deal with the Orient or the complexities of the interaction between colonial and sexual discourses within the texts, I concentrate on the interplay of desires attempting to break free from such binaries, despite the external pressures of social norms and politics.

PUBLIC SPACE

In "Body Politics" (1997),[12] Jan Jindy Pettman suggests that sex is associated with bodies which are not only sexualized but also nationalized, racialized, and culturalized. She asks how youngsters in the sex trade may move from a "bodily presence to a voice/voices, in circumstances where power relations are so often loaded against them" (104). The response to such a question may well lie in their use of public space. All males in Morocco are expected to participate in public space, since exploring it is part of their masculinity formation.[13] In fact, the streets and cafés are the places where boys and male youngsters spend most of their time when they are not in school or at work. In reference to the boys in the street from a Near Eastern perspective, Joseph Boone suggests in "Vacation Cruises: Or, the Homoerotics of Orientalism" (1995),

> The term underage sex carries little or no meaning and little of the sense of taboo or moral condemnation that it bears within Western constructions of sexuality as an adult activity; *a child*, particularly one of *the peasantry or working class*, is never a sexual innocent, indeed is a practicing adult from the time *he takes to the streets as his own*. (105, emphasis added)[14]

My intention is not to justify what Boone calls "underage sex" or to question this practice in the context of children's rights, but rather to stress the inferences in this passage concerning the cultural and socioeconomic realities in Morocco, as most of the children who take the streets on their own come from a disadvantaged socioeconomic position. Their use of the public space exposes them to the dangers of the street, among which is the allure of engaging in sex with the European gay tourist. While the initial intention is often merely to make financial gain when running errands, these minors nonetheless run the risk of being lured into taking on dubious activities, as suggested by André Gide's deliberate ambiguity as regards the events inside his protagonist's vacation home in Biskra.

SEXUAL TOURISM AS A CROSS-CULTURAL ENCOUNTER: WHEN HIS BODY MAKES THE MONEY

One of the first accounts of homosexual tourism in Moroccan literature is *Le pain nu* (1980) by Mohamed Choukri.[15] Considered by many critics one of the most controversial autobiographies in Arabic Literature, its frank tone relates a compilation of sexual and masturbatory experiences. The narrator describes the time when walking down the streets of Tangiers at sixteen years old, he is picked up by an older Spanish man in a car:

> Je me suis promené le long de l'avenue d'Espagne.... Les hommes regardent le cul des belles passantes. Une voiture s'arrête à mon niveau. Un vieillard me fait signe:

- « Monte! »

Je pris place à côté de lui. Que me voulait-il? C'était la première fois que je montais dans une aussi belle voiture. Il roulait lentement. Je lui demandai en espagnol où nous allions.

- « Faire un tour. » (Il fit un geste de la main.) « Un petit tour. »

Il allait certainement me demander quelque chose de ne pas très honnête. Enfin, je n'étais pas dupe. Je n'avais pas peur. J'étais capable de me défendre en cas de ... On se dirigeait vers les environs de la ville. Un pédéraste. J'en étais sûr. Il arrêta la voiture dans un coin sombre.... Il alluma la lampe intérieure de la voiture et passa sa main sur ma braguette. C'était donc ça, le petit tour! Le vrai petit tour commençait. Il déboutonna ma braguette avec lenteur, éteignit la lampe, se baissa sur moi ... [p]our aller plus vite, je m'imaginait en train de violer Assia. [Et une fois finie, je] fermai ma braguette et me croisai les bras comme si rien ne s'était passé.... En rentrant, on n'échangea pas un mot. Il m'arrêta au même endroit où il m'avait pêché et me rendit un billet de cinquante pésètes. Il me salua et me dit: « Au revoir! »... - « Au revoir! » Je respirai un air pollué et pensai: cinq minutes. Cinquante pésètes. Est-ce une pratique particulière aux vieillards? Un nouveau métier parmi d'autres, en plus du vol et de la mendicité. Je sortis le billet de cinquante pésètes et l'examinai. Ce sexe, lui aussi, doit contribuer à me faire vivre! Il travaille et prend du plaisir.... Suis-je devenu un prostitué? (85–86, parentheses in the original)

(I walked along the Avenue of Spain.... The men look at the ass from beautiful passersby women. A car stops at my level. An old man signals me: - "Get in!"

I sat next to him. What did he want from me? It was the first time I got into such a beautiful car. He drove slowly. I asked him in Spanish where we were going.

- "On a tour." [He made a hand gesture.] "A short tour."

He was certainly going to ask me something not very honest. Anyhow, I was not a fool. I wasn't afraid. I could defend myself if ... We headed for the outskirts of the city. A pederast. I knew it. He stopped the car in a dark corner.... He lit the lamp inside the car and put his hand on my fly. So that was it, the little tour! The real short tour began. He unbuttoned my fly slowly, turned off the lights, and stooped down on me...[t] o go faster, I imagined raping Assia. [And once finished, I] closed my fly and folded my arms as if nothing had happened.... On the way back, we did not exchange a word. He dropped me off in the same place where he picked me up and gave me a bill for fifty pesetas. He greeted me and said: "Goodbye!" ... - "Goodbye!" I breathed polluted air and thought: five minutes. Fifty pesetas. Is this a particular practice to older guys? A new profession among others, in addition to theft and begging. I took out the bill for fifty pesetas and examined it. This sexual organ of mine might, just as well, help me make a living! It works and takes pleasure…. Did I become a prostitute?) (85–86, parentheses in the original)

In this passage, the public space serves not only as the point of contact between the indigent Moroccan boy and the affluent Spaniard elder, but also as the intersection of socioeconomic differences in 1950s Tangiers. This cross-cultural encounter does not take place in an impoverished neighborhood inhabited mainly by local Moroccans, but rather the Avenue of Spain (*Avenue d'Espagne*), the artery to one of Tangiers's most fashionable neighborhoods inhabited predominantly by wealthy Europeans. Echoing the previous chapters, here we again find the binary us/foreigners as well as Moroccans/Europeans. Here too, the Moroccan is enticed by the sexual deviance of the European man attracted to underage passersby. The predatory character of the Spanish driver identifies the impoverished-looking Moroccan boy and seizes him for his sexual appetite. There are two inseparable implications to this episode: On the one hand, the public space acts as a dominant (European) male space; and on the other, the sixteen-year-old Moroccan boy becomes the racialized, othered object. In these respects, the novel recalls Jan Jindy Pettman's assertion which aligns "the public space and power with dominant group men [while] Other/othered men—working class, minority, racialized—might for certain purposes be … associated with physicality, dangerous sexuality, emotions, more of nature and less of reason" (94). As the Spanish driver's use of the imperative verb demonstrates, the dominance of the European male in public space yields to the perceived danger and sexual attraction. As soon as he reaches the boy, he commands him to "get in!" (*monte!*).

It is noteworthy that a jargon is used in gay cruising: a polite, welcoming one, even if it would be a simple greeting followed by a question, an invitation like "hello there, do you need a lift?" A question not a command: an invitation that would require a response and would also allow the youngster to have some decision-making in the process. I suggest that lacking such gesture to address sixteen-year-old Mohamed with whom the European wants to engage in a sexual activity dehumanizes the interaction. And his signaling (*me fait signe*) to get into the car increases the dehumanization, rendering the boy as a sexualized object. Mohamed's objectification is solidified by his physical appearance—as the previous passage recounts his walking barefoot with sticky hair in extreme hunger and exhaustion (80–84).[16] When considering the soci-oeconomic differences between the European driver and the Moroccan boy, we can determine that Mohamed gets picked up not *despite* but *because of* his impoverished-looking appearance—since the boy's dis-advantaged position does not challenge the privileged status of the Spaniard driver; on the contrary, it establishes it. This, indeed, corre-sponds to the public space and power of the dominant male group as suggested by Pettman. Although this incident occurs in North Africa, the Avenue of Spain seems to belong to the affluent European man. As Joseph Massad notes in *Desiring Arabs* (2007), Mohamed Choukri's encounter with the Spaniard takes "place in the early 1950s, while Morocco was under French colonial rule and European colonials roamed its streets like they owned the place" (316). In this scenario, the othered subject is not the actual foreigner but the native Moroccan: By walking down the Avenue of Spain, Mohamed enters into foreign territory and immediately becomes an othered, sexualized object—as his racialized, impoverished appearance cannot camouflage his vulnerability.

In addition, Choukri's passage also raises the question about homosex-ual contact as a paid activity (*métier*). If (in the narrative's previous pas-sage) after having walked for days, sixteen-year-old Mohamed wishes to have one peseta to satisfy his hunger with a bowl of soup, he now earns 50 pesetas for a five-minute-long fellatio performed by the Spaniard. He detaches himself completely from his own body and thinks about the women he is attracted to, and besides begging and stealing (which ech-oes Jean Genet's remark when referring to the racist stereotype of the Maghrebian as thieves), the sixteen-year-old protagonist learns about a new means of survival: selling his body to European tourists.

It seems that begging and stealing become, then, ordinary or expected activities for male teenagers from lower sectors of Moroccan society. Mohamed himself recounts,

> Je marchais. Égaré. Fatigué. J'avais peur de succomber sans pouvoir me relever.... Le soir, je m'étendis sur les marches face à la gare. Je proposais mes services aux voyageurs. Aucun ne me laissa porter ses affaires. Je n'en-tendis que des cris: « Fous le camp! Va-t-en! Maudit soit le vagin qui t'a mis au monde! Vous avez envahi cette ville heureuse, comme des sauterelles! »
>
> *Insulté, humilié, méprisé....* La seule fois où je réussis à porter une valise, je fus bousculé par un porteur plus grand que moi ...

Toute cette peine pour un peu de pain! Maudit soit ce pain! Le chat de tout à l'heure est plus heureux que moi.... Je deviendrai voleur et mendiant. Mais j'ai seize ans. Sebastoui avait raison! « C'est une honte pour un jeune homme de tendre la main. Il vaut mieux voler et laisser la mendicité pour les gosses et les vieillards. » (83–84, emphasis added)

(I walked. Misplaced. Tired. I was afraid of succumbing and not being able to get back up.... At night, I laid down on the steps facing the station. I offered my services to travelers. None of them let me take his affairs. I heard only cries: "Get the hell out! Go away! Cursed is the vagina that gave you birth! You invaded this happy city, like locusts!"

Insulted, humiliated, despised.... The only time I managed to carry a suitcase, I was jostled by a doorman taller than me ...

All this trouble for a little bread! Cursed be this bread! The cat from a moment ago is happier than me.... I will become a beggar and thief. But I'm sixteen. Sebastoui was right! "It's a shame for a young man to stretch his hand. It's better to steal and leave begging for kids and the elderly.") (83–84, emphasis added)

Although sixteen-year-old Mohamed finds begging shameful and thus hesitates about engaging himself into this particular activity, stealing seems a more suitable option. The fact that Mohamed's friend, Sebastoui, advises him about it suggests to me that stealing is a reality in which Moroccan boys must involve themselves, and thus, it is a more acceptable means of survival. That is, rather than mere stereotypes, begging and stealing are areas of social conditioning and expectations into which the young man must fall, eventually confirming the extent to which stereotypes and reality end up overlapping because no other outlet or agency is possible.

Does this mean, however, that this sixteen-year-old boy lacks agency and simply succumbs to his socioeconomic reality? At first glance, we see that his incapacity to control the situation while yielding his body to the Spaniard's desire, the boy appears to lack agency. Within the same context, women's lack of agency is also the focus of John Berger's analysis in *Ways of Seeing* (1972),[17] where he analyzes women's inability to own their bodies throughout art history. In relation to the female body in paintings, Berger claims,

Men look at women in paintings. Women watch themselves being looked at. The surveyor of woman in herself is male ... Thus she turns herself into

an object—and most particularly an object of vision: a sight.... Her body
is arranged in the way it is, to display it to the man looking at the picture. This picture is made to appeal to his sexuality. It has nothing to do
with her sexuality.... The woman's sexual passion needs to be minimized
so that the spectator may feel that he has the monopoly of such passion.
Women are there to feed an appetite, not to have any of their own. (47,
55, emphasis in the original)

Just as the image of the feminine body is designed to please the male
spectator, we can attest that in the European art form the painters and
spectator-owners were usually men and the persons treated as objects,
usually women. I suggest that this asymmetrical relationship is so embedded in European culture that it still structures the male consciousness,
be it heterosexual or homosexual. Such European male monopoly of
passion is also shown in Mohamed Choukri's passage—as sixteen-year-
old Mohamed's encounter with the older Spaniard has only one objective: to feed the man's sexual appetite, not to have any of the boy's own.
Treating Mohamed's homosexual encounter in isolation provides us
an account of the boy's lack of agency, with the seeming impossibility
of escape. If he has indeed become a prostitute, then does this *métier*
require that he resigns himself to his new situation and, thus, gives up on
striving for sexual agency of his own?

Because Mohamed's homosexual experience has little if anything
to do with his own sexual appetite, it represents less an opportunity to
develop homosexual agency than a challenge to his own (hetero)sexual
agency. Thinking about Assia (*je m'imaginais en train de violer Assia*)
while the older Spaniard touched him, Mohamed shows emotional
detachment. Fantasy becomes a site of resistance, where he is capable
of maintaining his (hetero)sexual agency in the midst of a homosexual encounter. The conscious effort to maintain self-control suggests
to me that the teenager is not a passive object of desire but a subject
with (hetero)sexual agency despite a challenging situation provoked by
his economic misery. Mohamed's separation of mind and body corresponds to survivor accounts of rape. Indeed, it seems no coincidence that
Mohamed extends this form of fantasy agency by specifically imagining
that he might force himself unto Assia. In other words, he transforms
his experience into a heterosexual encounter when mentally substitut-
ing Assia's body for his own, but takes his defensive daydream a step

further by intensifying the violence of the imagined rape. By pretending to be the perpetrator of such sexual aggression, he empowers himself and transfers the plight of victimhood back to a female body.

Mohamed nonetheless indicates that his sexual desire geared toward the opposite sex involves more than mere objectification. On the contrary, he recognizes the individuality and independent emotions of the women he loves. A year later, he explicitly tells us about the passion he feels toward Sallafa.

> On a fait l'amour quatre fois hier. J'ai envie d'elle à présent. Je coucherai avec elle si ... j'arrive à la cabane ... J'aurais voulu que Sallafa soit avec nous.... Je l'aimais? ... Je l'aimais quand elle était en colère ... Je l'aimais triste. Je l'aimais folle. (115)

> (We made love four times yesterday. I want her now. I would sleep with her if ... I get to the hut ... I wish Sallafa was with us.... Did I love her? ... I loved her when she was angry ... I loved her sad. I loved her crazy.) (115)

Seventeen-year-old Mohamed's expression of love for Sallafa allows us to attest not only to his more mature understanding of subjectivity, but also his (hetero)sexual agency. There is no mention of his homosexual intercourse with the Spanish man in this passage, suggesting that it in no way alters his heterosexual desire a year later. His unfilled desire to take Assia's virginity has become the source of his continuous masturbations, yet he no longer conveys aggression toward her.

> [J]e pensais tout d'un coup à Assia nue entre mes bras.... Je regrettais ce viol imaginaire. N'est-ce pas une forme de folie que d'imaginer le corps d'Assia, de la dépuceler, de l'aimer alors que je ne sais rien d'elle, si elle est morte ou vivante? J'aurais mieux fait de dormir dans la chaleur de Sallafa. Sa présence m'aurait suffi. Ses gestes, ses mouvements. Assia ... était l'objet de ma masturbation. (118–119)

> ([I] suddenly thought about Assia naked in my arms.... I regretted this imaginary rape. Isn't this a form of madness to imagine Assia's body, to deflower her, to love her even if I don't know anything about her, if she is dead or alive? I would have done better to sleep in Sallafa's heat. Her presence would have been enough. Her gestures, her movements. Assia ... was the object of my masturbation.) (118–119)

It is essential here to note the following from this passage: on the one hand, Mohamed's regret about the imagined violation, which reiterates the earlier discussion about this point; and on the other, the object of his sexual appetite is indeed the female body, attesting to this heterosexual subjectivity. Although his agency is challenged because of the homosexual encounter, he does not question his own (hetero)sexuality. His original quandary during his meeting with the Spaniard regarded whether he had become a prostitute, not a homosexual. With an unchallenged sexuality, Mohamed's main concern is to make a living for himself: Would prostitution be the only *métier* available to an illiterate, orphan teenager who has recently moved to the city of Tangiers?

Whereas Mohamed has tried, unsuccessfully, to use other body parts (like his arms, hands, and legs) to earn money, his genitals ultimately prove better capable of saving him from starvation. That is, treating his paid sexual encounter as yet another *métier* allows Mohamed to express a heterosexual agency that he had until then not managed to build in the work realm. Although his heterosexual agency is challenged by this homosexual act, he learns that his body will indeed allow him to earn a living. In this respect, his sheer amazement at the amount he earns from illicit acts in fact indicates a form of financial triumph. Not unlike the young men in Gide's *L'immoraliste*, Mohamed takes advantage of the European's homosexual desires in order to achieve economic success. What is perceived as dishonest behavior (theft, emotional detachment, etc.) by sexual tourists is in fact a defense mechanism that allows the young victims of coercive exploitation to maintain a degree of autonomy as subjects in a system that treats them as objects.

It is precisely within this context of survival that we can appreciate the teenager's potential for agency and subject formation. Mohamed is not a subservient boy that surrenders passively to his unforgiving reality. He is a subject with agency: As an orphan from the countryside of the Rif region who struggles to eke out a living in the city, he jumps from one tedious job to another. Regardless of his failed attempts, he insists on not giving up.

> La barque devait être tirée par le chalutier jusqu'au port de Tanger. Les deux porteurs dans l'eau poussèrent la barque vers la mer…. On mit deux caisses dans chaque sac. Kandoussi me dit:
> - « Si tu ne te sens pas capable de porter deux caisses, n'en porte qu'une. »
> - « Je suis capable d'en porter trois, si tu veux. »

Je lançais un défi à ma force et à mon âge. J'étais maigre, c'était pour ça
qu'il doutait de mes capacités.
Ce travail valait mieux que de mendier ou de voler. C'était mieux que de
livrer mon pénis à la bouche d'un vieillard ou d'aller vendre la soupe et
le poisson frit aux ouvriers et aux paysans dans le grand socco ou dans
Foundak Chajra. Ce travail me faisait vivre l'aventure et me donnait l'occa-
sion de mettre à l'épreuve ma virilité, à dix-sept ans. *Une nouvelle étape de
ma vie commençait en ce matin de brume.* (114)

(The boat had to be towed by the trawler to the port of Tangiers. The two
carriers in the water pushed the boat out to sea…. We took two boxes in
each bag. Kandoussi said to me:
- "If you don't feel capable of carrying two boxes, carry just one."
- "I'm able to carry three, if you want."
I threw a challenge to my strength and my age. I was thin, that was why he
doubted my abilities.
This work was better than begging or stealing. It was better than give my
penis to the mouth of an old man or sell soup and fried fish to the workers
and peasants in the main square or at Foundak Chajra. This work made me
live the adventure and gave me the opportunity to test my manhood, at
seventeen years old. *A new stage of my life began on the morning haze.*)
(114)

After having begged, stolen, sold his body, dished out soup, and fried
fish to laborers and peasants, the new opportunity before him seems
more promising than the rest precisely because it allows him to express
his budding virility. Mohamed understands that this new job at the ship
has a longer sense of durability despite its initial struggle. And although
the ship itself will be in a continuous move from port to port, it will
also give him, paradoxically, a sense of stability for the first time in his
life. His determination and sense of adventure to take on this job in the
ship not only indicates that he has finally taken control of his life and
future, but also attests to his agency and potential for subject formation.
Furthermore, after having worked in the ship for three years, his subjectivity begins to strengthen.

Le matin, en revenant du port j'achetai un livre pour apprendre à lire et
à écrire en arabe. Abdelmalek était au café…. Je lui montrai le livre:
- « Il faut que j'apprenne. Ton frère Hamid m'avait appris quelques let-
tres quand on était en prison. » Il trouvait que j'étais bien disposé pour
apprendre.

- « Et pourquoi pas? »
Hassan me proposa de partir avec lui à Larache pour entrer dans une école.
Étonné, je lui dis:
- « Moi? Comment serait-ce possible? J'ai vingt ans et je ne sais même pas
comment signer. »
- « Ce n'est pas important. Je connais bien le directeur de l'école. Je
t'écrirai une lettre de recommandation pour lui. Je suis sûr qu'il compren-
dra ton cas. Il a beaucoup de sympathie pour les gars seuls et pauvres qui
désirent apprendre. » (159)

(In the morning, returning from the port I bought a book to learn how
to read and write in Arabic. Abdelmalek was in the café.... I showed him
the book:
- "I must learn. Your brother Hamid had taught me a few letters when we
were in prison." He thought I was keen to learn.
- "And why not?"
Hassan asked me to go with him to Larache to enter a school. Surprised, I
said:
- "Me? How would that be possible? I'm twenty years old and I don't even
know how to sign."
- "It's not important. I know the school principal. I'll write a letter of recommendation for him. I'm sure he'll understand your case. He has great
sympathy for the poor single guys who want to learn.") (159)

The stability provided by his work on the ship for a period of three years
realizes Mohamed's potential for subject formation. It is only through
the stability of communities as well as the role of institutions that
Mohamed's subjectivity can be achieved. In the context of this novel, the
specificity of group solidarity is what provides Mohamed the ability to
express his individual subjectivity, as the ship grants him the mind-set to
solidify a network of friends as well as the opportunity to develop his
cognitive talents. Mohamed's organization of social life as well as the stability of his community allows him to benefit from the role of institutions
for the first time in his life.

Without the concern of scrapping for jobs, Mohamed begins to focus
on his own intellectual curiosities. While later in prison, his friend helps
him discover his talent for learning; he then takes the initiative to buy a
book in order to teach himself how to read and write in Arabic. Upon
meeting his friend in the café, he reiterates his own desire to learn. But
when he is given the suggestion to acquire formal instruction in school,
he hesitates, as he is not even capable of signing his own name. Then,

his friend offers him a letter of recommendation he should give to the school principal who, in turn, is sympathetic to help the disadvantaged with the desire to learn.

Thus far, I have attempted to illustrate that the harsh socioeconomic situation pushes Moroccan youth to engage in paid sex work. After sixteen-year-old Mohamed Choukri discovers as a narrator how to make quick cash by selling his body to older homosexual European tourists, he later uses his newfound strength of mind to obtain his position as a sailor, enabling him to eat on a daily basis. It is only following that three-year experience at sea that he begins to realize his own potential.

CONCLUSION

The sexual tourism of white European travelers portrayed in these narratives amounts to a new form of sexual imperialism with little if any long-term liberation for the impoverished boys who seek economic and affective stability. Similarly, the European tourist's sense of entitlement seems to remain untouched during his homosexual affair with the ethnicized. These texts follow a similar pattern, regardless of their narrative chronologies: The European male tourists continue to use, abuse, and then neglect the Moroccan boys, leaving Mohamed in this chapter or Youssr and Nouâmane in next chapter to fend for themselves once the Europeans' own wants and needs are satisfied. Whereas the contemporary reader might expect to find an evolution since the binary opposition of the European traveler and impoverished North African boy was first introduced in French literature in the nineteenth century, it has instead remained a literary dyad throughout the twentieth century, and into the twenty-first century, as well. While the background settings have changed, and North African writers have found their own voices, they describe a reality, which has not structurally changed since the colonial era.

NOTES

1. See Françoise Lionnet, *Postcolonial Representations: Women, Literature, Identity* (Ithaca: Cornell University Press, 1995), 23.
2. Homi K. Bhabha, *The Location of Culture* (New York: Routledge, 1994).
3. Robert J. Corber and Stephen Valocchi, *Queer Studies: An Interdisciplinary Reader* (Malden, MA: Blackwell, 2003), 1–20.

4. See for example Joseph A. Boone, "Vacation Cruises: Or, the Homoerotics of Orientalism," *PMLA* 110, no. 1 (January 1995): 89–107; and Jarrod Hayes, *Queer Nations: Marginal Sexualities in the Maghreb* (Chicago: University of Chicago Press, 2000).

5. All the translations in this book are my own.

6. Elisa Puvia and Jeroen Vaes, "Being a Body: Women's Appearance Related Self-Views and Their Dehumanization of Sexually Objectified Female Targets," *Sex Roles* 68 (New York: Springer Science + Business Media, 2013): 484–495.

7. www.larousse.fr, http://www.larousse.fr/dictionnaires/francais/souple/73719?q=souple#72891.

8. Nick Haslam, "Dehumanization: An Integrative Review," *Personality and Social Psychology Review* 10, no. 3 (2006): 252–264.

9. Fabio Fasoli, Maria Paola Paladino, Andrea Carnaghi, Jolanda Jetten, Brock Bastian, and Paul G. Bains, "Not 'Just Words': Exposure to Homophobic Epithets Leads to Dehumanizing and Physical Distancing from Gay Men," *European Journal of Social Psychology* 46 (2016): 237–248.

10. Although there is a fruitful discussion on André Gide's concept about the "unnamable," this chapter deals with André Gide's specific accounts about his cross-cultural encounters with local boys in North Africa. For a thorough analysis on the "unnamable" within André Gide's literature, see Leo Bersani's fourth chapter entitled "The Gay Outlaw" in his book, *Homos* (Cambridge, MA: Harvard University Press, 1995); as well as Michael Lucey's chapter entitled "Introduction: Referring to Same-Sex Sexualities in the First Person" in his book, *Never Say I: Sexuality and the First Person in Colette, Gide, and Proust* (Durham and London: Duke University Press, 2006).

11. Emphasis added.

12. Jan Jindy Pettman, "Body Politics: International Sex Tourism," *Third World Quarterly* 18, no. 1 (March 1997): 93–108.

13. Ibid., for a thorough analysis on public space in a broader sense of the so-called Third World, see Jan Jindy Pettman, 94–96.

14. Joseph A. Boone, "Vacation Cruises: Or, the Homoerotics of Orientalism," *PMLA* 110, no. 1 (January 1995): 89–107.

15. Choukri, Mohamed. *Le pain nu.* (Paris: Librairie François Maspero, 1980). However, the interesting fact about the book's editions is well worth telling—and I cite in its entirety from Joseph A. Massad's book, *Desiring Arabs* (Chicago: University of Chicago Press, 2007): "Shukri's Al-Khubz al-Hafi (Plain Bread) was published in French, English, and Spanish before coming out in Arabic in 1982.... Written sometimes in an ethnographic native informant style, the book became popular among

Western readers while remaining unavailable in Arabic. Paul Bowles translated it to English after Shukri orally translated it to him from classical Arabic to Moroccan vernacular and to Spanish.... The book was most recently made into a feature film (2005) in a Moroccan-Italian-French production directed by Rachid Benhadj" (314–315).
16. Je descendis au port pieds nus et fatigué. Je bus un verre d'eau ... Si j'avais eu une pésète, j'aurais avalé un bol de purée de fèves....Mes cheveux étaient gluants. J'avais la peau toute rouge à force de me frotter, mais j'étais un peu moins sale. (80–84).
17. John Berger, *Ways of Seeing* (New York: The Viking Press, 1972).

References

Berger, John. *Ways of Seeing*. New York: The Viking Press, 1972.
Bersani, Leo. *Homos*. Cambridge, MA: Harvard University Press, 1995.
Bhabha, Homi K. *The Location of Culture*. New York: Routledge, 1994.
Boone, Joseph A. "Vacation Cruises: Or, the Homoerotics of Orientalism." *PMLA* 110, no. 1 (January 1995): 89–107.
Choukri, Mohamed. *Le pain nu*. Paris: Librairie François Maspero, 1980.
Corber, Robert J., and Stephen Valocchi. "Introduction." In *Queer Studies: An Interdisciplinary Reader*, edited by Robert J. Corber and Stephen Valocchi, 1–20. Malden, MA: Blackwell, 2003.
Dollimore, Jonathan. *Sexual Dissidence: Augustine to Wilde, Freud to Foucault*. Oxford and New York: Oxford University Press, 1991.
Fasoli, Fabio, Maria Paola Paladino, Andrea Carnaghi, Jolanda Jetten, Brock Bastian, and Paul G. Bains. "Not 'Just Words': Exposure to Homophobic Epithets Leads to Dehumanizing and Physical Distancing from Gay Men." *European Journal of Social Psychology* 46 (2016): 237–248.
Gide, André. *L'immoraliste*. Paris: Mercure de France, 1902.
Haslam, Nick. "Dehumanization: An Integrative Review." *Personality and Social Psychology Review* 10, no. 3 (2006): 252–264.
Hayes, Jarrod. "Reading and Tourism: Sexual Approaches to the Maghreb." In *Queer Nations: Marginal Sexualities in the Maghreb*, 23–49. Chicago: The University of Chicago Press, 2000.
Larousse Dictionary. Online. http://www.larousse.fr/dictionnaires/francais/souple/73719?q=souple#72891.
Lionnet, Françoise. *Postcolonial Representations: Women, Literature, Identity*. Ithaca: Cornell University Press, 1995.
Lucey, Michael. *Never Say I: Sexuality and the First Person in Colette, Gide, and Proust*. Durham and London: Duke University Press, 2006.
Massad, Joseph A. *Desiring Arabs*. Chicago: The University of Chicago Press, 2007.

Pettman, Jan Jindy. "Body Politics: International Sex Tourism." *Third World Quaterly* 18, no. 1 (March 1997): 93–108.

Puvia, Elisa, and Jeroen Vaes. "Being a Body: Women's Appearance Related Self-Views and their Dehumanization of Sexually Objectified Female Targets." *Sex Roles* 68 (2013): 484–495.

CHAPTER 5

Moroccan Boys: Points of Resistance in Homosexual Tourism

Building on the previous analysis, this chapter focuses on the Moroccan boys' perception to homosexual tourism as a cross-cultural encounter. I will emphasize on the exoticization of the young brown body and the controversial relationships created with older Frenchmen in Rachid O.'s narratives *Chocolat chaud* (1998) and *Ce qui reste* (2003). These works illustrate the seemingly unavoidable reality of same-sex tourism among young Moroccan men. The spatial paradigm adopted here allows me to explore how sexual encounters for leisure occur in the street, coffee shop, and music boutique. In particular, the texts studied in this chapter reveal what I would call a progression of sexual tourism from *métier* to *façon d'être* in Morocco: The young boy begins by learning that he can earn cash for the use of his body and, thus, discovering the *métier* of sex worker as a paid activity; he then falls into this *métier* while working in another domain of the tourist industry; finally, he becomes absorbed by this way of life and gives into a romance or another form of emotional attachment to the European tourist who offers him an important affective bond.

Such affective experiences should neither be neglected nor granted excessive weight in the development of the local boy's agency, as he becomes entangled in a relationship beyond the mere exchange of pleasures for compensation. However, because he receives financial assistance from his lover, it remains impossible to overlook the socioeconomic differences between the privileged white sojourner and the impoverished

© The Author(s) 2019
L. Navarro-Ayala, *Queering Transcultural Encounters*,
Palgrave Studies in Globalization and Embodiment,
https://doi.org/10.1007/978-3-319-92315-4_5

brown boy: In many ways, their relationship may serve as a screen for a more banal form of homosexual prostitution. I am interested in exploring how these affective and pecuniary ties can either prevent or challenge sexual agency and subject formation.

Despite the importance of social ties in identity formation, it would be naive to portray these narratives as utopian spaces where cultural contexts grow to accommodate and support all the needs of the characters. Instead, mimicry plays an important role in their efforts to reach maturity. In "Of mimicry and Man: The ambivalence of Colonial Discourse" (1994),[1] Bhabha describes "a double articulation" which he considers to be a "complex strategy of reform, regulation, and discipline, which 'appropriates' the Other as it visualizes power" (126). For him, mimicry is also a "sign of the inappropriate," because of its potential to act as a defiance that joins together "the dominant strategic function of colonial power, intensifies surveillance, and poses an immanent threat to both 'normalized' knowledges and disciplinary powers" (ibid.). These two traits of Bhabha's mimicry become especially apparent in the body-changing efforts put forth by Youssr in *Chocolat chaud*, but they influence each main character to some degree.

In addition, Nouâmane's three-year relationship with Pierre in *Chocolat chaud* reflects the "gift-exchange relationship" explained by Marcel Mauss in his seminal work entitled *The Gift* (1990).[2] His idea that "[p]resents put the seal upon marriage" (19) is particularly crucial to understand Nouâmane's initial attraction for Pierre, which relies on the musical instrument the Frenchman holds during their first meeting. Whether the gifts transacted between Nouâmane and Pierre are material, economic, sexual, or affective, the logic of obligatory reciprocity between them obeys the Maussian model: "It also supposes two other obligations just as important: the obligation, on the one hand, to give presents, and on the other, to receive them" (13).

MALE CHARMS FOR HIRE: THE "*MÉTIER*" OF PAID SEX TOURIST GUIDE

Rachid O.'s novel *Chocolat chaud* (1998)[3] describes harsh socioeconomic conditions as a key element to male youth's sexual involvement with European homosexual tourists. It is through the character Youssr that Rachid learns about intimate contact with tourists. Youssr's illustration shows homosexual tourism as a well-established *métier* in Morocco, where the local boy falls into the profession of paid same-sex work while already employed in the tourist industry. Recalling his introduction to the coffee shop where his friend works as a tourist guide, Rachid O. writes, "Ce jour-là, je l'avais accompagné sur une terrasse de café où il avait l'habitude de passer du temps, c'était son lieu de travail où il essayait d'aborder les touristes pour qu'ils le prennent comme guide" (That day, I had accompanied him to a café terrace where he used to spend time; it was his workplace where he tried to approach tourists so that they would take him as a guide) (67).[4] The coffee shop is thus portrayed as the meeting place for this sector of the informal economy.

Here, it is noteworthy to emphasize that this chapter treats the coffee shop as a component of the public domain in the Muslim context of North Africa. In Morocco, it serves as the meeting point where males spend most of their time. Moroccan women rarely cross its threshold, allowing men and youngsters to interact with each other in a male-gendered space. It is not a place of obligatory consumption in the capitalist sense, as the proprietor—also a man—interacts with customers as friends. They discuss daily life, play cards or dominos, drink mint tea, or smoke a shisha[5]; however, the coffee shop's main role is that of a communal setting for the neighborhood. Rather than seeking profit only, the owner also expects such noncommercial relationships. As an accessible place to the public, men use it to establish their social network. When a neighbor chooses not to visit that communal space, he is seen with suspicion, as a man who may be concealing something. By not interacting with his peers, the individual seems disdainful. In this respect, privacy, as it is understood in the West, takes on a different form in Moroccan society. For this reason, Joseph Boone's words about the "boys in the street" who take the public space as their own at an early age may be extended to suggest that society goes so far as to create an expectation (even an obligation) of male participation in the public domain starting since childhood.

More precisely, the dynamics of tourism entails two divergent expectations of locals and tourists. Whereas the traveler may expect to have the most authentic experience of the country, the inhabitant anticipates generous compensation from that visitor. In order for this meeting to take place, both participants must engage willingly in the exchange. The description provided by writer Rachid O. suggests that false guides congregate in the coffee shop, with the hope of being hired by tourists, aware of the financial gain involved in the tourist industry. Although Youssr does not receive professional training, he uses the coffee shop as his workplace.

"Sur cette terrasse même, il y avait de nombreux guides professionnels et de faux guides [et] Youssr était d'ailleurs un faux" (On this same terrace, there were many professional guides and false guides [and] Youssr was, in fact, a false one) (66–67). Rachid O. also describes his friend as a street-smart youngster who moves around restlessly, looking for clients and establishing a solid network that assures his income, resulting in jealousy from the rest of those who are also based in that coffee shop in Tangiers.

Youssr seems well-aware of his physical beauty and the attraction he represents for European tourists, and so he uses them as tools to win over their trust and be hired for the day. Youssr's street smarts to make a living in the tourist industry show not only his agency but also his tactics of survival *vis-à-vis* the increasing process of globalization. On the one hand, he competes with the locals to be chosen by European tourists; on the other, his use of his own charm to attract the visitors shows his understanding of their desires. "Youssr était d'ailleurs un faux [guide] et, grâce à sa beauté et à la sympathie qu'il suscitait dès qu'il souriait, il n'y avait aucune inquiétude à se faire pour qu'il soit choisi par des touristes individuels ou en couple" (Youssr was, in fact, a false [guide] and, thanks to his beauty and sympathy he aroused when he smiled, there were no concerns to be chosen by individual tourists or in couples) (67–68). Although nowhere in the novel does the author specifically tell us that Youssr has the so-called typical Moroccan look, this description insists that he manipulates his eye-catching handsomeness to win over the tourists' attention.

Despite coming from an impoverished background, Youssr is a kind-hearted orphan whose job helps to support his blind adoptive father as well as himself. A self-taught guide among professionals, he is far from being intimidated by his rivals. On the contrary, he sees their presence as a competition that he is determined to win. To beauty, he adds charm, a detail suggesting that Youssr's successful manipulation of his good looks and enchanting gestures satisfy the stereotypical image expected by European travelers—he knowingly presents himself as the captivatingly handsome and serviceable Arab.

CLIMBING THE GLOBAL ECONOMIC LADDER THROUGH GOOD LOOKS

In addition, Youssr's ability to make a living in the tourist industry also encapsulates the dynamic between the global and the local. In this process of homosexual tourism, the white European man leaves an impact on the local brown boy. What begins as Youssr's skillful manipulation to attract European tourists in that coffee shop turns into a life-changing experience for the native youngster. Rachid O. narrates, "Youssr me disait que son rêve était de devenir monstrueux, de dépasser les cent kilos,... comme un taureau ... que cette idée lui était venue d'en rencontrant un Français qu'il avait guide et baisé ... que ce touriste était parfait à ses yeux" (Youssr would tell me that his dream was to become monstrous, to exceed one hundred kilos,... like a bull ... that this idea had occurred to him when he met a tourist Frenchman that he had guided and fucked ... that this tourist was perfect in his eyes) (65). While Youssr demonstrates personal initiative as a self-taught tourist guide, this job drives him to accept paid activities involving sex when he so skillfully manipulates its codes. By juxtaposing the verbs "*guider*" and "*baiser*" ("guiding" and a vulgar verb most equivalent to "fucking"), the narrator implies that Moroccan boys must be willing to lead the traveler in their exploration of the country, as well as to new sexual adventures. These verbs function as parallel components to Youssr's job description; if European travelers decide to hire his services, they obtain the option to discover not only the landscape in Morocco, but also Youssr's erotic body. The bodybuilder from Europe leaves an impact on him after just one sexual encounter because his obsession is thereafter to achieve "perfect" physical beauty, a masculine ideal of firm muscles, physically representing the socioeconomic strength he wishes he could achieve through his job.

Due to this cross-cultural encounter, the local and the global begin to intersect in Youssr's daily life: His earnings as a tourist guide helps him achieve his "dream body" since he also discovers, through contact with Europeans, the supplementary pills and protein powder that he must order from abroad. "Sa substance dorée, qu'il attendait avec impatience par la poste, étaient les protéines" (His golden substance, which he looked forward to by mail, were the proteins) (65). Thus, the ongoing consumption of Western dietary supplements as well as his daily workout regimen in Morocco will assist Youssr in becoming like the French tourist. In this manner, Youssr enacts Homi Bhabha's concept of mimicry, a body politic which involves "a writing, a mode of representation [that] repeats, rather than re-presents" (128). Youssr's journey to attain a perfect body like that of the Frenchman's involves reform and self-discipline on a daily basis; to this effect, Homi Bhabha (1984) suggests that "mimicry" is the "desire for a reformed, recognizable Other,... a complex strategy of reform, regulation, and discipline, which 'appropriates' the Other as it visualizes power" (126). Indeed, Youssr's determination to attain an ideal body requires reform and self-discipline on a regular basis. The fact that the Moroccan boy discovers the beautiful perfect body of the French tourist during the sexual encounter makes me consider Homi Bhabha's "site of interdiction" within the production of visibility of mimicry. That is, I believe Youssr's mimetic discourse originates at Bhabha's "inter dicta," at the point where the mimetic discursive utterance occurs, "a discourse at the crossroads of what is known and permissible and that which though known must be kept concealed: a discourse uttered between the lines and as such both against the rules and within them" (130). In this case, what is known and permissible corresponds to working as a guide in the tourist industry, while "that which though known must be kept concealed" involves prostitution, and the "discourse between the lines" is Youssr's seductive smile in the coffee shop.

From Strategic Confusion to Bodily Liberation: Agency in Youssr

Despite his acts of mimicry carried out on a daily basis, Youssr's desire to work toward adding muscles to his own body does not originate in passivity but in action, as a form of agency. Nowhere in the narrative does Youssr express shame for his body or a desire to replace it with the "look" of a European body; instead, he demonstrates a disposition to transform the body he possesses. Rather than trade his own body for that of his one-time lover, Youssr strives to reshape it; his desire for the muscled body is not an alternative, but a strategy to act in the real world. He must not merely be disciplined, but create a physical presence that outshines the so-called real guides formally trained in the tourist industry. In other words, Youssr must compensate his lack of training by his appearance. Further, he also benefits from his sexual encounter as a source of knowledge. Since only Youssr experiences full access to the chiseled body of the Frenchman—not any other Moroccan guide—he inverts the order of cultural symbols and creates an advantageous strategy for himself. Although he may manifest what Homi Bhabha calls an "interdictory desire" (130), he has strategic objectives: A muscular body will provide him a stable source of income in his competitive industry. Yet, nowhere in Youssr's account does emotional or economic repression connect him to the Frenchman. In fact, the Moroccan teenager remains completely independent; he expresses no affection for the muscled French tourist, nor does he fantasize about meeting another European tourist with a similar body. In many respects, the youngster uses his client simply to become a stronger incarnation of himself as he was before they met. In sum, he appropriates the *bodily* ideal of the tourist as means to achieve his own local success without accepting a *social* ideal prescribed by global power structures that otherwise dominate the terms of their interaction.

Moreover, Youssr's desire moves beyond fantasy as he sets his plan into action: His performative structure opens up a narrative strategy for the emergence and negotiation of those agencies he has access to—like experiencing full access to the muscled French body. If working out and dieting daily to attain a muscled body may create what Homi Bhabha calls "strategic confusion" as well as a "crisis for the cultural priority" within the hegemonic normality, the "discourse uttered between the lines" of what is "both and against the rules and within them" (130) is precisely what I believe allows Youssr to act upon agency.

My take on Youssr's agency performance stems from Homi Bhabha's understanding of "strategic confusion" in his article "Of Mimicry and Man" (1984) and solidifies on the idea of "contingencies" within "cultures of survival"—as defined in his chapter entitled "The postcolonial and the postmodern: The question of agency" (1994). Here, he suggests that contingencies are empowering strategies of emancipation that stage other social antagonisms, and as counterhegemonic strategies, they indicate the contradictory yet productive space (171–172). These new forms of identification may not only confuse the continuity of historical temporalities, but also confound the ordering of cultural symbols, traumatizing tradition (179). This process also allows objectified others to turn into subjects of their history and experience—and also proposes forms of defiant subjectivities that gain authority to erase the politics of binary opposition (ibid.). Youssr's counter politics to move beyond the polarities represented in his cross-cultural encounter with the Frenchman allows us to see the defiant conditions of his agency, resembling those ideally described by Homi Bhabha in "The postcolonial and the postmodern: The question of Agency."[6]

Nouâmane and Pierre: Sexual Tourism or Romance?

A similar culture of survival appears in Rachid O.'s novel *Ce qui reste* (2003).[7] Here too, the public space allows for a cross-cultural encounter to occur and illustrates the socioeconomic differences present within homosexual tourism in Morocco. Nouâmane, a teenage friend of the title character Rachid, engages in a homosexual relationship with Pierre, a French tourist sojourning in Morocco for three years. This ambiguity of their affair is of particular interest, since it is difficult to determine if Nouâmane takes part in the industry known as sexual tourism. The narrative plays with the uneasy distinction between gifts from a lover and the financial exchanges of prostitution. If the impoverished native boy cannot afford certain items, but receives them as presents from an affluent European male traveler, is their relationship no more than a thinly veiled disguise for sexual tourism? At what point does the steadiness of a continuous, but stable and permanent relationship, turn a commercial exploit into a romance? Does the longevity of the relationship matter in homosexual tourism? While taking into account this longevity, my analysis of Nouâmane's example explores the Maussian approach in gift relations in order to study the socioeconomic differences between Nouâmane and Pierre. This approach provides insights into the materiality of the object (in this case, a musical instrument), as well as the dynamic between the recurrent longing to give (in the case of the traveler) and the continuous need to receive (in the case of the native). Subsequently, I will examine how the affection potentially involved in this three-year relationship influences the basis for homosexual agency and subject formation in Nouâmane.

PIERRE'S ORGAN AND NOUÂMANE'S DESIRE: GIFTS NEVER GIVEN

Socioeconomic differences are established from the very beginning of Nouâmane's narration, as his impoverished background pushes him to venture out on his own. Nouâmane is born to a dysfunctional family, the only child of a widowed mother who remarries a violent man. This abuse forces him to leave his home and his native village, moving to the nearest big city, Tangiers. Like the examples studied above, his choice reflects Joseph Boone's assertion that boys take to the streets as a place of their own in Morocco.[8] Although all of the teenagers' examples used in this chapter share a similar marginal socioeconomic status, Nouâmane's case allows us to appreciate his individuality: He shows a highly developed interest in music, and he dreams of learning to play an instrument. Regardless of his indigent condition, this orphaned fifteen-year-old boy is attracted to the following items: "Je suis arrivé dans un beau magasin d'instruments de musique" (I arrived to a beautiful shop of musical instruments) (35). Despite his use of the verb "arriver," which indicates entry into a place, Nouâmane does not dare to enter the music shop that he admires, because he has no means to purchase its goods. As fascinated as he may be with these instruments, he stays in the street and looks in through the glass windows. This window-shopping illustrates how socioeconomic status impacts private and public spaces in the narrative: Self-aware about his poverty and, thus, his exclusion from the private space of the music shop, Nouâmane occupies instead the public space of the street, which provides the opportunity to nourish his dream to learn how to play music. Amidst this reverie within the public space, fifteen-year-old Nouâmane meets Frenchman Pierre in Rachid O.'s *Ce qui reste* (2003).

> Quand Pierre est sorti du magasin avec un orgue sur le bras, il m'a fait savoir qu'il attendait mon aide et je l'ai porté avec lui jusqu'à sa [voiture]. À quinze ans, j'ai compris qu'il ne me lâchait pas des yeux, et moi, j'étais aguiché par l'instrument ... Le soir, j'ai dormi pour la première fois dans un beau lit. (36)

> (When Pierre exited the store with an organ on his arm, he made me understand that he was expecting my help and I carried it with him to his[-car]. At age fifteen, I realized that he would not let me go off his eyes, and me, I was led on by the instrument ... At night, I slept for the first time in a beautiful bed.) (36)

This quote first echoes a colonial discourse. As Pierre exits the music shop with the organ in his arms, he notices Nouâmane and immediately signals him to give him a hand (*il m'a fait savoir qu'il attendait mon aide*) with a dominant presence. Interestingly, the Frenchman, as a colonizer, considers himself superior and sees the locals as people whose main role is to serve him. In this context, Pierre need not use spoken language to command the native boy to help; Nouâmane clearly understands the order and moves quickly to assist him. The first sentence of the passage therefore situates the French traveler and Moroccan boy within the historical context of colonial discourse. Even if Nouâmane does not speak French at the time when he meets Pierre, the communication between both of them occurs through body language based on a hierarchical system linking the white Frenchman and the ethnicized Moroccan boy.

The second level of communication in this cross-cultural encounter reflects what is commonly referred to as queer language. As the Moroccan teenager clearly recounts, even at fifteen years old, he understands perfectly the homoerotic gaze coming from the Frenchman (*À quinze ans, j'ai compris qu'il ne me lâchait pas des yeux*). Whether the youngster has experienced this gaze before or not remains unstated, just like the manner in which he has learned to identify it. His ability to recognize Pierre's homoerotic gaze is for that reason all the more significant. Understanding the homoerotically charged gaze is one of the first (and most important) skills to have when communicating in queer language within a cross-cultural context. Nouâmane's awareness of sexual appeal to Pierre allows him to conceive the possibility of making his dream a reality: Whereas Pierre cannot stop staring at him, the boy is seduced by the instrument (*j'étais aguiché par l'instrument*). The fact that he does not reciprocate a sexual attraction for Pierre, but expresses an interest for the newly purchased possession shows his own individuality.[9]

However, the choice of words to describe Nouâmane's interest for music also leads to some ambiguity and, thus, to a queer interpretation: Is the boy seduced primarily by the hand-held organ or by Pierre's sexual organ? An ellipse in the narration again leaves readers without clear answers. They learn only that, for the first time in his life, he sleeps on a beautiful bed the night he meets the Frenchman (*Le soir, j'ai dormi pour la première fois dans un beau lit*). Such a declaration suggests that author Rachid O. joins Mohamed Choukri from Chapter 4 in raising collective awareness about the unavoidable realities confronting Moroccan male youth who engage sexually with older European male tourists.

Taken literally, Nouâmane's initial potential for subject formation (shown in his appreciation for music) is reduced to sexual objectification in the eyes of the European traveler in Morocco. Despite some ambiguity in the narrative, it seems that the boy's lack of purchasing power, alongside his musical interests, are the factors that lead him to engage sexually with Pierre. His attraction to music leaves him vulnerable to sexual exploitation precisely because he views it as incidental to his own goals; the older man therefore determines the terms of their relationship and controls its progression, like bribery. On the one hand, the European male tourist maintains his privileged status; on the other, the native Moroccan boy perpetuates his socioeconomic marginality. In this context, the advantageous economic position enjoyed by the white

European traveler allows him to retain his self-perception of superiority when engaging sexually with the underprivileged youngster.

While sexual satisfaction is arguably part of subject formation, the socioeconomic conditions here prevent Nouâmane from fully developing sexual agency. He essentially *works* for a soft bed to sleep in for the first time in his life, and he may well take as much pleasure from the experience as from its results. Yet the absence of comment on his physical gratification in the narrative implies that the rewards outweigh his means of achieving them.

Nouâmane's encounter with Pierre suggests the traces of a colonial past and their transfer into a homosexual framework in the current era. At first level, the historical superiority enjoyed by the European is shown in the figure of Pierre—whereas the "eternal" obedience of the local seems to correspond to the figure of Nouâmane. The second level corresponds to the transfer of the colonial traces within a contemporary homosexual context in a cross-cultural encounter. I suggest that the accustomed behavior of superiority from White Europeans in colonies is still present when discussing homosexual tourism in Morocco. And Nouâmane's "natural" instinct to follow Pierre's body language attests to this point. Whether this is due to the teenager's indigent appearance, which the Frenchman quickly identifies, or not is irrelevant for my argument. What is significant is Nouâmane's reality: His low socioeconomic background forces him to venture out to the streets on his own and, hence, places him in vulnerable situations, like meeting and engaging sexually with Pierre. Upon entering the homosexual paradigm, the colonial past solidifies its binary system: The colonizer becomes the older European man of economic privilege while the colonized transforms into the poor and ethnicized local boy.

However, Nouâmane describes Pierre as a Frenchman sojourning for an extended period of time in Morocco, where they live together and, hence, maintain an ongoing relationship. While their relationship is first and foremost sexual in nature, its longevity allows readers to appreciate the phenomenon of homosexual tourism through a different lens. What are the effects of an affair that begins as sexual, continues to occur, and subsequently stabilizes? Does it become romantic? At what point, does it morph into a supportive system, where the affluent European traveler financially (and, perhaps, emotionally) supports the impoverished native youngster?

I suggest that Nouâmane's and Pierre's relationship corresponds to the Maussian model of gift exchange: Whereas Nouâmane contributes with companionship and acquiescence, Pierre provides financial support, as well as the promise of gifts. In the long term, they grow to share affection as well as sex. In his classic description of gift exchange within a relation, Marcel Mauss's *The Gift: The Form and Reason for Exchange in Archaic Societies* (1990) claims the following:

> The exchange of presents ... represents an intermingling. Souls are mixed with things; things with souls. Lives are mingled together, and this is how, among persons and things so intermingled, each emerges from their own sphere and mixes together. This is precisely what contract and exchange are. (19–20)

I understand the Maussian view of gift as any object or service exchanged as essential to establishing social relations. At the core of the gift relationship is reciprocity and the mutual understanding of the transactions in question. As the essay entitled "Gifts, Commodities, and Social Relations: A Maussian View of Exchange" (1991) by James Carrier suggests, the objects exchanged are "inalienably associated with the giver, the recipient, and the relationship that defines them" (121).[10] The gifts transacted between Nouâmane and Pierre can be thought of in terms of the two following paradigms: material (economic) and sexual (affective). The economic axis includes financial support (a musical instrument, a bed, daily sustenance, etc.) while the affective axis involves companionship, acquiescence, promises, and sex. While Pierre contributes with both axes, Nouâmane brings only affective wealth to this gift relationship. Regardless of the order in which the transaction occurs, there is the clear mutual understanding of the gifts, objects, and services involved in the exchange. To this effect, James Carrier insists upon the reciprocity of gifts and mutual obligation uniting those who exchange them.

> [The] elements that underlie the Maussian view of gifts [are] that gift exchange is (1) the obligatory transfer of (2) inalienable objects or services between (3) related and mutually obligated transactors. These elements identify the key dimension in terms of which transactions are understood. These are the degree and manner of the obligation to transact, of the link between what is transacted and those who transact it, and of the link between transactors. (122–123)

The Maussian model clearly outlines that giving and receiving are obligatory in the gift relationship. From this perspective, the gift and the obligations embedded in their transactions generate and regenerate the relationship between the giver and recipient. Nouâmane and Pierre's first encounter marks out the gifts that will be shared in their relationship. What are initially material gifts—the musical instrument and the bed—will later become the points of intersection of many additional gifts and services involved in their relationship. Whereas the bed might seem to lend itself to stronger affective ties, the musical organ surpasses it in terms of influence on Nouâmane's (homo)sexual agency and subject formation (this question will be fully explored in the last part of this section). I consider the materiality of the bed itself to require immediate study. As I have previously suggested, Nouâmane sleeps on a beautiful bed for the first time upon meeting Pierre. This has a twofold implication: The first reminds us about the boy's socioeconomic marginality as well as the gift of financial assistance in the relation; the second clearly evokes the sexual/affective aspect of their rapport. Here, it is significant to make a parenthesis in my analysis and state that the overlapping paradigms—or in Maussian terms, the gift to transact: economic (material) and sexual (affective)—may also overlap even when discussing them separately.

From the outset, Rachid O.'s *Ce qui reste* (2003) shows how Pierre uses his intuition about Nouâmane's homelessness to his advantage, as he quickly invites the teenager to live with him. Nouâmane recounts, "À partir du matin qui a suivi, il m'a toujours dit 'Je t'aime.' Il me le répétait dans chaque pièce et le jardin, je répondais 'Moi aussi'" (As of the following morning, he would always tell me "I love you." He would repeat it in every room and the garden; I would say "Me too") (37). Telling someone "I love you" in English right from the first encounter would make it more credible than saying it within the French cultural context—as the French in France do not confess their love (like Americans would) after spending the first night with someone. This near-immediate attachment on the part of Pierre might strike as more or less genuine, depending on the perspective of the reader. While some could argue that his *coup de foudre* (love at first sight) proves the sincerity of his emotions, others could affirm that it appears artificial due to their lack of previous relationship. Above all, it is quite possible that Pierre says "*Je t'aime*" to Nouâmane after their first night together because he is not saying it to a white French youngster in France, but to a Moroccan boy in Morocco. Similar to French writers from the nineteenth and twentieth centuries—who would travel to North Africa to engage in homosexual fantasies—Pierre also sojourns there to create a fantasy world of homosexual love with a teenager.

Can this desire to live an illusion be the cause of the Frenchman's inability to find love in his native country? Or is it a genuine feeling that he
is free to express in exile from the Hexagon? Another incident suggests
that Pierre legitimately cares for the local youngster. Nouâmane states,
"Ma mère, chanceuse, [car notre maison s'était] écroulée un jour par un
violent orage [et] Pierre nous a aidés avec de l'argent à en construire une
autre" (My mother, lucky, [because our house had] collapsed one day by
a violent storm [and] Pierre helped us with money to build another one)
(40). According to this passage, Pierre's attention for the boy's well-be-
ing extends not only to the boy himself, but also to his mother, his only
family. His goal to help the Nouâmane by building another house for the
mother corresponds to an act of affection, as he is providing shelter and
security to this Moroccan family.

Sexual Mimicry: Emphatically Not to Be French

This affection indeed seems reciprocal, since Nouâmane also expresses
emotional attachment for Pierre. The boy declares, "Je me suis attaché
réellement à Pierre" (I became very attached to Pierre) (37). He
recounts how his own development seems intrinsically linked to living
with the Frenchman. "J'étais devenu un autre Nouâmane qui me plai-
sait. Je parlais plus le français que l'arabe, moins timide et apeuré, je ne
tremblais plus devant les gens" (I had become another Nouâmane that
I liked. I spoke more French than Arabic, less shy and frightened, I
would no longer tremble in front of people) (ibid.). Being happy with
himself, the Moroccan boy goes so far as to become more comfortable
as a Francophone than an Arabic-speaker during the three-year relationship with Pierre. He also manifests sexual satisfaction, "je faisais l'amour
sans m'apercevoir que c'était tous les jours" (I would make love without realizing it was everyday) (ibid.). Pierre's idyllic world of homosexual
love seems to convene as well for the Moroccan teenager, who also finds
pleasure—if not love—while living in it.

> [Pierre] me considérait comme un garçon facile, pas compliqué, adorable,
> il le disait à ses amis avec un profond soulagement, comme une évidence
> qui faisait du bien, enfin le genre de garçon avec lequel il fallait vivre, pas
> comme ceux qui le volaient. J'ai l'impression que je me suis déjà entraîné
> pour parler comme je fais. Ça me rendait fou de joie d'être un garçon de
> promesse. (37–38)

([Pierre] saw me as an adorable, uncomplicated, and easy-going boy, he would say this to his friends with deep relief, as evidence that felt good, anyhow, the kind of boy with whom he needed to live, unlike those who would steal from him. I feel as if I have already been trained to talk like I do. It would make me ecstatic to be a promising boyfriend.) (37–38)

This side-by-side self-account of Nouâmane seen by Pierre as "adorable" and "uncomplicated," like a sexual object, but worthy of more consideration than a boy toy or thief illustrates the ambivalence of their relationship. The domestication that Nouâmane undergoes during his relationship with Pierre merges into one individual with two distinct stereotypes: It recalls Gide's image of the charming *"petit Arabe,"* yet it reiterates Genet's stereotype of the dishonest Arab boy. In *L'immoraliste,* Gide compares the *"petit Arabe"* to a *"petit chat"* to portray the Arab boy as a domesticated animal because of his tender and affectionate attributes.[11] In addition, the image of the "noble savage"[12] also appears in Nouâmane's self-perception. In fact, the youngster himself expresses tremendous joy for possessing the characteristics, which render him a *"garçon de promesse"* (a boyfriend with potential) for Pierre—and, presumably, for other homosexual European travelers. Aware of his own communication skills, he seems to have learned to communicate according to the Frenchman's design—in relation to not only *how* he speaks but also *what* he says. He manages to describe himself as though it is not himself speaking, but rather Pierre. He offers an echo of Pierre's words, confirming his own assertion: "je me suis déjà entraîné pour parler comme je le fais" (37).

Nouâmane's intention to obtain Pierre's approval through the imitation of French customs and language corresponds to Homi Bhabha's figure of mimicry in "Of Mimicry and Man" (1984). Just as Bhabha argues that mimicry is perceived as a means to attain integration but falls short in that it can only ever be imitation, rather than authenticity—"to be Anglicized," he affirms, "is empathetically not to be English" (128),[13] so, too, Nouâmane's intention to be accepted as French ends up reinforcing his status as Other. Nouâmane's desire to turn into a recognizable French Other resonates with Bhabha's "subject of a difference that is almost the same, but not quite" (126). This incomplete transformation, which the critic calls the "ambivalence of mimicry," fixes the colonial subject as a "partial presence." In Bhabha's words, "'partial' ... mean[s] both 'incomplete' and 'virtual.' It is as if the very emergence of the 'colonial' is dependent for its representation upon some strategic limitation or prohibition *within* the authoritative discourse itself" (127, emphasis in the original). Nouâmane's impossibility to fully become French, as well as his continuous quest for Pierre's approval, reduces him to the "partial presence" found in the ambivalence of mimicry. To transpose Bhabha's claim within Nouâmane's situation, I would contend that *to be Frenchified is empathetically not to be French.*

Furthermore, the second implication within Nouâmane's statement evokes Jean Genet's racist stereotype that treats the Arab boys as thieves and deceitful. As Nouâmane's self-awareness is built under Pierre's tutelage, he manifests sympathy for Pierre, who claims to have been robbed by young (and handsome), but deceitful Moroccan boys. Here, Pierre seems to praise Nouâmane for not resembling the rest of those who steal, which appears to be one of the reasons why Pierre chooses him. Although a compliment, it echoes Genet's racist stereotype and seems a point of discussion between Pierre and his friends. The idea that the Frenchman talks about Nouâmane and compares him with other Moroccan boys (from his sexual past) suggests a sort of gamesmanship among the European homosexual crowd in Tangiers. They share their experiences with the youth they encounter amidst their search of their homoerotic adventures in Morocco like trophy tales. Although others might encounter handsome thieves, these European men seem hopeful that some day they too will fulfill their fantasy by building a homosexual paradise like Pierre's—and come across an adorable and uncomplicated boy like Nouâmane. Simply put, Nouâmane gives him bragging rights.

With the exception of the specific reference provided by Nouâmane, nowhere else in Rachid O.'s novel *Ce qui reste* (2003) do we learn about the details regarding the personalities of the other Moroccan boys Pierre dates prior to him. Moreover, Nouâmane's reference to the Moroccan boys as thieves has absolutely nothing to do with his own interests: He is not the one who has been robbed by other Moroccan boys. Unlike Mohamed Choukri's impoverished character, he does not inform readers that he is (or has been) himself involved in stealing. In fact, despite half a century between Mohamed Choukri's and Nouâmane's same-sex encounters with European tourists, both of them allude to the phenomenon of stealing as part of the Moroccan boy's upbringing. As if Nouâmane overheard Mohamed Choukri's statement (*un nouveau métier parmi d'autres, en plus du vol et de la mendicité*),[14] this protagonist strives to prove to the Frenchman that he will take no part in such an underhanded activity.

Keeping this objective very clear, Nouâmane continues to speak for Pierre, further reinforcing his discursive mimicry. Whereas his ability to speak could otherwise be taken as an indication of agency, Nouâmane's verbalization about the "Moroccan boys who would rob Pierre" (*ceux qui le volaient*) above all suggests that Pierre has repeatedly discussed the topic with his European friends. Interpreted as indirect discourse, this retelling attests to Nouâmane's knowledge about his own differentiation from the stereotypical Moroccan boys. This distinction is not essentialist but constructed according to Pierre's design. Through continuous self-work, Nouâmane succeeds in becoming partially French and, most importantly, he succeeds in obtaining approval not only from Pierre, but also from other European men. Not unlike the Lotmanian boundary figures from Chapters 2 and 3 in this book, Nouâmane develops what Homi Bhabha calls a "discriminatory identity." He builds an "identity between stereotypes which, through repetition, also becomes different; the discriminatory identities constructed across traditional cultural norms and classifications" (130). This identity is based less on the emotional ties between the two men than on the economy of the gift.

In many ways, Frenchness could be considered the most valuable affective commodity that Pierre shares with Nouâmane. For this reason, their gift relationship ultimately seems to benefit both: Pierre constructs an idyllic world of homosexual love, whereas Nouâmane seeks to gain knowledge and cultural capital in order to learn to play a musical instrument like the Frenchman. Pierre takes the role of provider; interestingly, however, Nouâmane narrates that Pierre pays all the expenses to build another house for his mother—not for him. He does not consider Pierre's generosity an act addressed toward him, but towards his mother; hence, he describes her as "lucky" for benefiting financially from his own relationship with the Frenchman. That is, the youngster does not want a house, but the organ that Pierre had just bought before their first meeting. The boy's desire to possess this object is nourished throughout the time he spends living with the Frenchman; he claims to be "hypnotisé avec de la musique dans les oreilles" (hypnotized with the music in my ears) (37). His only hope is that he will inherit the organ when Pierre returns to France.

But this promise is never carried out, as the tourist takes the organ home with him. Nouâmane remembers, "Je pleurais en voyant ces trois années emportées par le vent, je le voulais cet orgue" (I would cry to see these three years gone in the wind, I wanted that organ) (40). This statement suggests that the organ seems to be one of the chief reasons why Nouâmane lived with Pierre during the time he stayed in Morocco. This unfulfilled promise reinserts the Maussian dynamics of exchange in a winding narrative where it sometimes seemed that the couple may have truly verged on a full-scaled love affair. Whereas Nouâmane brings sex and company to the Frenchman, Pierre provides financial support and the promise to leave the instrument to the Moroccan boy. Since this gift is not transacted, the break of their relationship ensues. Marcel Mauss claims,

> To refuse to give, to fail to invite, just as to refuse to accept, is tantamount to declaring war; it is to reject the bond of alliance and commonality. [Further,] these presents do not serve the same purpose [: their] goal is above all a moral one, the object being to foster friendly feelings between the two persons in question.... If the exercise failed to do so, everything had failed. (13–19)

If transactions create and maintain the gift relationship, Pierre's refusal to give the organ to Nouâmane forces a clear rupture in the bond of their alliance. The promised object represents Pierre's ethical values as well as his inalienable obligation to their relationship. His failure to fulfill a commitment clearly severs the ties between him and Nouâmane. This failure to follow through creates an asymmetrical effect on both of the characters. Similar to an unbalanced trading system that involves two partners, the one at a disadvantaged position will remain marginal, while the one in a superior position will continue to profit. As the figure of Nouâmane shows, Moroccan youth who engage sexually with European men also come from a lower socioeconomic sector of society; thus, their disadvantaged position not only makes them vulnerable to sexual exploitation but also perpetuates their marginality when they participate in the sexual tourism industry—even if their interactions with clients grow into more complex relationships.

Nouâmane's feelings of abandonment take us back to the metaphor of historical colonial discourse mentioned at the beginning of this section. Just as the colonizer comes to the unclaimed land, exploits it, and then returns to his homeland, taking with him the valuable goods he subtracts from this land, Pierre resides in Morocco, maintains a sexual and romantic relationship with Nouâmane, and then returns to France, taking with him the musical instrument already promised to the youngster. By doing so, the Frenchman is stealing not only the material object that the Moroccan boy considers "his" throughout their relationship, but also his dream. Completely lucid about his own impoverished situation, Nouâmane also seems aware that without Pierre's gift, he will never learn to play. In this context, Nouâmane can no longer envision his educational pursuits in music as a means to struggle out of poverty. This deceit leaves the teenager feeling not only regretful and hopeless, but also deceived and robbed by Pierre. Nouâmane's feelings of abandonment after his long-lasting relationship with Pierre attest perhaps the most firmly to a phenomenon that I would call homosexual imperialism.

Furthermore, this situation effectively reverses Genet's racist stereotype of Arab boys as deceitful thieves. In Nouâmane's experience with Pierre, it is difficult not to wonder: Who is the thief here? Who deceives whom in the relationship between them? On the one hand, Pierre's departure with his prized possession reflects his lack of commitment and respect for the youngster. On the other, it attests to a crucial point in homosexual tourism in Morocco, which is the Frenchman's sense of entitlement to use, abuse, and neglect the native.

Pierre lives an idyllic romance with Nouâmane for three years and then abandons it, turning on his heels to trace back his colonial steps. Pierre's extended stay in Tangiers recalls Jarrod Hayes's idea about the nineteenth-century French traveler who also expected to have sex with a stereotype from Chapter 1. In "Homosexuality and Islam" (1993), Khalid Duran adds that "Morocco has become a favorite playground for European gay men" (186) and that these travelers hope to find "potent men—the 'noble savages'" (186). Duran argues that the gay tourists more recently seeking sexual partners (performing the active role) in North African countries are usually unaware of the hostile attitude toward them on the local scene, as they represent the nations that once were colonial masters. In Duran's words, "To sodomize a Westerner provides a kind of psychological relief for some people from among the former 'subject races' who now have a chance to take it out on their oppressors. This also holds true of some other African regions; to do it to a white man is like taking revenge, along with having a source of income" (189). Such hostility toward the West can also be considered "a symptom of "Westernization," as Muslim fundamentalists in particular are fond of rejecting all "'imported ideologies' and 'foreign isms'" (194).

THWARTED MATERIAL AMBITION: (HOMO)SEXUAL
AGENCY IN NOUÂMANE

In the end of *Ce qui reste* (2003), Moroccan writer Rachid O. alludes that Nouâmane fails to reach full sexual agency partly because his goals are material, rather than affective. Without specifying how long it is since Pierre's departure from Morocco, Nouâmane simply tells readers that he is on his honeymoon in France. His trip is a wedding present for marrying Faïda. Because the entire country is in mourning for the king's death, they have not been able to consummate their marriage in Morocco. However, the first night they spend in Paris, he finds himself completely restless and unable to sleep. Thus, he goes out for a walk, without specifying if they have already "consummated" the marriage in their Parisian hotel. He declares, "C'est avec elle que j'aurais dû me réveiller ce matin" (47). The ambiguity as to where or with whom he has slept that night—if he has slept—influences the depiction of his sexuality. Rather than searching for a Western classification that would encapsulate his ambiguous heterosexuality, the narrative focuses on his unfulfilled homosexual agency.

> Mais une fois ici [à Paris], je ne pouvais pas passer un instant sans que Pierre me vienne en tête. Brusquement je me suis dit: « Tu es là maintenant, Nouâmane, tu ne vaux pas grand-chose … si tu n'es pas capable de lui rendre visite. » Son adresse n'avait jamais quitté mon portefeuille. Je sais, ma conduite est lamentable de faire ça à ma femme Faïda … Depuis qu'il était parti, je me réveillais souvent triste le matin, ce n'était pas normal, et ce n'était pas qu'une histoire d'orgue, c'était aussi toute la tendresse dont il me couvrait et tout d'un coup je me suis retrouvé seul. (47–48)

> (But once here [in Paris], I couldn't be without a moment Pierre coming to my head. Suddenly I thought: "You're here now, Nouâmane, you're worth nothing … if you don't dare to give him a visit." His address had never left my wallet. I know my behavior is appalling to do that to my wife Faïda … Since he was gone, I would often wake up sad in the morning, it wasn't normal, and it wasn't only a story about an organ, it was also all the tenderness which he covered me with and suddenly I found myself alone.) (47–48)

Rather than spending the night with his new bride, Nouâmane seems to be overwhelmed by Pierre's presence. Although he had never been to Paris before, the entire city reminds him of his old flame, the only homosexual love he claims to have experienced in his life. Nouâmane's representation of Paris as a homosexual space has two especially relevant implications. On the one hand, it proves analogous to the representation of France (and, more specifically, Paris) as a queer space in the Latin American imaginary from Chapters 2 and 3. On the other hand, it inverses the image of the Frenchmen in search of homosexual encounters in North Africa, since Nouâmane enacts that process in reverse. To return to André Gide's *L'immoraliste* in Chapter 4, Nouâmane comes to resemble Michel, the protagonist, who chooses to leave his wife at home in his quest to meet Arab boys in the parks of Biskra.

Nowhere in the narrative does Nouâmane affirm that he manages to collect himself emotionally and carry out his desire to search for Pierre in Paris. Nouâmane's hesitation to see Pierre, as well as to consummate his marriage with Faïda, reflects his frustrated sexual agency. Since Pierre's departure from Morocco, Nouâmane has mainly experienced a sense of sexual and affective incompleteness. The void left by the unfulfilled promise of receiving a musical instrument from Pierre leaves him in difficulty, unable to conceive other ways to achieve his broken dream. While he acknowledges that Pierre also provided affection and tenderness in their gift relationship, he realizes the importance of these offerings only once they are withdrawn. This reflects the permanence of gifts, which, according to Mauss, "are never completely separated from the men who exchange them; the communion and alliance they establish are well-nigh indissoluble" (32). Once in Paris, Nouâmane cannot stop thinking about the relationship he once had with Pierre. Both the person and the place become inalienably associated with the provider, the recipient, and the gift relationship that once bound them together in Nouâmane's own eyes.

Conclusion

The preceding analysis explores homosexual tourism in Morocco as a cross-cultural encounter in Rachid O.'s novels, *Chocolat chaud* (1998) and *Ce qui reste* (2003), which illustrate the stories of the author's friends Youssr and Nouâmane, respectively. Joined by Mohamed Choukri's autobiography, *Le pain nu* (1980) from the previous chapter, Rachid O. also underscores the harsh socioeconomic realities experienced by Moroccan youth, which lead them to succumb to the sexual advances of affluent foreign tourists. My interpretations have highlighted two main points: the socioeconomic differences which determine relationships between the privileged European traveler and the impoverished Moroccan boy on the one hand; and on the other, the spatial paradigm that establishes the public space as a predominantly male space where contact occurs. The focus of Chapters 4 and 5 has been the public space, where all the local teenagers have their encounters with homosexual European tourists: the street, the terrace of a café, and the window in front of the music shop. The narratives follow a progression of same-sex tourism as a paid activity for underage males: Firstly, in the previous chapter, Choukri describes how a five-minute encounter ends the starvation of a youngster; secondly, this chapter shows how Youssr seeks to transform into a bodily-ideal while already working in the tourist industry; and lastly, this chapter also demonstrates how Nouâmane becomes involved in a three-year-long relationship with Pierre that changes, if only temporarily, his socioeconomic status. In particular, this example brings to light questions about the blurry dividing line between sexual tourism and romantic relationships abroad, as well as financial support as a disguise for compensation for sex. In this manner, the challenging socioeconomic situation in Morocco draws into question the ability for local young men to engage in sexual activity with European travelers while still maintaining individual agency. Although it might be tempting to suppose that they use sex to move up the social ladder, or that they turn to Europeans as a safe alternative to break local cultural taboos, these youths in fact find their greatest sources of agency outside the bedroom—that is, in heterosexual romance, bodybuilding, music, and other self-enhancing forms of development less entangled in (post)colonial power imbalances.

The next two chapters will therefore examine the expectations of the ethnicized local boy who voluntarily plans to encounter the French Other. It will analyze Rachid O.'s childhood allegory about the blond-haired, blue-eyed French boy by paying particular attention to two main realities in a North African country like Morocco: (1) The (traditional) French presence in the country, where children learn from an early age about the existence of the French Other; and (2) the prestige and allure of all things French. Rather than entering into the realm of colonial discourse (that reflects the history of French colonialism in Morocco), my book will continue to focus on young Moroccans' imaginary in relation to the French. Moving away from the privileged Frenchman and marginal Moroccan boy as a pair, the next two chapters will concentrate on intimate moments and explore the ethnicized body in relation to subjectivity formation as well as homosexual awakening in Rachid O.'s writing.

NOTES

1. Homi Bhabha, "Of Mimicry and Man: The Ambivalence of Colonial Discourse," *Discipleship: A Special Issue on Psychoanalysis* 28 (Spring 1984): 125–133.
2. Marcel Mauss, *The Gift: The Form and Reason for Exchange in Archaic Societies*, trans. W. D. Halls (New York: W. W. Norton & Company, Inc., 1990).
3. Rachid O., *Chocolat chaud* (Paris: Éditions Gallimard, 1998).
4. All the translations in this book are my own.
5. "Shisha," also known as "hookah" is a "waterpipe or narghile, is single or multi-stemmed (often glass-based) instrument for smoking in which the smoke is cooled by water. The tobacco smoked is referred to as shisha (sheesha) in the United Kingdom, United States and Canada." However, the term 'Shisha' Shisha (شيشة), from the Persian word shīshe (شیشه), meaning glass, is the common term for the hookah in Egypt, Sudan and the Arab countries of the Persian Gulf (including Kuwait, Bahrain, Qatar, Oman, UAE, and Saudi Arabia), and in Algeria, Morocco, Tunisia, Somalia and Yemen." http://en.wikipedia.org/wiki/Hookah.
6. Homi K. Bhabha, "The postcolonial and the postmodern: The question of Agency," in *The Location of Culture* (New York: Routledge, 1994), 245–283.
7. Rachid O., *Ce qui reste* (Paris: Éditions Gallimard, 2003).
8. See full citation in this chapter.
9. As suggested previously in Nouâmane's inability to enter the music shop because he cannot afford to purchase any of the instruments, his interest for the organ also shows the question of the possession of material objects and the needs to those who lack the means to have them.
10. James Carrier, "Gifts, Commodities, and Social Relations: A Maussian View of Exchange," *Sociological Forum* 6, no. 1 (March 1991): 119–136.
11. See Chapter 4 in this book, where I analyze the comparisons of the Arab boys to a cat and a dog in André Gide's *L'immoraliste* (1902).
12. See my use of this concept and its different suggestions by critics Joseph Massad, Khalid Duran, as well as Jarrod Hayes.
13. For a thorough analysis of Homi Bhabha's claim, see pages 127–128 in his article "Of Mimicry and Man" (1984).
14. This statement can be found in Mohamed Choukri's passage on the previous chapter.

References

Bhabha, Homi K. "Of Mimicry and Man: The Ambivalence of Colonial Discourse." *Discipleship: A Special Issue on Psychoanalysis* 28 (Spring 1984): 125–133.

———. *The Location of Culture*. New York: Routledge, 1994.

Carrier, James. "Gifts, Commodities, and Social Relations: A Maussian View of Exchange." *Sociological Forum* 6, no. 1 (March 1991): 119–136.

Duran, Khalid. "Homosexuality and Islam." In *Homosexuality and World Religions*, edited by Arlene Swidler, 181–197. Valley Forge, PA: Trinity Press International, 1993.

"Hookah," Wikipedia, Google, accessed on July 5, 2017, http://en.wikipedia.org/wiki/Hookah.

Mauss, Marcel. *The Gift: The Form and Reason for Exchange in Archaic Societies*. Translated by W. D. Halls. New York: W. W. Norton, 1990.

O., Rachid. *Chocolat chaud*. Paris: Éditions Gallimard, 1998.

———. *Ce qui reste*. Paris: Éditions Gallimard, 2003.

PART III

Transcultural Information Media and Technology in Morocco

Rachid O.'s Homosexual Awakening: The Allegorical Representation of the Blond-Haired, Blue-Eyed French Boy

In much literature dedicated to homosexual awakening, the subject physically traverses sexual, ethnic, and cultural boundaries in search of homosexual fulfillment. Whether a Latin American character crosses into French cultural space in search of homoerotic freedom, or a Frenchman seeks adventures with local youth engaged in European homosexual tourism in Morocco, the individual is often motivated to cross over cultural and national boundaries to find partners. In most of these cases, homosexual fantasy motivates travel and postcolonial paradigms directly influence power dynamics in the more or less developed relationships (e.g., the privileged European tourist *vis-à-vis* the impoverished Moroccan boy). However, not all travels need be tangible in order to facilitate homosexual awakening. In this chapter, I focus on young Rachid's experiences with photography and television as information and media technology. I study how these means of transcultural communication become a source of homosexual fantasy, which awakens desire in the local Moroccan boy to search for a partner with ethnic and racial differences—more specifically, a blond-haired, blue-eyed French boy. I explore how the young protagonist materializes his homosexual fantasy with boys of his own age and develops homosexual agency by skillfully manipulating his internalization of the cultural contexts around him.

This chapter analyzes Rachid O.'s narrative *Chocolat chaud* (1998), where the childhood allegory about the blond-haired, blue-eyed French boy shows how photography and television produce Rachid's affective

© The Author(s) 2019
L. Navarro-Ayala, *Queering Transcultural Encounters*,
Palgrave Studies in Globalization and Embodiment,
https://doi.org/10.1007/978-3-319-92315-4_6

experience. It traces a progression throughout the chapter based on the senses of sight, touch, and taste. Whereas Rachid's intimate moments initially remain confined to the domestic sphere, seeing Noé's photograph for the first time awakens his desire to touch the image; subsequently, he succeeds in possessing a copy of the blond boy's image at home. I emphasize Rachid O.'s perception of the world: its relation to intimacy and the form it takes through embodiment, identities, and imaginaries, especially due to the relationship between himself, as a thirteen-year-old youngster, and Noé, a French boy who has moved away from North Africa with his family. I also examine the broader use of intimacy as related to personal affect, as Rachid's intimacy becomes inseparable from transcultural information and media technology produced within both the intimate and public spheres.

Intimacy in Cultural Context

I use the term intimacy as defined by Lauren Berlant in her essay entitled "Intimacy: A special Issue" (1998).[1] She explains that intimacy is "a narrative about something shared, a story about oneself" which is usually set within zones of familiarity and comfort, such as friendship, couple, and family. "Yet the inwardness of the intimate is met by a corresponding publicness" (281). This publicness refers to the process that personalizes the public sphere by reproducing a fantasy that private life is real in contrast to collective life. She continues by asking how attachments in different spaces produce personal identities. Rethinking intimacy calls for the redescription of the rhetorical and material conditions that enable lives to make sense. In Rachid O.'s case, intimacy reveals itself to be a relationship associated with tacit fantasies, rules, and obligations.

This intimacy, however, is manifested in many ways other than through the official publics of opinion, culture, and state, or through privatized forms normally associated with sexuality. In particular, intimacy, as described by Lauren Berlant and Michael Warner in their essay "Sex in public (Intimacy)" (1998),[2] is strictly connected with queers and other rebels who have long struggled, often dangerously or scandalously, to cultivate what hegemonic discourse refers to as criminal intimacy. These are the developed relations and narratives "that are only recognized as intimate in queer culture: girlfriends, gal pals, fuckbuddies, [and] tricks" (532). Queer culture, Berlant and Warner observe, "has learned not only how to sexualize these and other relations, but also to use them as a context for witnessing intense and personal affect, while elaborating a public world of belonging and transformation" (ibid.). In this sense, Rachid experiences intimate moments even while he remains surrounded by his friends: He may use coping mechanisms that enable him to belong according to outward appearances despite the sexual difference that he fosters in his most private thoughts.

Yet, Rachid's affective experience never becomes divorced from his contact with the world. In "Bitter After Taste: Affect, Food, and Social Aesthetics" (2010),[3] Ben Highmore draws on the post-structuralist idea that cultural research should turn toward materialism, recognizing that the body acts as "a nexus of finely interlaced force fields." In an effort to focus on the concrete existence of bodies, he calls for studies of emotions and affects that highlight "the senses, the sensorial, and the human sensorium" (119). This methodology is particularly useful to demonstrate how Rachid's affective experience is a densely "woven entanglement" that involves substances and matter, as well as feelings and affect. It is also central to understanding Rachid's contact with the technological world that provides him access to French male figures. Moreover, Highmore warns against a "critical untangling (the scholarly and bureaucratic business of sorting categories and filing phenomena)," claiming instead that "a critically entangled contact with affective experience" is required to capture the complexities of such phenomenon (ibid.). This approach entails finding the connections between senses and emotions in Rachid's encounter with the French boy: His sensual interconnection with the Other (seeing and craving to taste hot chocolate = homoerotic desire) resonates with Highmore's idea about "cross-modal networks that register links between perception, affect, the senses, and emotions" (120). Whereas synesthesia reflects direct ties between the senses—sound inspiring taste or shapes associated with colors—this longing for the Other inspired by the senses might be considered more akin to a daydream. Sight and taste inspire a great longing to touch, but Rachid does not perceive his senses interchangeably. Instead, he uses his imagination to fill the gaps between his reality and desires, until he ultimately manages to reach a much sought-after experience of touch.

That said, Rachid's universe reveals a specific kind of feeling that relates to the sociocultural status of his body. To describe his emotions, it is helpful to refer to the intersections of affect and ethnicity as presented by queer Latino critics in the USA. In "You Can Have My Brown Body and Eat It, Too!" (2005),[4] Hiram Perez claims that queer theorizing "as it has been institutionalized, is proper to—and property to—white bodies. Colored folk perform affect but can never theorize it" (174). According to Perez, this situation leads to shame for ethnicized others in the queer community. He criticizes that "U.S. race discourse stipulates that gay shame, as an experience both visceral and self-reflexive, be recuperated for whiteness" (ibid.). Continuing with a binary opposition, he disapproves of the failure to discuss shame in relation to other forms of difference at a national academic conference on the subject.

> For a conference devoted to theorizing shame, there was curiously little scholarship specifically addressing affect. Despite the conference theme, the proceedings reproduced an opposition between theory and affect, particularly in its gendered and raced foundations: theory is to affect as masculine is to feminine; civilized to primitive; rational to paranoid; white to other. The brown thug and the sentimental feminine find themselves unlikely compatriots in this opposition. (179)

Hiram Perez's strong criticism clearly suggests that a gay or lesbian identity fails to prevent some queer theorists from reinstituting masculinist biases and patriarchal privileges. The critic's frustrated experience among his peers suggests the need to explore affect production in greater depth. Extending Perez's concern outside academia in the USA, it could be further argued that the affect manifested by the queer body requires an even more careful theorization, other than dominant Western scholarship, in postcolonial contexts like North Africa. Rachid's intimate moments provide noteworthy material to examine this topic because of his fascination with the white European male figure and his refusal to give into social pressures to feel shame concerning his sexual preferences and his attraction for racial and ethnic differences.

According to several scholars, the brown subject gives shape to a unique affect intrinsically linked to his or her subject formation. This is what queer Latino critic José Esteban Muñoz dubs "feeling brown" in his essay "Feeling Brown: Ethnicity and Affect in Ricardo Bracho's 'The Sweetest Hangover (And Other STDs)'" (2000).[5] Muñoz begins his argument on affective difference by returning to Jean-Paul Sartre's paradigm of emotions. For the purpose of defining his argument, Muñoz adopts the Sartrian description of emotion as an extension of consciousness, a humans' comprehension of the world that makes demands upon them. Muñoz notes,

Life in this existentially and phenomenologically oriented description consists in a set of tasks, things we need to do. We encounter routes and obstacles to the actualization of certain goals, and make a map for ourselves of the world which includes these pathways and blocks to these goals. But when we are overwhelmed by this map of the world, a map replete with obstacles and barriers to our self-actualization, we enact the "magical" process that Sartre describes as emotions. When facing a seemingly insurmountable object, we turn to emotion. (71)

Muñoz's interest on this Sartrian description lies primarily in the phenomenological concept of emotion as the reaction to reality in a world that overwhelms us. He considers Sartre's definition to be deeply relational and argues that Sartre's paradigm subsequently regresses to the magical realm of emotions when under pressure. As a result, Muñoz considers the Sartrian definition of emotion a "typically misogynist gender logic that positions men as reasonable and better suited to deploying the world of utensils whereas women (and men who are overly feminine) are cast as a weaker" (71). In such a scenario, members of the queer community—whose maps often include more obstacles than open routes—would find themselves faced with emotionality as a psychological state almost inevitable at every turn.

Furthermore, the idea that emotion becomes a last resort for those deprived of reason strikes a disharmonious chord with people of color, often historically perceived as primitive who regret to expressing themselves through feelings due to limited rationality. If emotions surface when losing distance in relation to the world, as Sartre proposes, then, by contrast, minority subjects often find themselves already distanced from a world that is far from ideologically neutral. Muñoz explains,

Because stigmatized people are presented with significantly more obstacles and blockages than privileged citizen-subjects, minoritarian subjects often have difficulty maintaining distance from the very material and felt obstacles that suddenly surface in their own affective mapping of the world. (72)

Simply put, this organization of social space corresponds to cultural registers of normativity that favor citizen-subjects. However, Muñoz believes minoritarian subjects can still use the Sartrian affective sketch and think of it in terms of "the working of emotion." According to him, this type of mapping can potentially provide a "critical distance that does not represent a debunking of emotion but, instead, an elucidation of emotion's 'magical' nature within a historical web" (ibid.). In other words, his theory recognizes that emotions can result from processes other than a breakdown in rational thinking, or a visceral response to reality. Instead, they may continue to uphold a critical distance between the self and the world. This line of thought consequently demystifies the Sartrian magic of emotion; "and this in and of itself is an important contribution to a theory of the affective nature of ethnicity" (ibid.).

Muñoz develops a "minoritarian theory of affect" by calling attention to projects initiated by radical women of color, but continued by gay men from a similar background. He observes that the affective overload that is *latinidad* (Latino/a identification) manifested in politics, performance, and other passions is no longer represented as "stigmatized excess."[6] Muñoz's ethnic affect becomes another basis by which to grasp the working of emotion: Here, race and ethnicity also represent an "affective difference," in which "various different groups feel differently and navigate the material world on a different emotional register" (70). Muñoz's powerful argument cites affective performances that reject the *modus operandi* of white normativity, instead of sketching alternative economies of culture. To further his point, he alludes to Cherríe Moraga's poem entitled "Dreaming of Other Planets" (1993)[7] in which she develops a theoretical formulation in terms of dreaming of other planets in order to represent the type of utopian planning necessary to imagine "other ways of being and doing within the world" (93). Muñoz reimagines that this is not only a dream "of other spaces but of other modes of perceiving reality and 'feeling' the world ..., feeling brown" (74).

José Esteban Muñoz's minoritarian theory of affect is particularly useful for the understanding of Rachid O.'s affective experience. The notion of imagining and feeling other temporalities and spaces occurs in Rachid O.'s childhood allegory through his interactions with the figure of the blond-haired, blue-eyed French boy. In order to grasp how affective difference influences his fictional world, it is necessary to examine in detail the ways in which his senses and affect combine to invoke homosexual awakening. This process unfolds in two main spheres—intimate and public—which often overlap, as demonstrated in previous chapters.

Lalla's Sharing Love: Noé

Initially, the only sense that dominates the narrative is sight, when Rachid's longing for the French boy begins in the intimate setting of home, with his Lalla. Nowhere in the narrative do we learn her real name; however, Lalla literarily means "auntie" in Moroccan Arabic and is used as an affectionate term for a maternal figure. She becomes Rachid's stepmother after the death of his biological mother when he was two years old. Lalla tells playful Rachid stories in order to keep him entertained and quiet inside the house.

> Ma Lalla continuait à me raconter des histoires dans le but de me garder tranquillement à la maison.... Ce que j'adorais dans ses récits, c'est qu'elle revenait sur des histoires et me répétait ce qui me plaisait, comme son histoire avec la famille française chez qui elle avait travaillé. Je l'accompagnais, me disait-elle, quand j'étais tout petit.... [E]lle me répétait tout cela en me caressant le long de la joue. Je passais mon temps immobile sur ce fauteuil, à regarder Noé, ce Français dont elle était la gouvernante, et avec qui je jouais parfois. Ce sont ses souvenirs à elle sur lesquels je mets des images. (*Chocolat chaud*, 30)

> (My Lalla would continue to tell me stories in order to keep me quietly at home.... What I would love in her stories is that she would return to stories that I liked, just like the history about the French family with whom she worked. I used to accompany her, she would tell me, when I was little.... [S]he would repeat all of this while she caressed my cheek. I would spend my time motionless on the chair, watching Noé, the French boy she used to look after, and with whom I used to play at times. These are her memories on which I put on some images.) (*Chocolat chaud*, 30)[8]

Lalla's affection for the young boy she cares for professionally becomes shared by little Rachid, whose imagination begins to marvel at the French. When the French family decides to return to France in order to provide an "authentic" French education to Noé, they give Lalla a photograph of him as a souvenir. Her feelings for Noé are maternal; hence, she often misses him after his departure. Whenever she finds herself in such an emotional state, she shares her feelings with Rachid, a receptive and compassionate child.

> Par moments, j'avais l'impression qu'elle évoquait cette période de son travail chez cette famille juste pour parler à son aise et *avec beaucoup d'amour*

de Noé. Il était comme son deuxième fils, rajoutait-elle à chaque fois qu'elle avait le nez dans ses affaires et qu'elle tombait sur la photo de Noé, mais moi j'étais sûr qu'elle faisait exprès de faire du rangement dans son armoire pour déballer tous ses souvenirs. (*Chocolat chaud*, 31, emphasis added)

(At times I would feel she evoked this period about her work with this family just to talk at ease and *with much love for Noé*. He was like his second son, she would add back every time she had her nose in her business and she would fall on Noé's photo, but I was sure she would do it deliberately in her cleaning the cabinet to unpack all her memories.) (*Chocolat chaud*, 31, emphasis added)

Here, the nanny, a loving Moroccan woman, directs maternal affection toward the blond-haired French boy. Such affection between a nanny from a Third-World culture and children from First-World parents corresponds to the feelings expressed by those interviewed in Arlie Russell Hochschild's essay entitled "Love and Gold" (2003),[9] where the author discovers that "First World parents [describe] a nanny's love of her employer's child [as] a natural product of her more loving Third World culture, with its warm family ties, strong community life, and long tradition of patient maternal love of children" (22–23). Although Rachid O.'s narrative shares no detailed information about the French family, these French parents may aim to express gratitude in giving Lalla a photograph of Noé.

Yet, subsequent cross-cultural encounters with the French boy represented by Noé's photograph move far beyond this maternal scene. If Rachid's viewing of the photograph produces curiosity at first, the affective register soon transforms into a more sensual feeling, which in turn induces a desire to touch.

Ça faisait du plaisir de pouvoir toucher cette famille indirectement, et moi comme elle, c'était Noé qui m'intéressait.... Je commençais à adorer m'asseoir auprès d'elle, et petit à petit je voyais que je pouvais me permettre de toucher cette photo et ces cartes postales, tenir Noé dans mes mains. (*Chocolat chaud*, 32)

(It pleased me to be able to touch this family indirectly, and like her, I was interested above all in Noé.... I began to love to sit next to her, and gradually I saw that I could afford to touch this photo and these postcards, to hold Noé in my hands.) (*Chocolat chaud*, 32)

Despite the enjoyment Rachid derives from touching the image, his feelings for Noé become stronger, provoking a desire to possess Noé's photograph for himself.

> J'étais tellement mal sur mes genoux à ne pas trouver une position confortable pour regarder Noé à mon aise.... J'étais mal et ça m'était difficile parce que je commençais à aimer Noé autant qu'elle. Elle, elle pouvait le regarder autant qu'elle voulait du matin au soir et mettre sa photo sous son oreiller même, et s'endormir avec.... Je me perdais dans mes sentiments et aussi dans les siens pour Noé, je ne savais pas si notre amour pour lui était semblable. (*Chocolat chaud*, 32–33)

> (I was on my knees so bad to not find a comfortable position to look at Noé at ease.... I was wrong and it was difficult for me because I began to love Noé as much as her. She, she could see him as often as she wanted all day and put the photo under her pillow even, and fall asleep with it.... I would get lost in my feelings and also in hers for Noé, I did not know if our love for him was similar.) (*Chocolat chaud*, 32–33)

Here, the relationship between Noé and Lalla turns into a sort of love triangle including Rachid, whose childlike affection for a maternal figure gradually blossoms into the romantic interest of a young adult for another boy. In addition, the materiality of the photograph and its viewing conditions impact the immateriality of Rachid's affect. It seems that the discomfort he experiences on his knees imitates a form of self-sacrifice that only deepens his attachment to Noé. The difference between his love for the boy pictured and the emotions felt by Lalla reinforces the impression that he may already be beginning to recognize how the body influences affect.

In Lalla's Closet: Rachid's Postcolonial and Homosexual Agencies

The development of Rachid's feelings for Noé continues to manifest in the increasing risks he takes to hold the photograph. Further along in the narrative, he transgresses the most intimate space of his Lalla: her closet. This is where she stores Noé's photograph inside her jewelry box.

> J'allais chercher la photo délicatement pour ne pas défaire le rangement de toute cette soie qui glissait facilement, je devenais égoïste à accaparer ces moments pour moi tout seul, sans ma Lalla. J'aimais le regarder, lui

sourire, *son visage aux yeux bleus et étroits* qui ne voyaient que moi me souriait aussi et *cette peau tellement blanche*. Je craignais que ma Lalla soupçonne mon obsession à voir cette photo, me surprendre fouillant dans ses affaires l'énerverait. (*Chocolat chaud*, 34–35, emphasis added)

(I would go get the photo gently so as to not disturb the organization of all this silk that glided easily, I would become selfish to capture these moments for myself, without my Lalla. I loved watching him, smile at him, *his face with narrow, blue eyes* that only saw me would smile as well and the *skin incredibly white*. I would fear that my Lalla suspected my obsession to see this picture, surprise me rummaging through his stuff would irritate her.) (*Chocolat chaud*, 34–35, emphasis added)

Rachid's transgression within the intimate sphere of the family's home is just the beginning of his journey for subject formation and homosexual agency. It is precisely the desire to appreciate the image that pushes him to invade the most intimate space of his caretaker and surrogate mother.

Moreover, it is noteworthy to highlight Rachid's descriptions of Noé based on eye and skin color. Whereas he rarely names the object of his affection in the text, he insists on possessive and demonstrative adjectives (*ma Lalla, son visage, cette soie, cette peau*) that express belonging and proximity. Rachid's fascination for the blond boy with blue eyes is, indeed, a fascination with ethnic difference. To put it in Muñoz's terms, Rachid's reactions can be considered a working of emotion, where racial and ethnic differences have the potential to be transposed to an affective difference. As a minority subject in formation, Rachid navigates the material world through a unique emotional register. In touching the photograph, he already refuses to obey normativity and begins to shape his own homosexual subjectivity.

Furthermore, Rachid's attraction becomes an expression of his homosexual agency. His ingenious strategy to possess his own copy of the photograph, in a personalized form, acts as an expression of creativity as well as subversion.

J'ai pris la photo de Noé plus une de moi où j'ai *le même âge*, je les ai posées sur le comptoir. Le photographe était atterré par *mon assurance* tellement précise de ce que je voulais faire de ces deux photos. Il ne faisait que me regarder et écouter *mes explications*. *J'avais oublié de dire que le plus blond n'était pas mon frère vu qu'on se ressemblait très peu....* Je voulais qu'il *reproduise les deux photos en une, avec moi aux côtés de Noé*. Il fallait que je passe deux jours plus tard pour les récupérer chez lui et j'avais pris soin de ne pas dépenser l'argent. Ma crainte, c'était que ma Lalla ait besoin d'aller regarder Noé pendant ces deux jours, je ne la quittais pas d'une semelle, *je faisais un effort énorme pour l'occuper* jusqu'à ce que je remette la photo dans son placard. (*Chocolat chaud*, 36, my emphasis)

(I took Noé's photo, alongside one of mine where I'm also *the same age*, I put them on the counter. The photographer was appalled by my confidence about what I wanted to do these two photos. He was just looking at me, listening to *my explanations. I had forgotten to say that the blonder boy was not my brother given that we did not look alike....* I wanted him to reproduce the two photos into one, *with me alongside Noé.* I only had to stop by two days later to retrieve them at the camera shop and I had to avoid spending money. My fear was that my Lalla had to go look at Noé during these two days, I never left her an inch, *I made a huge effort to keep her busy* until I placed the photo back in her closet.) (*Chocolat chaud*, 36, my emphasis)

This description shows a very creative boy who, just like in the previous scene, transgresses his Lalla's intimate space in order to hold the photograph. Taking the image in order to appreciate it alone no longer suffices to satisfy Rachid's longing to possess Noé. He embarks upon a journey to build a composite image that illustrates a relationship between the two of them. Without getting caught, he manages to transport the image, combine it with another, and return the original to its usual place. Although such a fusion of images could easily be interpreted as sexual, his motivations seem to be based on the physical traits of ethnicity, as well: Rachid's homosexual awakening fixates on Noé because he represents the Other. His ingenuity lies partly in finding a way to unite these two images without needing to explain to the photographer *why* their fusion appeals to him, despite the visible differences in physiognomy that show they share no blood ties.

This is just the boy's first success. The second and last occur during the two following days, when he must prevent his Lalla from noticing the photograph's absence by diverting her attention from the missing item. The strategies that he deploys to conceal and reproduce the photograph attest to two distinct forms of agency at play: homosexual agency and postcolonial agency. By homosexual agency, I mean Rachid's ability to fully engage in pursuing his own intuition about sexual preference, manifested in his desire to possess the image for himself. Although this desire does not necessarily have a sexual end, it does seek satisfaction through a (visual) relationship with another subject of the same sex. In managing to carry out his plan, Rachid asserts homosexual agency that will enable him to spend time alone with the picture of Noé whenever he so wishes. Whereas a Sartrian description of affect would affirm that emotions arise against obstacles, Rachid overcomes a hurdle in order to explore his emotions more freely.

Rachid also demonstrates postcolonial agency in his artistic license with the image. His photographic reproduction is not an exact replica, but a creation of his own. By choosing to add his own likeness next to Noé's, Rachid places himself in parallel to the French boy. Such equal pairing indicates that Rachid's homosexual subjectivity is distanced from the binary opposition between the privileged white Frenchman and the impoverished native Moroccan boy. In spite of his desire for the blond figure, he does not fail to assume a position of equality. Here, both boys have a similar age and share equivalent status within the photograph collage. That is, Rachid's cross-cultural encounter with the French Other is a radical revision of the colonial past. His deliberate act to choose an early photograph of himself and his specific instructions to the photographer serve as an indication of postcolonial as well as homosexual agency.

While such a synthesis between sexual and political forms of agency may appear natural—and, even, necessary—it often failed to surface in earlier fictions. For example, Mohamed Choukri's heterosexual agency proves to be at odds with his homosexual experiences as a heterosexual male in *Le pain nu* (1980).[10] While treating his sexual acts with a Spanish tourist as part of his *métier* in tourism, the protagonist manages only with difficulty to protect his heterosexual agency through continuous fantasies of sexual encounters with women. In *Ce qui reste* (2003), also written by Rachid O., Nouâmane encounters a still greater conflict of goals and experiences: His incomplete homosexual agency is based on an inability to recover emotionally from his relationship with an older European man. Nouâmane attempts to use their relationship to gain subjectivity and social status, but is left with only broken dreams in Morocco when Pierre returns to France.[11] Hence, his postcolonial subjection prevents him from pursuing his own sexual agency. In this sense, Nouâmane becomes the antithesis of Rachid. Thanks to constant creativity, Rachid makes his homosexual desires fully compatible with postcolonial authority; his postcolonial agency transfers itself onto homosexual agency and vice versa.

The productions of meaning that Rachid extracts from transcultural media further allow him to develop his subjectivity: As a postcolonial agent, he succeeds in negotiating differential meanings and values. Despite the assumption of unequal power dynamics that might undermine any postcolonial relationship between a European and a North African, Rachid builds the relationship through his own imagination, leaving room to be free from such historically determined relationships. His fascination for the blond-haired, blue-eyed French boy corresponds to Homi Bhabha's statement in *The Location of Culture* (1994), "Postcolonial critical discourses require forms of dialectical thinking that do not disavow or sublate the otherness (alterity) that constitutes the symbolic domain of psychic and social identifications" (173).[12] It is precisely within these forms of dialectical thinking that Rachid decides not to disavow the French Other; on the contrary, he possesses him in his own terms. Such a revisionist approach to his own homosexuality attests to his postcolonial agency.

By distancing himself from any colonial past, Rachid moves into a new era where different cultures come into contact. He is a visionary who understands that the new technological era produces new imaginaries, new ways of feeling. The photograph with the fused images in fact represents a queer world that Rachid builds for himself around the pale French boy with narrow blue eyes. After having carried out the mission to possess his own photograph, Rachid is able to continue exploring his homosexual subjectivity in the intimacy of his own bed.

> Sur le tirage de la photo, Noé et moi on était chacun dans un cercle. Je pouvais enfin l'avoir toujours sur moi, dans mon cartable, du matin au soir et du soir au matin. Quand la nuit je la tenais dans mes deux mains, allongé sur mon lit, j'adorais dresser mes bras et puis la rapprocher de mon visage et regarder en plein dedans jusqu'à avoir les larmes aux yeux. (*Chocolat chaud*, 37)

> (On the print of the photo, Noé and I were each in a circle. I could finally carry him with me in my satchel, from morning to night and from night to morning. At night I would hold him with both of my hands, lying on my bed, I would love to embrace it and then get it closer to my face and look right into it until I had tears in my eyes.) (*Chocolat chaud*, 37)

When the Moroccan boy is supposed to prepare for sleep, he literally takes the photograph to bed with him. Rachid is not a passive subject, but an agent with strong feelings geared toward the French boy, whose photographic presence moves him. The ability to embrace Noé's image interlaces Rachid's physical and affective experience in his most intimate moments. Hence, the photograph pushes him to transgress social norms in both domestic and public spaces: After having visited the camera shop to reproduce Noé's photograph, this spatial transgression that originated at home turns into a philosophical transgression, as well, by which he debunks a colonial past.

Rachid's narrative indeed goes beyond the paradigms of colonial homoerotic literature in the Orient. Through the concrete act of possessing Noé's photograph, he also evokes a more transcendental concern, namely faith. His fascination with Noé allows him to reconcile his homosexual subjectivity and Islam.

> [Les nuits] je n'avais plus peur des «djnouns», les diables ... et je ne savais pas encore réciter des prières du Coran, je disais juste: «Ô Dieu protège moi.» Je me sentais rassuré avec la photo de Noé. (*Chocolat chaud*, 37–38)

> ([In the nights] I no longer had fear of "*djnouns*," evil spirits ... and I did not yet know how to recite the prayers from the Koran, I would just say: "God protect me." I felt reassured with Noé's photo.) (*Chocolat chaud*, 37–38)

Noé's image is as powerful as nightly prayers for Rachid, implying a reconciliation between homosexuality and religion. Whereas these nightly moments allow Rachid to be at peace with himself, his homosexuality, and religion, José-María's evening trysts in Alfonso Hernández-Catá's *El ángel de Sodoma* (1928) morphed into an overwhelmingly destructive force.[13] In Chapter 2, I show that José-María's realization about his homosexuality engulfs him in a self-perception of disgrace, where he embarks upon a psychological battle of gender construction that he ends up losing. In contrast, Rachid uses his intimate moments to gain emotional strength and reconcile his homosexuality with his religion. In this respect, I agree with Jarrod Hayes, who affirms in "Rachid O. and the Return of the Homopast: The Autobiographical as Allegory in Childhood narratives by Magrebian Men" (1997)[14] that the author "participates in a recent trend of efforts to deny fundamentalists a monopoly on Islam" (522). The critic suggests that Rachid's narratives correspond to Assia Djebar's *Loin de Médine* (1991) and Fatima Mernissi's *The Veil and the Male Elite* (1992), works that rewrite Islamic history from a feminist perspective. Similarly, Jarrod Hayes indicates that Rachid O. writes a "Muslim identity that embraces instead of marginalizing his homosexuality," bringing "homosexuality into a present Muslim subject" (1997, 522). Rather than compete, Rachid's faith in God and his longing for Noé come together to reassure him in times of emotional need.

VENTURING OUT: THE MOROCCAN STREETS AND FRENCH T.V.

Rachid's feelings for Noé are never limited simply to the home; they soon become stronger and soon accompany him out into the public sphere. As illustrated by regular stops outside the Hitachi store in his day-to-day routine, Rachid's reconfiguration of the intimate branches out thanks to information technology.

> *Ces images* que je passais mon temps à regarder chez [le magasin] Hitachi pendant mes allés-retours entre chez moi et l'école ne faisaient que provoquer en moi *un désir qui augmentait et me liait à Noé....* J'aimais de plus en plus *aller me plonger dans cette atmosphère et voyager dans tous ces écrans. Je n'entendais qu'à peine le son à travers la vitrine. La France et les Français étaient pour moi partout,* et aucun de *ces garçons scotchés* comme moi devant les télés ne pouvait se douter que *j'avais plus de raisons qu'eux* d'aimer *cet univers qui me liait encore à Noé.* (*Chocolat chaud*, 34, emphasis added)

> (These images that I would spend my time looking at Hitachi [the store] on my way back and forth between home and school would just provoke in me *a desire that was growing and bounding me to Noé.... I liked more and more to dive into this atmosphere and travel in all of these screens. I could barely hear the volume through the window. France and the French were everywhere for me,* and none of *these boys glued* like me to the televisions could have imagined that *I had more reasons than them to love this world that bounded me to Noé.*) (*Chocolat chaud*, 34, emphasis added)

In this passage, the static figure of Noé transforms into a movable image on television, which Rachid employs to enrich his imaginings about France. In this scene, he seems to contribute at least a partial response to the question asked by Elizabeth A. Povinelli and George Chauncey in "Thinking Sexuality Transnationally:"[15] "where are the intimate and proximate spaces in which persons become subjects of embodied practices and times of desire?" (1999, 443). Rachid himself explicitly admits that the images on the television cause him an increasing desire for Noé; he also acknowledges that he is not the only one watching the television, as other boys are likewise "glued" to the screen.

Does this mean that he is just like the rest of those boys, a passive spectator? Is he simply absorbed by globalized television programming? Most approaches to the television set as information technology focus on subjectivity formation as an effect of globalization. That is,

French programming in Morocco shapes public and intimate spheres, thus producing desire. I suggest quite the opposite: Rachid in fact performs homosexual agency while watching French television. This point is illustrated by Rachid O.'s verb choices: "*plonger*" (to dive) and "*voyager*" (to travel). Both are verbs of action that imply a continuous movement. In stating that he likes "to dive to this atmosphere" (*aller plonger dans cette atmosphère*) as well as "to travel in all of these screens" (*voyager dans tous ces écrans*), Rachid, the character, uses images that entail mobility. Whereas the atmosphere moves at a slow but steady pace, the television screen quickly jumps from one image to the next. Because of this fictional mobility, Rachid imagines himself an active—albeit imaginary—participant in globalized television programming. Despite his inability to hear the television (or perhaps, in part, thanks to this lack of sound), he takes on a dynamic role and performs his own homosexual affect to accompany the broadcast. The French characters on the show not only remind him of Noé, but also afford him the opportunity to envision other scenarios where he might interact with them.

Moreover, Rachid's statement "I could barely hear the volume through the window" (*Je n'entends qu'à peine le son à travers la vitrine*) deserves special attention. While the window forms no visible barrier between the television and its viewers, it does modify their experience by muting the sound. Although Hitachi is a privately owned television store, Rachid describes it as a space accessible to the public: All the children in the neighborhood watch television programs as often as they wish. However, the glass blocks their access to the shops and marks a socioeconomic divide. Just like the window panes that exclude Nouâmane from the music shop in Chapter 5, this barrier likewise separates Rachid from a world to which he would like to belong. Instead of portraying the exclusion as hurtful, in this case, the author suggests that it actually leaves more room for Rachid to develop his thoughts, to adapt the television program to his own dreams, and to invent unforeseen uses for media images as a make-believe part of his intimate life. Whether his family owns a television set or not is irrelevant; Rachid neither condones nor praises lacking or possessing one. The significant aspect of the Hitachi store for him lies in his exposure to French television programming and, therefore, French culture.

Conclusion

Lastly, the passage quoted above at length brings into question the imaginary universe that Rachid creates solely for himself. Because of his emotional attachment to Noé, he connects with the televised representation of French culture in ways that he considers specific to himself. By contrast, his friends lack intimate contact with Europeans and, thus, have a less thorough understanding of the shows. Rachid thus cherishes self-awareness about what he considers to be his first-hand understanding of the French. As a result, he gains a special appreciation of television and believes that his connection to this type of media proves stronger than in others. As George Chauncey and Elizabeth A. Povinelli state, "the intimate grammar that every subject has ... unperceived, migrates, so to speak, with persons as they enter and transgress public and intimate spheres, orienting their expectations and demands" (1999, 444). Rachid's affective experience that begins with Noé's photograph and develops with televised programs allows him to feel especially connected with French culture. In this sense, the Moroccan boy in the midst of subject formation finds familiarity with the imaginary community that is France. As an avid boy in development, Rachid finds his "intimate grammar" by identifying new homoerotic words, which will later help him to write full homosexual sentences—as he does in the soccer field in the next chapter.

Notes

1. Lauren Berlant, "Intimacy: A Special Issue," *Critical Inquiry* 24, no. 2 (Winter 1998): 281–288.
2. Lauren Berlant and Michael Warner, "Sex in Public. (Intimacy)," *Critical Inquiry* 24, no. 2 (Winter 1998): 547–567.
3. Ben Highmore, "Bitter After Taste: Affect, Food, and Social Aesthetics," in *The Affect Theory Reader*, eds. Melissa Gregg and Gregory, J. Seigworth (Durham: Duke University Press, 2010), 118–137.
4. Hiram Perez, "You Can Have My Brown Body and Eat It, Too!" *Social Text* 23 (Fall–Winter 2005): 171–192.
5. José Esteban Muñoz, "Feeling Brown: Ethnicity and Affect in Ricardo Bracho's 'The Sweetest Hangover (And Other STDs),'" *Theatre Journal* 52, no. 1, *Latino Performance* (March 2000): 67–79.
6. Muñoz refers to "stigmatized excess" as the ethnic affect. In this instance, Latino affect, as "inappropriate" *vis-à-vis* the "official" national affect, is the "mode of being in the world primarily associated with white

middle-class subjectivity," positioning itself as the law. He observes that the affect of Latinos is often "off-white" in relation to the hegemonic protocols of North American affective behavior. The understanding of the Latino/a as "affective excess" is derivative of the predictable clichés of Latino/a as "hot 'n spicy" or simply "on fire" (69–70).

7. Cherríe Moraga, *The Last Generation* (Boston: South End Press, 1993), 33.
8. All the translations in this book are my own.
9. Arlie Russell Hochschild, "Love and Gold," in *Global Woman: Nannies, Maids, and Sex Workers in the New Economy*, eds. Barbara Ehrenreich and Arlie Russell Hochschild (New York: Metropolitan Books, 2003), 15–30.
10. See Chapter 4 in this book.
11. See Chapter 5 in this book.
12. Homi Bhabha, "The Postcolonial and the Postmodern: The Question of Agency," in *The Location of Culture* (New York: Routledge, 1994): 171–197.
13. See Chapter 2 in this book.
14. Jarrod Hayes, "Rachid O. and the Return of the Homopast: The Autobiographical as Allegory in Childhood Narratives by Maghrebian Men," *Sites* 1, no. 2 (1997): 497–526.
15. George Chauncey and Elizabeth A. Povinelli, "Thinking Sexuality Transnationally: An Introduction," *GLQ* 5, no. 4 (1999): 439–450.

REFERENCES

Berlant, Lauren. "Intimacy: A Special Issue." *Critical Issue* 24, no. 2 (Winter 1998): 281–288.

Berlant, Lauren, and Warner, Michael. "Sex in Public. (Intimacy)." *Critical Inquiry* 24, no. 2 (Winter 1998): 547–567.

Chauncey, George, and Elizabeth A. Povinelli. "Thinking Sexuality Transnationally: An Introduction." *GLQ* 5, no. 4 (1999): 439–450.

Bhabha, Homi. "The Postcolonial and the Postmodern: The Question of Agency." In *The Location of Culture*, edited by Homi Bhabha, 171–197. New York: Routlege, 1994.

Hayes, Jarrod. "Rachid O. and the Return of the Homopast: The Autobiographical as Allegory in Childhood Narratives by Maghrebian Men." *Sites* 1, no. 2 (1997): 497–526.

Highmore, Ben. "Bitter After Taste: Affect, Food, and Social Aesthetics." In *The Affect Theory Reader*, edited by Melissa Gregg and Gregory J. Seigworth, 118–137. Durham: Duke University Press, 2010.

Morraga, Cherríe. *The Last Generation*. Boston: South End Press, 1993.

Muñoz, José Esteban. "Feeling Brown: Ethnicity and Affect in Ricardo Bracho's 'The Sweetest Hangover (And Other STDs)." *Theatre Journal* 52, no. 1 (March 2000): 67–79.

O., Rachid. *Chocolat chaud*. Paris: Éditions Gallimard, 1998.

Perez, Hiram. "You Can Have My Brown Body and Eat It, Too!" *Social Text* 23 (Fall–Winter 2005): 171–192.

Russell Hochschild, Arlie. "Love and Gold." In *Global Woman: Nannies, Maids, and Sex Workers in the New Economy*, edited by Barbara Ehrenreich and Arlie Russell Hochschild, 15–30. New York: Metropolitan Books, 2003.

CHAPTER 7

Interracial Attraction: Male Bodies on Television and in the Soccer Field

As we saw in the previous study, a spatial transgression allows thirteen-year-old Rachid to reproduce Noé's image at a photography shop. This chapter, however, explores the modes of attachment that cause young Rachid to face the public space, even as he resituates collective activities within intimate spaces. Moroccan writer Rachid O.'s narratives *Chocolat chaud* (1998) and *L'enfant ébloui* (1995) show how the teenager turns to television in the process of subjectivity formation as an effect of trans-culturalism, since he watches French programming in Morocco. I ana-lyze the internalization that turns a collective scene into an intimate space, which reveals the evolution of the Moroccan boy's sensual per-ception and affective register, eventually developing into a homoerotic desire. Focusing on Rachid's ingenious ways of engaging in homosex-ual encounters and sustaining relationships, I demonstrate how affec-tive experience is produced by his cross-cultural contact with the French Other whereby affect and the senses nourish one another to result in his subject formation and homosexual agency. Rachid's attraction for the blond-haired, blue-eyed French boy he meets through transcultural information technology materializes into a real encounter in the soccer field. Here, the sense of touch dominates and solicits a strong emotional response that shows an interconnectedness of private desires and public behavior.

© The Author(s) 2019
L. Navarro-Ayala, *Queering Transcultural Encounters*,
Palgrave Studies in Globalization and Embodiment,
https://doi.org/10.1007/978-3-319-92315-4_7

CRAVING HOT CHOCOLATE: RACHID'S
HOMOSEXUAL SUBJECT FORMATION

Rachid's individual relationship to television programming begs the question how intimacy occurs within a collective setting, since his media moments effectively turn a collective scene into an intimate space. Deepening the sensorial understanding from the previous chapter, the following key scene in the novel continues to illustrate intimacy in front of a television set; this time, however, Rachid's affective experience is produced by homoeroticism, involving the sense of taste as well as sight. Rachid explains,

> Le garçon au torse nu et complètement échevelé qu'on voyait sur l'écran se réveillait, je suis incapable de dire par quoi j'étais réellement marqué à ce point-là, c'est juste que je le voyais tenir son bol de chocolat chaud qu'une femme venait de lui proposer.... Le chocolat débordait autour de sa bouche. Une chose était sûre, c'est que je n'avais jamais été autant frappé avant par ce que je voyais. (*Chocolat chaud*, 40–41)

> (The boy totally disheveled that one could see on the screen was waking up, I am unable to say what I really was attracted to at this point, it's just that I saw him holding his bowl of hot chocolate that a woman had just offered him.... The chocolate was overflowing around his mouth. One thing was certain, it was that I had never before been so struck by what I was watching.) (*Chocolat chaud*, 40–41)[1]

Prior to this scene, Rachid reveals feelings for Noé and an increasing interest for France; this time, however, he does not take interest in the screens because they show an image representative of French daily life. In this passage, which is by far the most detailed description Rachid offers of his television viewing, Rachid appears preoccupied by the body—more precisely, the nude torso and mouth. Whereas other television episodes are individually unimportant for the Moroccan boy—whose main reason to watch French programming is to nourish his affection for Noé—this half-naked French male provides him for the first time with an intimate moment of intense and personal affect.

The process that personalizes the public sphere by reproducing a fantasy that private life is real, in contrast to collective life, has been astutely theorized by Lauren Berlant in "Intimacy: A Special Issue" (1998). On this subject, she affirms, "the inwardness of the intimate is met by a corresponding publicness" (281). This correspondence entails that intimacy for Rachid becomes inseparable from transcultural information and media technology. Whether inspired by the photograph (Chapter 6) or television (Chapter 7), intimacy is produced simultaneously within both the domestic and public spheres. Indeed, Rachid seems to experience an intimate revelatory moment of homoerotic desire even while he remains surrounded by his friends in front of the Hitachi store. His initial affection for the blond-haired, blue-eyed boy in the photograph turns into a broader homoerotic desire for the actor on French television.

As a result, Rachid could participate in what Lauren Berlant and Michael Warner term "a queer counterpublic" in their essay, "Sex in public (Intimacy)" (1998). By their definition, a queer counterpublic manifests itself in many ways, but it always presents an alternative to the official publics of opinion culture or the privatized forms of public existence associated with normative sexuality. Members of this counterpublic cultivate a space in which queers and others (including girlfriends, gal pals, and fuck-buddies) have to maintain what hegemonic discourse refers to as "criminal intimacy" (558). That is, Rachid belongs to a "queer counterpublic" because he reacts to collective stimuli in ways that the bulk of society might disapprove. His unconventional take on television puts him in the category of a group that manipulates public space to employ it for private purposes, some of which are deemed transgressive or criminal by the majority.

While this experience may be far from isolated as a social phenomenon, I would add that Rachid experiences this revelatory form of intimacy as self-discovery. Berlant and Warner indeed observe that queer culture "has learned not only how to sexualize these (intimacies) and other relations, but also to use them as a context for witnessing intense and personal affect" (532). Whereas the notion of a queer counterpublic often presupposes social (or sexual) activities involving more than one participant, Rachid uses media technology as a surrogate for the Other. The revelatory intimacy that he develops at the Hitachi store fits the model of a subject in formation who may go on to participate in a queer counterpublic, but who first and foremost undertakes the process of finding himself.

As it is evident in all of the passages related to his homoerotic awakening, Rachid relies heavily on his senses of sight and touch to foster his budding homosexual subjectivity. The television programming presents a shirtless, unkempt, sensual French hot chocolate drinker. His physical appearance is disheveled due not only to his morning hair (*complètement échevelé*), but also to the fact that he spills hot chocolate around his mouth (*le chocolat débordait autour de sa bouche*). While the assumed audience for this commercial is expected to desire the warm beverage on his upper lip, Rachid instead focuses on his body itself. Without recourse to a graphic image, Rachid remains in the realm of sensual, rather than sexual description. His homoerotic desire is therefore not quite criminal by social standards, allowing the author to highlight *emotions inspired by physicality*, instead of physical traits alone.

Thus far in the narrative, Rachid's homosexual awakening had been intrinsically connected with Noé (the blond-haired, blue-eyed French boy from Chapter 6). Yet, this scene transforms his curiosity for any-thing French into a homoerotic desire that becomes ubiquitous in his mind (*Et l'image du garçon au chocolat chaud ne me sortait pas de la tête*). Similar to the curiosity produced by Noé's photograph, Rachid's affective experience is homoerotically charged and motivates his other desires in daily life. As a result, Rachid craves the chance to taste hot chocolate in the morning, just like on French television. Whereas the commercial is designed to make viewers identify with the actor drinking—in the hopes that they will want to reproduce the experience he is having—Rachid instead longs for contact with him. Ultimately, if the commercial succeeds in seducing the Moroccan boy, it is because he wants to be with or near the "*garçon au chocolat chaud*" (the guy with the hot chocolate), whose designation in the text also portrays *him* like a delicacy to be consumed.

Rachid's homosensual association between seeing the commercial and craving to taste hot chocolate creates "cross-modal networks" like those identified by Ben Highmore in "Bitter After Taste" (2010). Highmore shows the inefficiency of institutionalized studies that separate the sen-sual, experiential, and cognitive modes of experience. He infers that "a world of touch separable from a world of sight" produces an incomplete picture of the affective experience. Eating food might privilege taste, "yet to concentrate on taste to the exclusion of other senses means to fail to recognize that the experience of eating is also dependent on the haptic sensitivity of tongues and mouths, on our olfactory abilities, and on sight and sound" (119). In his conclusion, he proposes that cross-modal net-works "register links between perception, affect, the senses, and emo-tions." Here, senses and affect nourish one another. "This is where every flavor has an emotional resonance" and the "bio-cultural arena … simul-taneously invokes a form of sensual perception, an affective register" (119–120). Highmore's proposed framework concerning cross-modal networks helps to understand Rachid's sensorial affective experience. His bio-cultural craving to taste hot chocolate invokes an interconnection: The homoerotic image about the chocolate trickling onto a half-naked man's face accentuates Rachid's sensual perception and affective register. Since emotions are produced by flavors, hot chocolate gives Rachid a premonitory taste of his homoerotic desire, although he has yet to experience either in reality.

While Rachid learns about the hot chocolate through transcultural information and media technology in a collective setting, he brings his own referential specificities to the experience and adds to them. His frequent visits to the Hitachi store contribute to the development of latent feelings he already began to nurture while viewing the photograph of Noé. As a matter of fact, his continuous quest to explore such emotions further leads him to connect each newly acquired knowledge of his desires to other aspects of his life. Therefore, the television commercial is precisely what persuades him to ask his Lalla for hot chocolate on a morning when he awakes feeling splendid.

> Quelques jours plus tard, je me suis levé aux aurores, avant que ma Lalla me prépare mon petit déjeuner. Je n'avais pas prévu le moment où je me trouverais nez à nez avec elle. Comment le lui demander, lui expliquer que ce matin je voulais du chocolat chaud? Je pensais que pour elle ça devrait être normal, que sûrement elle en avait déjà préparé à Noé petit, et imaginer tout ça m'émouvait. En voyant la tête qu'elle avait faite, j'ai vite changé d'avis et me suis contenté de mon thé à la menthe, sans qu'elle ait besoin de dire quoi que ce soit. (*Chocolat chaud*, 40)

> (A few days later, I got up feeling splendid, just before my Lalla prepared my breakfast. I had not anticipated the moment when I found myself face to face with her. How to ask her, explain to her that this morning I wanted hot chocolate? I thought that for her it should be normal, that most likely she had already prepared some for Noé, and imagine all of that moved me. Seeing the face she had made, I quickly changed my mind and contented myself with my mint tea, without needing to say anything else.) (*Chocolat chaud*, 40)

Rachid rapidly returns to the traditional mint tea upon garnering a refusal; however, this does not mean that he represses his new thirst. On the contrary, it becomes increasingly strong, while Noé's static image gradually loses its significance. Although Rachid's sensorial affective experience allows him to change his object of desire (moving from Noé's image to the televised shirtless Frenchman), his fascination for the original French figure that drew his attention continues to influence his nascent subjectivity. Each of these internalizations suggests that Rachid is able to build his sense of self independently, by merging what he sees and wants with what he actually experiences in daily life. This compromise between fantasy and reality is precisely what disrupts the postcolonial binary between self and Other that might otherwise continue to distance Rachid from his homosexual identity in formation.

His subversion of observed norms questions the Western paradigm of homosexuality, more specifically the idea of "being in the closet." Rachid knows he shares the same profound feelings as his Lalla, who earlier introduced him to Noé's image. Sharing this affective experience allows Rachid to believe his feelings for the French boy are harmless and natural. Because his homosexual awakening begins at home, he does not stigmatize his own homosexual feelings. His decision to make a collage of the photograph, and his evening habit of holding it close in bed, effectively pulls his homosexual desires *out* of the closet, while respecting them as intimate and private.

However, this interpretation does not deny his awareness of the social stigmatization about homosexuality in Morocco. He becomes aware of his blatantly effeminate traits, which he acknowledges he had previously tried to "standardize," but affirms that he will no longer oppress as follows:

> Désormais je devenais maître de moi, j'aurais ma propre assurance, je sortirais bien habillé et ne me décoifferais plus jamais, je ne me noircirais plus les mains exprès avec de l'encre pour rester *un garçon normal aux yeux de mes camarades*, ils trouvaient tous que j'étais d'une propreté étonnante et trop élégant pour un garçon, et tout l'effort que ma Lalla faisait pour mon apparence était pour eux comme *un signe qui me rendait efféminé*. (*Chocolat chaud*, 58–59, emphasis added)

> (Now I became master of myself, I would have my own confidence, I would go out well dressed and would never again undo my hair, I would no longer blacken my hands with ink on purpose in order to be *a normal boy in the eyes of my classmates*, they all thought I was of an astonishing cleanliness and too elegant for a boy, and all the effort that my Lalla made for my appearance was to them *a sign that would make me effeminate*.) (*Chocolat chaud*, 58–59, emphasis added)

Rachid's work to masculinize his appearance in order to conform to the heteronormative Moroccan society manifested in the classroom echoes José-María's attempt to erase his delicate features analyzed in Chapter 2. Whereas Rachid blackens his hands with ink and ruffles his hair, José-María works out every morning, learns how to smoke, and foregoes shaving. Although Rachid is several years younger than José-María, they both experience a self-imposed process of gender construction: Each works toward eliminating all feminine traces and enhancing his masculine qualities. According to their self-descriptive plan, both characters hope to achieve supposedly "normal" masculine characteristics. In this manner, Rachid would no longer look effeminate to his classmates and José-María would conceal his intrinsic femininity.

Just as José-María carries out these changes to disguise his sexuality and prevent family shame, Rachid's attempt to standardize his feminine appearance is due to his awareness about gay stigmatization in Morocco. Because male effeminacy translates as the passive role in same-sex activities within Moroccan culture, Rachid's effeminacy would also make him sexually available to men and boys, who, in turn, would perform the active role in a potential homosexual encounter.

> [C]'était à son tour à lui aussi de faire l'amour avec moi ... J'ai évidemment refusé en ne disant rien, juste en faisant semblant de dormir profondément et de rien sentir de ses frôlements contre moi, j'avais peur de devenir un graffiti sur les murs du quartier me traitant d'enculé de service. (*Chocolat chaud*, 56–57)

> ([I]t was his turn also to have sex with me ... I obviously refused by saying nothing, just pretending to sleep soundly and feel those touches against me, I was afraid to become graffiti on the neighborhood walls calling me an ass hole for service.) (*Chocolat chaud*, 56–57)

The "heterosexual" boys' disposition to engage sexually with Rachid suggests that homosexual activity is not what Rachid fears as a source of stigmatization in Moroccan society, but rather public acknowledgment that he might perform the passive role. In reference to the sexual roles performed during same-sex acts, Andreas Eppink's essay, "Moroccan Boys and Sex" (1992), claims, "for [male] youth, sex with other boys is a more likely sexual outlet and is accepted as an initial experience" (38). The response toward the active role is positive, whereas the passive role inspires "tolerant pity," and, for penetrated adults, "scorn" (ibid.).[2] Although Rachid does not specify the homosexual role he performs, his fear to make public his homosexual encounter indicates that he is the one who takes on the passive role. If, as Eppink suggests, "In the Moroccan cultural pattern genital (homosexual) penetration is the most highly valued form of sexuality, since it is considered to be the most active" (ibid.), then penetrating another boy actually reaffirms masculinity in Moroccan society. Therefore, if Rachid had performed the active role in this homosexual encounter, he might not hesitate to make it known; on the contrary, he could publicize it himself.

Several scholars have stressed the importance of this distinction between active and passive roles publicly recognized as different, including Arno Schmitt in "Different Approaches to Male-Male Sexuality" (1992).

> A man should not allow others to bugger him. Otherwise he loses his name, his honor, that is if others know it and are known to know. The decisive line is not between *the act kept secret and the act known* by many, but between only talking behind one's back and saying it in your presence, *between rumors and public knowledge*.... As long as nobody draws public attention to something everybody knows, one ignores what might disrupt important social relations. (7, emphasis added)[3]

Similarly, in "The Will Not to Know: Islamic Accommodations of Male Homosexuality" (1997), Stephen O. Murray points out that "everyone successful avoids public recognition" of deviations from heteronormative norms in Arab and Islamic societies (15).[4] His research shows that although the established customs of Islam are theoretically respected by the majority of Muslim societies, in practice, "it is only public transgression of Islamic morals that is condemned.... In a way, concealment is advised, because to disclose a dreadful sin would be a sin in itself" (ibid.). In keeping with such practices, Rachid knows that performing the passive role during homosexual activities would stigmatize him. Even in this challenging situation, he knows that he ought to remain as discrete as possible. He protects himself from society's scorn through yet another ingenious strategy that remains compatible with his homosexual agency.

This discretion essentially relies on the margin of ambiguity separating knowledge from suspicion and discursive recognition from rumor or suggestion. In fact, Rachid describes his friends and family members as aware of his sexual difference. The crucial aspect of their understanding is that it remains unspoken. Despite growing suspicions about his homosexual behavior, his father mentions nothing when he learns that, rather than sleeping at home, Rachid spends the night at his French teacher's home.

> Le lendemain, on est rentrés tous les deux chez mes parents en leur demandant si je pouvais l'accompagner à Tangier pour un mois. Mon père ne pouvait rien dire, il a accepté. Heureusement que je n'étais pas une fille, ça aurait fait un scandale, on aurait pu le tuer. J'ai de la chance d'être un garçon. Mon frère était contre ce que je parte mais il ne pouvait rien dire non plus. (*L'enfant ébloui*, 76–77)[5]

> (The next day we got back to my parents and asked them if I could accompany him to Tangiers for a month. My father could not say anything, he agreed. Luckily, I was not a girl, it would have made a scandal, people could have killed him. I'm lucky to be a boy. My brother was against that I went but he could not say anything either.) (*L'enfant ébloui*, 76–77)

This passage lends itself to interpretation as a cross-cultural encounter and an Oedipal event by which the son defies the father.[6] Yet, even more significantly, Rachid's open manifestation of his homosexuality in front of his family subverts the dominant Western understanding of homosexuality. That is, Rachid's homosexual awakening to the blond boy's image enables his relationship with his French teacher and overcomes the Western gay dominance in the metaphoric representation of "coming out of the closet."

This narrative clearly shows that Rachid, as a homosexual, refuses to place himself inside a closet. Nowhere does the gay rite of passage known as "coming out of the closet" appears, as it does in so many Western stories, particularly those that first opened up discourse about homosexuality in Western literatures. As Jarrod Hayes observes in "Rachid O. and the Return of the Homopast" (1997), "Rachid O. differs from this type of narrative, however, in that he never occupies what one might describe as a closet; Rachid was never ashamed of his sexuality; and he never had to hide it" (522–523). Even more importantly, perhaps, he views his homosexuality as a trait that enables him to act on his desires with fewer conflicts than heterosexuality, rather than more. The overwhelming taboos that surround male–female relationships in Morocco make male–male bonds an ironically safe alternative, seemingly immune to sexual surveillance from society.

Rachid's deliberate self-exclusion from the Western gay closet is a subversive act that also clearly illustrates a situation of concern to queer critics working on race and ethnicity. Chief among them, Hiram Perez writes in "You Can Have My Brown Body and Eat it Too!" (2005),

> The closet, as the primary cultural canon of mainstream gay and lesbian politics, is a spatial metaphor, yet there is insufficient consideration of how that figurative space presupposes specific material conditions. The closet metaphor spatially and temporally suggests access to privacy not collectively experienced by all sexual minorities. The privacy this metaphor takes for granted requires specific economic, cultural, and familial circumstances. Likewise, the "coming out" metaphor suggest a kind of mobility not universally available. (177)

Whereas this approach suggests that factors may make it outright impractical to have a closet of one's own—especially due to poverty or collective family living—Rachid's story instead suggests that such a space may simply not provide a relevant or necessary hiding place. Material conditions present less of an obstacle to him than those encountered by other Moroccan boys analyzed in the preceding chapters. Instead, Rachid needs only to fetch the photograph out of the closet in order to bring it into his life.

That said, the allegory of the blond-haired, blue-eyed French boy is crucial to understanding the affective uniqueness of a young man growing up in Morocco who is exposed to the traditional French cultural presence. Whereas Chapter 6 demonstrates Rachid's fascination for the outward traits of Noé captured on film, Chapter 7 establishes how his homosexual imaginary and affect are associated with the French on television. He explicitly demonstrates his racial awareness in the explanation he provides the photographer when he observes that Noé and himself have very distinctive physical characteristics (*j'avais oublié de dire que le plus blond n'était pas mon frère vu qu'on se ressemblait très peu*) (*Chocolat chaud*, 36). Racial difference is precisely what Rachid finds attractive. Undeterred from pursuing Noé, he performs affect in search of a homosexual encounter even when he knows that he is encroaching upon unfriendly territory. In this manner, Rachid turns apparently disadvantageous situations into powerful homoerotic scenes, attesting to his homosexual agency and using the closet as no more than a storage space.

RACHID'S APPROPRIATION OF QUEER SPACE

Rachid's masterful subversion is also present in the only scene where he describes himself on a soccer-playing field, a virile context in which he displays an unexpected degree of homosexual agency. Here too, the sense of touch solicits a strong emotional response that shows an inter-connectedness of private desires and public behavior public.

> Je suis tombé amoureux d'un garçon qui était en tête de foot, qui était *blond et avait des yeux bleus*.... [L]es enfants de mon âge [ne faisaient] pas appel à moi pour que je joue au foot avec eux. J'avais dû jouer une fois et j'avais été nul, et plus personne ne me réclamait dans son équipe. Ça m'était égal sauf que tout le monde a envie de jouer au foot. Alors *ils jouaient au foot et moi au médecin*, j'étais habillé en short comme eux et *je m'étais fait un cartable en bois*, avec la croix rouge et blanche comme la Croix-Rouge et je me précipitais sur lui dès que quelqu'un était blessé. Ils me prenaient pour un crétin, les enfants. Quand quelqu'un était tombé, j'insistais pour venir *le masser, le toucher*, et ils finissaient par accepter. J'étais le crétin, vraiment. *Je les massais*, réellement, c'était invraisemblable qu'ils me laissent. Mais, entre enfants, tu ne penses à rien, *j'étais le plus vicieux. (L'enfant ébloui*, 46–47, emphasis added)

> (I fell in love with a boy who was the captain of the soccer team, who was *blond and had blue eyes*.... [T]he kids my age [would] not call me to play soccer with them. I played once and did horribly; since then no one claimed me on his team. I did not mind except that everyone wants to play soccer. While *they were playing soccer and me to the doctor*, I was dressed in shorts like them and *I made a binder in wood*, with a red and white cross, just like the Red Cross and I so rushed over him as soon as some-one was injured. They took me for a fool, the boys. When someone had fallen, I insisted on coming to *massage him, touch him*, and they ultimately accepted. I was the idiot, really. *I massaged them*, really, it was unlikely they would let me. But, between children, you don't think of anything, *I was the most vicious*.) (*L'enfant ébloui*, 46–47, emphasis added)

The clever strategy that Rachid employs to negotiate his homosexuality within a space of exclusion follows a progression from emotional response to homosexual agency. Firstly, Rachid expresses his feelings for another blond-haired, blue-eyed boy not unlike Noé. This time, how-ever, the object of his affection is not merely an image but an able-bod-ied boy in the flesh, whose role as the team captain garners him attention and respect. The only way to be near him is by playing soccer, which puts Rachid at a disadvantage given his lack of athletic talent. Rather than give up to his isolation, he turns the scenario around to create an advanta-geous situation for himself. Not only does he become part of the game, but he succeeds in expressing homosexual affect under conditions that make it socially acceptable. Hence, Rachid subverts one of the spaces most characteristically associated with masculinity—a sports-playing field—and turns it into a homosexual paradise.

Not content to sit out as spectator of the soccer match, Rachid penetrates into the game. His insistence to play the doctor while the rest of the boys are playing soccer gives him even more occasions to touch others than he would have as an athlete, even justifying why he should massage them. As this narrative episode shows, the boys initially see no need for a "doctor" in their game, which is for them a very serious matter in and of itself. Rachid's role-playing is nonetheless tolerated because he is not drastically changing the sport, even if he alters the dynamics of the game. His "doctor" essentially plays by the rules, since the other boys have doubtless seen equivalent medical treatment in televised soccer matches.

Closer attention to the points of comparison between Noé and the soccer team captain likewise suggests that Rachid grows in sexual and emotional maturity through the course of the narratives. He claims to be "in love with" the soccer player and expresses a desire to be near him. However, he does not insinuate that he wants to touch him, unlike his desire to touch and possess Noé's photograph. Because the boy is not a static image, but an actual human being, Rachid must build up the confidence to reach out to him. Such a gesture is not even within his frame of thinking at first, but Rachid never insinuates that such a deliberate omission of intention is due to shyness or fear. Knowing that he is attracted to the leader of the sport he is unable to play might be intimidating for him. Ultimately, however, he manages to play the significant role of doctor, who has access to not only the idealized blond-haired, blue-eyed boy, but to all the players.

Thus, the initial exclusion from the soccer-playing field turns into a homosexual encounter for Rachid, who simply wants to be in close proximity to the players. Modifying this heteronormative social space for his own homoerotic satisfaction is a "queer appropriation of space" as defined by Gordon Brent Ingram, Anne-Marie Bouthillette, and Yolanda Retter in "Strategies for (Re)constructing Queer Communities" (1997),

> The transformation of formerly homophobic and heteronormative social and physical space (whether public, private, or derived from the electronic media) for social relations that support or enhance opportunities for homoerotic and allied communality and eroticism. (449)[7]

In order to fully understand the analogy of the soccer field as a homosexual paradise, it helps to examine the progression in affective intensity of the verbs that describe Rachid's role as a doctor: "*toucher*" (to touch) and "*masser*" (to massage). Unlike his earlier encounters with Noé's image and the hot chocolate commercial, his role as a doctor relies little on sight and concentrates almost exclusively on touch.

However, the act of touching entails a nearly infinite array of affect. Massaging a human body requires more than brushing the body with the fingertips; it should penetrate the muscles, an experience by which the masseur creates sensations in the body of the athlete. While the receiver is commonly expected to obtain the greatest sensual satisfaction from this activity, Rachid's account suggests that he is the one enjoying it most. As the "doctor," he puts himself in the position of the active participant in this sensual exchange. The boy's skillful maneuver not only shows originality and agency, but also appropriates the soccer field as queer space. Furthermore, it puts him in a surprisingly dominant position, since he uses the bodies of his peers as stand-ins for others who might willingly engage in homosexual acts, taking on the more dynamic role in each pairing.

Moroccan writer Rachid O. associates the soccer field with homoeroticism just as the Latin American writers analyzed in Chapters 2 and 3 of this book associate French places with queer space. However, the main character here acts less like the frightened and hesitant characters in those narratives than like the French tourists examined in Chapters 4 and 5. Like them, he enters new terrain in search of homoerotic adventures.

RACHID'S STRATEGIC INGENUITY

In the end, Rachid develops his affect based on societal norms within Morocco and cultural impressions imported from France only to the degree in which he reinterprets them for his own individual purposes. Far from simply accepting behaviors prescribed by his entourage, his religion, or his society, Rachid picks and chooses what he wants to retain from various cultural practices. Although he outwardly appears to play by the implicit rules regarding homosexual encounters for young men in Morocco, he inwardly creates a rich imaginary life that allows him to interact with others according to his own desires. His ingenious strategies to transform disadvantageous situations into advantageous ones correspond to those described by Michel de Certeau in *The Practice of*

Everyday Life (1984).[8] For de Certeau, cultural practices are mainly gra-
tuitous, a means of achieving power rather than bidding for it. From the
photograph collage of Noé's image, to his chocolate fantasies, and his
successful role as a doctor in the soccer match, Rachid manages to resist
and thereby redefine acceptable expressions of sexuality. His secret plot
to touch the team captain brings to mind the following de Certeau's
notion of strategy:

> I call *strategy* the calculation (or manipulation) of power relationships that
> becomes possible as soon as a subject with will and power … can be iso-
> lated. It postulates a *place* that can be delimited as its *own* and serve as
> the base from which relations with an *exteriority* composed of targets or
> threats can be managed. As in management, every "strategic" rationaliza-
> tion seeks first of all to distinguish its "own" place, that is, the place of its
> own power and will, from an "environment." A Cartesian attitude, if you
> wish: it is an effort to delimit one's own place in a world bewitched by the
> invisible powers of the Other. (36, emphasis in original)

The "invisible powers of the Other" are here represented by the hegemonic space of soccer as a sport, as well as the soccer field. Whereas
Rachid's inability to play the sport well positions him at the margins of
the game, he develops a strategy that gives him power over that environment. Similar to the characters examined in the Chapters 2 and 3
of this book, Rachid enters into the public space as part of his masculinity formation. Yet, he initially finds himself in the position of the
boundary figure described in both of these chapters, since he experiences both inclusion and exclusion from national culture. Like them, his
privileged status as a young man from a respectable family grants him
access to society at large, but his homosexual desires threaten to exclude
him from a nationalist agenda. The Moroccan boy resembles the Latin
American boundary figures as defined in previous chapters because
he is encouraged to take part in the masculine identity-formation process in Moroccan society, but lacks the desire or capacity to perform as
expected.

Contrary to the Latin American boundary figures who commit suicide
in French cultural space—and, thus, prove unable to reach full homosexual agency—Rachid manages to enact homosexual agency on the soccer
field by using de Certeau's strategic manipulation of power relationships.
To put it in de Certeau's words, Rachid grips firmly and effectively onto

his goal to remain a subject with "will and power," despite the factors stacked against him. Through his role as a doctor, he rationalizes his own place on the soccer field, which then becomes the justification by which he is capable of influencing power relationships. When Rachid succeeds in living out his homoerotic fantasy to touch and massage the captain and other team players, he covertly takes on an almost domineering role. Since he cannot beat them at their game, he makes them play along with his. In the process, Rachid appropriates his milieu and creates his own space around, against, and within the male hegemonic representations of the soccer field.

Moreover, Rachid's imaginative role-playing game is not necessarily incompatible with the rules of the soccer match. Instead, it corresponds to what Pierre Bourdieu in an interview with Pierre Lamaison (1986) calls the strategies of a "double game,"

> I have described for example the strategies of a double game which consists in playing according to rule, in being legitimate, in acting in conformity with one's interests while giving the appearance of obeying the rules. (113)[9]

As befits this model of the strategic double game, Rachid manifests a "practical sense of a particular social game," which, Bourdieu suggests, is "acquired beginning in childhood ... through participation in children's games" (112). He adds that the good player as "the embodiment of the game, is continually doing what needs to be done, what the game demands and requires," even as the game changes and demands adaptation to new rules (ibid.). However, Bourdieu argues that such improvised creation "cannot be achieved by mechanical obedience to explicit, codified rules (when they exist)" (123); it relies on "strategies of a double game" that anticipate flexibility. Rachid demonstrates his strength as a player in managing to portray a credible "doctor" on the soccer field, right down to the detail of carrying a "satchel," which Rachid himself describes "in wood, with a red and white cross, just like the Red Cross" (*un cartable en bois, avec la croix rouge et blanche comme la Croix-Rouge*) (*L'enfant ébloui*, 47). The Moroccan boy pretends to obey the game's rules and even goes as far as to establish his legitimate status as a health professional; but, all along, he succeeds in acting in conformity with his own homosexual interest and leads the others to play along with his game, as well.

HOMOSEXUAL AFFECT IN THE MALE
HEGEMONIC SPACE OF SPORTS

Research about the importance of soccer for Islamic North African countries has primarily focused on the question of nationalism and national
identities according to their native populations, as well as immigrant
communities in several European nations.[10] Rather than concentrate
on national identity as it relates to postcolonial politics of Françafrique
relations, my research explores the portrayal of this sport as a space of
male hegemony. I argue that, growing up in Morocco, Rachid is expected
to partake in soccer matches as part and parcel of becoming a young man
in Moroccan society. As a homosexual subject in the process of identity formation, Rachid initially feels uncomfortable when he attempts to
play soccer. This point was proven earlier, where he claims in *L'enfant
ébloui* (1995) that kids his age would not call him to play soccer with
them because he had played once and did horribly (46). His ability to
overcome this feeling suggests that the author aims to reveal subtle
undercurrents of diversity in Moroccan public spaces, where homosexual
intimacy may be publicly performed as an expression of virility.

I treat soccer as a male hegemonic space as defined by Eric Anderson
in his article "Openly Gay Athletes: Contesting Hegemonic Masculinity
in a Homophobic Environment" (2002).[11] Summarizing the research
done by several sociologists having worked on the issue of gays in sports,
who largely agree that organized sports present highly homophobic institutions, Anderson highlights,

> Messner (1992, 34) said, "The extent of homophobia in the sports world is
> staggering. Boys (in sports) learn early that to be gay, to be suspected of being
> gay, or even to be unable to prove one's heterosexual status is not accept-
> able." Hekma (1998, 2) stated that "gay men who are seen as queer and
> effeminate are granted no space whatsoever in what is generally considered
> to be a masculine preserve and a macho enterprise." And Pronger (1990, 26)
> agreed, saying, "Many of the (gay) men I interviewed said they were uncom-
> fortable with team sports … Orthodox masculinity is usually an important
> subtext if not *the* leitmotif" in team sports. (860, emphasis in original)[12]

In keeping with such affirmations, one of the main reasons that Rachid
is excluded at first from the soccer matches may be his effeminate traits,
more than his lack of soccer skills. In the passage that follows this

confession, he provides one of the few utterances that clearly portrays him as effeminate, a trait that his friends begin to notice.

> Les garçons ont eu leur dimanche de foot. Ils ont formé les équipes. On ne m'a pas proposé de jouer, un petit pédé féminin ne peut pas maîtriser le ballon. Je ne le prenais pas mal car je me foutais de leur gueule en les voyant jouer en y prenant plaisir. (*L'enfant ébloui*, 70)

> (The boys had their Sunday soccer. They formed teams. No one invited me to play, a little feminine queer cannot master the ball. I would not take it badly because I made fun of them as I took pleasure in watching them play.) (*L'enfant ébloui*, 70)

Here, Rachid attempts to laugh off the social alienation and stigmatization that results when a boy takes on passive roles. Despite his exclusion from the collective setting, Rachid's homoerotic desires help him to gain inner strength and create an intimate moment of homoerotic pleasure. Regardless of his homosexual agency, the soccer field remains a masculine hegemonic space. That is, sports offer a place not only where hegemonic masculinity is reproduced and defined, but also where masculine privilege and the patriarchal system are established. Within this context, homophobia in sports represents, according to Anderson, a "form of resistance against the intrusion of a gay subculture within sports" (861).

A still larger body of research focuses on the way dominant gender relations are structured and reinforced among adolescents in athletic-related activities. To this effect, Robert E. Washington and David Karen in "Sport and Society" (2001) report in their sociological study that "athletic-related activities ... tended to reinforce dominant notions of gender because sports usually gave the male athletes ... high visibility and social status" (199).[13] Such claim certainly resonates with Rachid's attraction to the blond boy who happens to be the team captain. While this player shows the physical characteristics that Rachid finds attractive, he seems most intimidated by his rank above the other players. In sum, Washington and Karen explain that sports participation cements and reinforces social standing, granting higher social status to the players with a higher level of competitiveness. Alluding to such a competitive spirit, the boys deliberately exclude the unskilled effeminate body because they do not want to lose the game or put their masculinity in question.

Rachid's initial experience of exclusion brings to light the connection between sports and homosexual affect. It is the first situation in which his sexual preference openly threatens his social relationships and will not be overlooked by others to avoid confronting a taboo. In "Sporting Bodies: Dynamics of Shame and Pride" (2003),[14] Elspeth Probyn emphasizes that sports reveal the commonly known connections between pride and shame through what she terms "straight" or "mainstream" sport. As she points out, sport, as a sociological object, "highlights that bodies do something" (13) and that its promiscuous nature renews attention to the subversive disruptions that bodies may perform. Probyn writes,

[Shame] as a very *bodily affect* has the potential to focus attention on the body as a vehicle of connection. As a frequently *shamed entity*, the *sporting body* fundamentally connects with class and race matter in ways that may embarrass white middle-class sensibilities. *Sporting bodies also compete, and remind us of the visceral dynamics of pride, shame and bodily affect* in ways that have been notably missing within much feminist and cultural analysis. (14, emphasis added)

It is crucial to remember from *L'enfant ébloui* (1995) that Rachid's affective intuition is not necessarily shame, but some sort of regret at not being able to play. He cannot be considered a shamed entity about to enter into the competitive terrain of playing soccer with his Moroccan friends, since he is not chosen to participate. In acknowledging his inability to play, Rachid seems to turn instead toward his strengths. His refusal to compete is also a resistance to enter into the realm of "visceral emotions." He chooses rather to invent an entirely different—and relatively more intellectual—scenario in which he can excel. If the adjective "visceral" also insinuates here "primitive," "animal," or "primeval" feelings, then Rachid decides to act with a powerful and rational strategy in their stead. It would best be described in Probyn's words as one of the "positive material and conceptual effects" indirectly provoked by shame (23). In other words, Rachid's regret for his lack of athleticism is precisely what allows him to manipulate the situation and acquire control of the power relationships. He transforms what was at the outset a negative feeling and turns it into a strategic tool to reach an affective goal in *L'enfant ébloui*. By writing within the same paragraph of his narration both of the statements, "nobody would claim me in their team" (*Personne ne me réclamait dans son équipe*) and "I was the most vicious one" (*J'étais le plus vicieux*), Rachid implies that he is both the most dishonest and most intelligent, although he lacks athletic skills. Because of his strategy to subvert power relations, he becomes a skillful manipulator who infiltrates the virile setting of a national pastime and creates a space for homosexual desire in male hegemonic Moroccan culture.

CONCLUSION

My hope is that the focus on the allegory about the blond-haired, blue-eyed French boy has established the character of Rachid as a decolonized homosexual subject within Francophone literature. Rachid O.'s subversive approach to establishing subject formation and homosexual agency as intimately connected with the French Other offers a revision of the colonial past that moves beyond its traditional power dynamics. In spite of his preference for blonds, Rachid does not fail to put himself in an equal, if not superior, position in relationship to those he desires. The productions of meaning that he extracts from transcultural media and information technology allow him to develop his subjectivity and agency, such that they are not merely an effect of globalization, but also an element actively interpreted in the development of personal affect. Rachid's individual approach to the intimate and collective settings—which, it should be mentioned, is not portrayed as voluntarily revisionist, but simply independent from typical postcolonial concerns—enables him to create Noé's photograph collage in Chapter 6 and to reappropriate the soccer field as a space for homosexual autonomy in this chapter. Consequently, the Moroccan boy succeeds in gaining control of his sensorial needs and affective experiences in a national context where social relationships are otherwise expected to conform to predetermined norms.

Further, Rachid's attraction for ethnic and racial difference corresponds to José Esteban Muñoz's concept of the "working of emotion." His unique perception helps him to navigate the ever-changing transcultural technological world on a self-sufficient emotional register. He does not get absorbed in outside media influences; on the contrary, he transforms them and creates an autonomous psychological space. This reimagining constitutes a different engagement with reality, where there are other ways of being and doing in the world. As a visionary designing his own transcultural project, Rachid fits the description provided by Joane Nagel's conclusive argument in her book *Race, Ethnicity, and Sexuality*

(2010),[15] where she declares, "there are individuals who will challenge ethnosexual hegemonies ... and reach across racial and ethnic boundaries to form families and create communities. These are the ethnosexual resisters, innovators, and revolutionaries" (261). Rachid's innovation manifests itself in his strategic manipulation to transform the dynamics of male hegemonies in order to make his homoerotic fantasies a reality.

NOTES

1. All the translations in this book are my own.
2. Andreas Eppink, "Moroccan Boys and Sex," in *Sexuality and Eroticism Among Males in Moslem Societies,* eds. Arno Schmitt and Jehoeda Sofer (Binghamton, NY: The Haworth Press, 1992), 33–42.
3. Arno Schmitt, "Different Approaches to Male-Male Sexuality / Eroticism from Morocco to Usbekistan," in *Sexuality and Eroticism Among Males in Moslem Societies,* eds. Arno Schmitt and Jehoeda Sofer (Binghamton, NY: The Haworth Press, 1992), 1–24.
4. Stephen O. Murray, "The Will Not to Know: Islamic Accommodations of Male Homosexuality," in *Islamic Homosexualities: Culture, History, and Literature,* eds. Stephen O. Murray and Will Roscoe (New York: New York University Press, 1997), 14–55.
5. Rachid O., *L'enfant ébloui* (Paris: Éditions Gallimard, 1995).
6. On this topic, see Jarrod Hayes's article "Rachid O. and the Return of the Homopast: The Autobiographical as Allegory in Childhood Narratives by Maghrebian Men," *Sites* 1, no. 2 (1997): 497–526.
7. Anne-Marie Bouthillette, Gordon Brent Ingram, and Yolanda Retter, "Strategies for (Re)Constructing Queer Communities," in *Queers in Space: Communities, Public Spaces, Sites of Resistance,* eds. Anne-Marie Bouthillette, Gordon Brent Ingram, and Yolanda Retter (Seattle: Bay Press, 1997), 447–457.
8. Michel De Certeau, *The Practice of Everyday Life,* trans. Steven Rendall (Berkeley and Los Angeles: University of California Press, 1984).
9. Pierre Lamaison, "From Rules to Strategies: An Interview with Pierre Bourdieu," *Cultural Anthropology* 1, no. 1 (February 1986): 110–120.
10. See, for instance, Dominic Thomas, *Black France* (Bloomington: Indiana University Press, 2007), 200–205. Here, Thomas examines France's policies of integration as they relate to the French national soccer team. By tracing the history of Franco-African relations from the position of players with multiple ethnic origins, he also contextualizes national identity and sports within the broader context of globalization.

11. Eric Anderson, "Openly Gay Athletes: Contesting Hegemonic Masculinity in a Homophobic Environment," *Gender and Society* 16, no. 6 (December 2002): 860–877.
12. In relation to these references, see Gert Hekma, "'As Long as They Don't Make an Issue of It…': Gay Men and Lesbians in Organized Sports in The Netherlands," *Journal of Homosexuality* 35, no. 6 (1998): 1–23 (title appears in lower case letters in original publication); Michael Messner, *Power at Play: Sports and the Problem of Masculinity* (Boston: Beacon, 1992); and Brian Pronger, *The Arena of Masculinity: Sports, Homosexuality, and the Meaning of Sex* (New York: St. Martin's Press, 1990).
13. David Karen and Robert E. Washington, "Sport and Society," *Annual Review of Sociology* 27 (2001): 187–212.
14. Elspeth Probyn, "Sporting Bodies: Dynamics of Shame and Pride," *Body & Society* 6, no. 13 (2000): 13–28.
15. Joane Nagel, *Race, Ethnicity, and Sexuality: Intimate Intersections, Forbidden Frontiers* (New York: Oxford University Press, 2003).

REFERENCES

Anderson, Eric. "Openly Gay Athletes: Contesting Hegemonic Masculinity in a Homophobic Environment." *Gender and Society* 16, no. 6 (December 2002): 860–877.

Bouthillette, Anne-Marie, Gordon Brent Ingram, and Yolanda Retter. "Strategies for (Re)Constructing Queer Communities." In *Queers in Space: Communities, Public Spaces, Sites of Resistance*, edited by Anne-Marie Bouthillette, Gordon Brent Ingram, and Yolanda Retter, 447–457. Seattle: Bay Press, 1997.

De Certeau, Michel. *The Practice of Everyday Life*. Translated by Steven Rendall. Berkeley and Los Angeles: The University of California Press, 1984.

Eppink, Andreas. "Moroccan Boys and Sex." In *Sexuality and Eroticism Among Males in Moslem Societies*, edited by Arno Schmitt and Jehoeda Sofer, 33–42. Binghamton, NY: The Haworth Press, 1992.

Hekma, Gert "'As Long As They Don't Make an Issue of It…': Gay Men and Lesbians in Organized Sports in The Netherlands," *Journal of Homosexuality* 35, no. 6 (1998): 1–23.

Karen, David, and Robert E. Washington. "Sport and Society." *Annual Review of Sociology* 27 (2001): 187–212.

Lamaison, Pierre. "From Rules to Strategies: An Interview with Pierre Bourdieu." *Cultural Anthropology* 1, no. 1 (February, 1986): 110–120.

Messner, Michael. *Power at Play: Sports and the Problem of Masculinity*. Boston: Beacon, 1992.

Murray, Stephen O. "The Will Not to Know: Islamic Accommodations of Male Homosexuality." In *Islamic Homosexualities: Culture, History, and Literature*, edited by Stephen O. Murray and Will Roscoe, 14–54. New York: New York University Press, 1997.

Nagel, Joane. *Race, Ethnicity, and Sexuality: Intimate Intersections, Forbidden Frontiers*. New York: Oxford University Press, 2003.

O., Rachid. *L'enfant ébloui*. Paris: Éditions Gallimard, 1995.

———. *Chocolat chaud*. Paris: Éditions Gallimard, 1998.

Probyn, Elspeth. "Sporting Bodies: Dynamics of Shame and Pride." *Body & Society* 6, no. 13 (2000): 13–28.

Pronger, Brian. *The Arena of Masculinity: Sports, Homosexuality, and the Meaning of Sex*. New York: St. Martin's Press, 1990.

Schmitt, Arno. "Different Approaches to Male-Male Sexuality / Eroticism from Morocco to Usbekistan." In *Sexuality and Eroticism Among Males in Moslem Societies*, edited by Arno Schmitt and Jehoeda Sofer, 1–24. Binghamton, NY: The Hawthorh Press, 1992.

Thomas, Dominic. *Black France*. Bloomington: Indiana University Press, 2007.

CHAPTER 8

Conclusion: Frenchness as a New Transcultural Identification

The history manuals perpetually promote what are called typically French values,
or typically French temperaments. We are told, for example,
that Joinville is typically French, and what is French is
—General de Gaulle gave us a definition—*"regular, normal, national."*
"Reflections on a Manual"[1]

The reflection by Roland Barthes (1997) on childhood memories about the teaching of literature in France cited above depicts Frenchness as intimately tied to a national identification. Having studied manuals about the history of French literature throughout his school days, he investigates the nationalistic myths that have enabled France to invent and protect its own identity. "Classicocentrism," as Barthes describes it, associates the French language with a perfect incarnation of monarchical power, "Literature is the monarchy, and we irresistibly construct our schooldays image of literature around the names of certain kings … in such a way that we finally have a polished image in which the king and literature are reciprocal reflections of each other" (74). These manuals thus enable Barthes to draw two specific conclusions about French values. On the one hand, Barthes recalls that, in the Middle Ages, Jean de Joinville (1224–1317) embodied Frenchness due to his "literary genius, religious fervor, military valor, and political steadfastness. To call him typically French is to endow the French people with a broad range of

© The Author(s) 2019

L. Navarro-Ayala, *Queering Transcultural Encounters*,
Palgrave Studies in Globalization and Embodiment,
https://doi.org/10.1007/978-3-319-92315-4_8

virtues" (75). On the other, Barthes brings his audience back to contemporary times, in the summer of 1969, when he wrote this essay, by mentioning de Gaulle's more recent but no less powerful definition. As Christie McDonald and Susan Rubin Suleiman point out in *French Global: A New Approach to Literary History* (2010), "Barthes wrote [the essay] in the aftermath of May 1968, the historical event that shook De Gaulle's definition of Frenchness to its core" (xv).[2] Just as the notion of Frenchness has evolved over time within the boundaries of the nation, responding to historical as well as cultural change, it has similarly been modified around the globe.

The ongoing debate about the question of French identity not only concerns the Hexagon, but also becomes a curious object of exploration for those who come in contact with it. More precisely, the opening question of my introduction (Chapter 1) of this book counters de Gaulle's definition of Frenchness as "regular, normal, national" by suggesting that French-inspired spaces are associated in significant ways with queer identities outside of the Hexagon.[3] In this sense, my chapters' analyses have taken on Barthes's call for a "counterhistory" to France's classicocentrism. Barthes proposes that a new "literature to be written, a counterhistory, an obverse of the standard history: the history of censorship" (73). Among his responses to the rhetorical question, "What is censored?" He lists sexuality as an "act of censorship" in France (73). This book has in many ways sought to queer de Gaulle's regular, normal, and national definition of what is French. My research suggests that Frenchness is often perceived as queer when it exits the Hexagon. As such, my project distances the concept of French national identity away from the standardized, hegemonic, and nationalistic portrayal it carried with de Gaulle. That is, Frenchness, whether imagined or real, becomes queer and transcultural in the Latin American and North African contexts.

For instance, I have established the Latin American representation of Frenchness as sexually deviant by using Yuri Lotman's approach to culture. The Lotmanian concept of the semiosphere has served to identify national culture in terms of the boundary's mechanisms that include or exclude un/desirable citizens. I have taken this approach to the exclusion of the Other in order to show how these Latin American narratives represent Frenchness as homosexually threatening and, thus, unwanted. In the North African context, I have shown how transcultural encounters originated both in the public and intimate settings. Drawing on Joseph

Boone's studies of "the boys in the street," I explored how the public space produces encounters with the French Other.

Although an age differential places Moroccan boys in a socioeconomic disadvantage *vis-à-vis* European tourists, the works of Marcel Mauss and Homi Bhabha helped identify the social conditionings that either contribute to or challenge sexual agency and subject formation on these youngsters. Marcel Mauss's concept of the gift illustrated the contrasts in economic and romantic expectations between the tourist and local guide. Using the logic of reciprocity, I categorized the presents transacted between characters as material, economic, sexual, or affective. Furthermore, Homi Bhabha's idea of cultures of survival allowed me to move beyond both canonical cultural aesthetics and tragic victimization in analyzing how Moroccan characters participate in homosexual encounters with Europeans. I contend that possible sites of resistance—which initially appear to be signs of the inappropriate, because of the individual's mimetic component through self bodily manipulations (or the strategic confusing character, as Bhabha would claim)—provide an unexpected agency to the teenagers involved in homosexual tourism in Morocco.

By combining key ideas from Homi Bhabha, Lauren Berlant, Michael Warner, Ben Highmore, Hiram Pérez, and José Esteban Muñoz, I have further demonstrated how Rachid O.'s childhood allegory about the blond-haired, blue-eyed French boy has contributed to his homosexual agency and subject formation. Here, the intimate interaction with the French Other allows the author to not only erase former colonial traces, but also propose postcolonial subversion and new transcultural identifications, where the queer subject from marginal areas becomes an active participant in the global arena.

Finally, in conclusion to this project, I consider Barthes's citation a fitting way to draw attention to new modes of engagement for the transcultural queer subject: Frenchness is no longer a purely nationalistic idea, as viewed by the Gaullism that dominated the latter half of the twentieth century, but a queer transcultural project that involves Latin American and North African subjectivities. Future research on nations and nationalism would doubtless be enriched by further studies comparing cultural visions of former colonial powers by postcolonial subjects, who reinterpret not only the past, but also the present through contemporary transcultural encounters.

NOTES

1. Barthes, Roland. "Reflections on a Manual," trans. Sandy Petrey, *PMLA* 112, no. 1. (January 1997): 69–75, 74. Emphasis in original.
2. Christie McDonald and Susan Rubin Suleiman, "Introduction: The National and the Global," in *French Global: A New Approach to Literary History*, eds. Christie McDonald and Susan Rubin Suleiman (New York: Columbia University Press, 2010), ix–xxi.
3. See Chapter 1 in this book.

REFERENCES

Barthes, Roland. "Reflections on a Manual." *PMLA* 112, no. 1. Translated by Sandy Petrey (January 1997): 69–75.

McDonald, Christie, and Susan Rubin Suleiman. "Introduction: The National and the Global." In *French Global: A New Approach to Literary History*, edited by Christie McDonald and Susan Rubin Suleiman, ix–xxi. New York: Columbia University Press, 2010.

INDEX

A

Acts
  sexual, 95, 144, 159
  unnamable, 88, 90
Affect
  body and, 136, 141, 165, 170. *See also* Body
  ethnic, 138. *See also* Ethnicity
  experience, 136
  feelings and, 19, 135
  homosexual, 148, 162, 163, 168, 170. *See also* Homosexual
  minoritarian theory of, 138
  physical and affective experience, 145
  register, 135, 156
Agency
  heterosexual, 98–100, 144
  homosexual, 15, 75, 98, 114, 119, 126, 133, 142–144, 148, 153, 160, 162, 163, 166, 169, 171, 177
  postcolonial, 143–145
  sexual, 3, 98, 108, 117, 126, 127, 144, 177

Allan, Graham, 59, 63, 77, 78
Ambiguity
  sexual, 37, 116, 126
Anarchist beliefs, 66, 69, 70, 73
Anceau, Eric, 20
Anderson, Eric, 168, 169, 173
Andrews, Edna, 27–30, 51
Art history, 97
Athletes
  gay, 168, 173

B

Bachelard, Gaston, 35, 36, 52
Barthes, Roland, 175–177
Bejel, Emilio, 25, 38, 42, 45, 47, 50–52, 77
Berger, John, 97, 105
Bergero, Adriana, 63, 64
Berlant, Lauren, 134, 149, 154, 155, 177
Bersani, Leo, 104
Bhabha, Homi K.
  double articulation, 108
  mimicry, 108, 111, 121, 129

© The Editor(s) (if applicable) and The Author(s) 2019   179
L. Navarro-Ayala, *Queering Transcultural Encounters*,
Palgrave Studies in Globalization and Embodiment,
https://doi.org/10.1007/978-3-319-92315-4